Access and Equity

GLOBAL PERSPECTIVES ON HIGHER EDUCATION

Volume 20

Higher education worldwide is in a period of transition, affected by globalization, the advent of mass access, changing relationships between the university and the state, and the new Technologies, among others. *Global Perspectives on Higher Education* provides cogent analysis and comparative perspectives on these and other central issues affecting postsecondary education worldwide.

This series is co-published with the Center for International Higher Education at Boston College.

Access and Equity

Comparative Perspectives

Heather Eggins
Editor

For Chris & Bobbie
With our thanks
for a delightful stay
And our love
Heather

April 11 2013

SENSE PUBLISHERS
ROTTERDAM/BOSTON/TAIPEI

A C.I.P. record for this book is available from the Library of Congress.

ISBN: 978-94-6091-184-2 (paperback)
ISBN: 978-94-6091-185-9 (hardback)
ISBN: 978-94-6091-186-6 (e-book)

Published by: Sense Publishers,
P.O. Box 21858,
3001 AW Rotterdam,
The Netherlands
http://www.sensepublishers.com

Printed on acid-free paper

DEDICATION

This book is dedicated to
the memory of
Soleà
the little daughter of *Gaele Goastellec*

TABLE OF CONTENTS

ACKNOWLEDGEMENTS

This book could not have been written without the Fulbright Commission, who honoured each of the authors with a New Century Scholarship in 2005/6. We worked together during that period on the topic of 'Access and Equity', examining it as a major challenge to higher education systems worldwide, and one that benefited from comparative approaches. We have continued to work together on the issue, which remains as important as ever in a world where demand for higher education continues to expand exponentially, just as the finance available for it appears to shrink in the face of the financial crisis.

We owe special thanks to the Rockefeller Foundation that enabled us to spend a week in the magnificent and nurturing environment of the Bellagio Conference Center in May 2008. This week made it possible for us to engage in intense discussions and collaborative writing, and consolidate all the separate chapters into a comprehensive book.

We wish to thank many individuals who have offered help and support, not least Michaela Iovine, Phil Altbach and Patti McGill Peterson and also the group of lifelong Fulbright friends we have made as a result of working with them all during 2005/6. It was an extraordinary opportunity for us all.

We are all most grateful for the patient support and encouragement of our partners and families during the Fulbright year and the period of the writing of this book: Tsehay Berhane, Åine Clancy, Philippe Losego, Abraham Rosenblit and Jack Simmons.

I, as Editor, wish to give particular thanks for the valuable assistance given by Diana Tlupova in gathering data during 2005–6, my colleagues at Staffordshire University, and those at the Pell Institute for the Study of Opportunity in Higher Education. I remain greatly indebted to my family, Jack Simmons and Rosanne Eggins, who have given time and effort in helping me to prepare and format the manuscript in its final form.

Lastly, I would like to thank my fellow authors personally: I have enjoyed working with you: I hope each of you will be satisfied with the outcome.

JANUARY 2010

FOREWORD

It is a pleasure to write this foreword since the present book has special significance. Its origins are in the 2005–6 Fulbright New Century Scholars Program which presented the findings of its research on higher education at a seminar held at UNESCO in October 2006 with support from the UNESCO Forum on Higher Education, Research and Knowledge.

The present volume tackles one of the major areas of the current debate and action in higher education, issues of equity and access continue to be located centre stage in the analysis of higher education as both national and institutional policy-makers and concerned social stakeholders ponder options for the future orientations of these systems and their role in the Knowledge Society and in its main engine, the Knowledge Economy.

Over the past fifty years, higher education has devoted priority attention to the reality of massification whereby more than 50% of the age cohort are enrolled in some type of post-secondary educational provision. By 2007, the global figure for this phenomenon was 26% compared with 19% in 2000. Further growth is expected as the Knowledge Society and Economy depends on highly skilled human capital endowed with a broad range of sophisticated competences, including strong IT capacity.

Equity and access are complex domains which present urgent challenges for all countries, whatever their levels of socio-economic development. Their scrutiny poses crucial prior questions, namely equity for whom and access to what type of provision? It is worth revisiting these questions as an introduction to this rich collection of specialised studies.

Equitable Entry to Higher Education

The principle of equal access was proclaimed by the *World Conference on Higher Education* convened by UNESCO in 1998. The principal statement from that meeting reaffirmed Article 26 (1) of the *Universal Declaration of Human Rights* which states that "Everyone has the right to education…higher education shall be equally accessible to all on the basis of merit."

The original intention of this declaration targeted specific groups: middle and low income countries where higher education enrolments represented much smaller percentages of the age cohort, minority segments of the population such as immigrants and second chance learners, students with disabilities, and women. To respond effectively to these challenges, many countries implemented a diverse range of policies such as affirmative action, reserved admission, special funding schemes, tutoring programmes, promoting continued study after secondary education, the wider use of CIT provision for teaching and learning and strategies to open international mobility and opportunities for academic research careers to a much broader student public.

Certainly participation in higher education has increased exponentially in all regions of the world. Female enrolment has witnessed spectacular rises, along with the resulting impact of women's role in and contribution to social development.

While this is cause for satisfaction, the gains have often been uneven and the root causes of exclusion for certain social strata indicate that special intensive strategies will be needed to eliminate the continuing barriers and their attendant attitudes.

Promoting Access to Tertiary Education for All

Moreover, the goal of equitable access is more complex than it may first appear. The changes of the past decades and advent of the knowledge society and economy have further qualified this goal because of the global need for skilled citizens and professionals in virtually all areas of the labour market. This poses the question of access to what type of provision, thus evoking the terminology of tertiary education to denote diversified systems and institutions. Equitable access to teaching, to training and to research are all important. This variety of mission is both justified and necessary, hence value and status are equal and the twin pillars of quality and relevance should be reinforced.

Also in 1998, the Organisation for Economic Cooperation and Development (OECD) published its seminal report entitled *Redefining Tertiary Education.* This forecast the expected profound changes in this area of the system, notably increased demand, varied learner profiles and the general requirement for a more skilled workforce. A decade later, the OECD presented *Tertiary Education for the Knowledge Society* based on 24 reviews of this sector both in OECD countries and beyond. Essentially, this sets out the parameters of the modern academy and proposes policy directions to achieve these.

Equity and access constitute a key domain for action which should include identifying the origins of inequality, reinforcing career guidance, recognising the particular obstacles related to cultural differences, providing incentives for transfer amongst varied types of institutions, responding to the needs of adult learners, considering alternative ways to acquire eligibility for tertiary education, ensuring that young intellectual talent is not excluded from entering the field of sophisticated research and endorsing the varied learning outcomes from tertiary provision. The proposals constitute a new framework suited to the needs of the global society and economy in the 21st century. For this reason, they are pertinent for countries in all regions which are seeking the rapid modernisation of their post-secondary systems and institutions.

These remarks have sought to emphasise that equity and access are multi-faceted issues which concern all missions relating to higher education. The chapters in this book explore this complex reality in depth due to the expertise of the authors regarding the numerous aspects involved. This publication should generate wide interest due to the actuality of its outstanding scholarship and foresight.

Mary-Louise Kearney,
Consultant, Institutional Management of Higher Education (IMHE) Programme, OECD
Director, The UNESCO Forum on Higher Education, Research and Knowledge (2006–2009)

INTRODUCTION: ACCESS AND EQUITY: THE ISSUES

Changing Inequalities: The Necessity for Research

The massive expansion of higher education across all continents is one of the defining features or our time. The pressures generated by the impact of globalisation and the desire to take part in the knowledge society have had the effect of making governments much more aware of their higher education systems as a tool to advance the prosperity of their countries. Simultaneously the expansion of communications, with television, mobile phones, and email and internet providing ever easier access to knowledge and being available in far flung locations, has had the effect of heightening the demand for higher education worldwide. It is no surprise that the fastest expanding higher education systems are those in the less developed but rapidly rising nations. The importance of the proper management of access to higher education as a tool of government policy has been increasingly recognised in recent years. Research continues to be essential in understanding how inequalities are engendered and what can be done to enable countries to move towards equality of access. The development of meaningful data can provide a basis for government policy decisions which have an influence on the shape of their societies, particularly in terms of opportunities for social mobility. Koucký et al. (2009), for instance, have developed a model for defining and calculating an Inequality index for Europe. Their analysis indicates that, within Europe, there has been a change in the character of inequalities: they are becoming 'more subtle and less discernible as they changed from quantitative to qualitative characteristics. Today they affect predominantly access to preferred fields of studies and to prestigious institutions, and later on, to positions in the labour market'. However, studies which consider access in non-European and developing countries, along with Koucký's work, all indicate that the problems of inequitable access to higher education are inextricably linked to low levels of attainment and high levels of non-completion at second level. As is pointed out in the OECD Thematic Review of Tertiary Education (2008) "Equity in tertiary education is affected by inequities in preceding levels of education".

MAPPING THE ISSUES

The importance of the history and culture of the individual countries and groups is fundamental to an understanding of the question of access to higher education. Sarah Guri-Rosenblit examines the historical and cultural contexts which give rise to the shapes of particular education systems. Unique patterns in the historical development of higher education systems can be discerned, some of which are able to adapt quickly to new circumstances, and others are much more rigid, so that change is difficult and slow. Some countries, which have come under the influence of successive dominant nations, exhibit characteristics in their higher education systems drawn from a number of different national models. These unique features of national systems arguably affect the formation of access policies and retention patterns. There are thus different national patterns of widening access, which can bring about the formation of new higher education institutions (public and/or private), influenced by the impact of political rulers, and of different academic cultures.

The massification of higher education (with between 15 and 40% of the relevant age group attending higher education) is now a common factor in much of the world; universal higher education, where over 40% of the relevant age group attend higher education, is an expanding phenomenon. However the level of flexibility, which can ensure greater equality of opportunity, is clearly affected by cultural contexts, as is the attitude to diversification. Some countries are able to diversify their institutions in such a way as to expand access and support social mobility: others have systems either with little diversification or with compartmentalised systems where there is little movement between institutions. Historical and cultural contexts can also affect attitudes towards the retention of students in higher education institutions. Some cultures such as the UK provide appropriate infra-structures for high retention rates, while others, like Germany, Italy and France, do not. Yet conversely one can get virtually open access in some countries, but difficult entry hurdles in others.

The investigation of the effects of different cultures is explored in relation to two key ideas: merit and equality – in the chapter by Gaele Goastellac. She notes that the tension between meritocratic access to higher education and equity in access can not only be explored in national distinctive histories of access but also in the range of definitions of equity in different national contexts. Her chapter examines the shifts in meaning of both 'merit', particularly 'inherited merit' and of 'equality'. She argues that four distinctive rationales have affected attitudes to the old, dominant idea of 'inherited merit'; namely human capital theories, democratisation, the impact of the knowledge society, and knowledge production. The concept of 'the knowledge society', explored in Manuel Castells' work, carries with it a 'dimension of social, cultural, economic, political and institutional trans-formation' which creates, in Goastellec's words "a symbolic pressure on public bodies to increase access".

The evolving norm of equality of opportunity, in Goastellec's view, has led to two different mainstream conceptions of equality: one is a formal equality of identical treatment for all; the other is the view that inequalities are acceptable if they produce advantages for the less favoured members of society. The differentiation of higher education systems and the development of databases can be viewed as expressions of social categories and national priorities. Yet the tension between merit and equality continues, exemplified by the expectation of governments that their universities should simultaneously provide high quality graduates drawn from socially diverse backgrounds and provide a fair range of degrees based on merit.

The underlying concept of globalisation, touched on in previous chapters, is examined in detail by Teshome Yizengaw and Heather Eggins, and considered particularly in terms of its impact on access. Globalisation, like equity, is a complex concept to which are ascribed different meanings. However, its impact on access has been huge, in a number of respects. Non-governmental organisations, such as UNESCO, and the World Bank and Commission for Africa, have all argued for the necessity to expand higher education which must 'promote development of the whole person and train responsible, informed citizens, committed to working for a better society in the future'. (UNDP 1999 Human Development Report).

Thus it is now accepted that higher education has important implications for the economic, political and socio-cultural development, sustainability and global competitiveness of nations. The processes of globalisation enable cross-border connections and international networks to be established, and further the integration of economies and cross-cultural interactions. The major actors in developing countries such as Vietnam and Ethiopia are drawn from the bilateral and multilateral agencies. They are able to provide funding for the higher education system and influence the direction of policy. In these countries, policies are also significantly informed and influenced by what is happening in countries such as the USA, UK and Australia. Agendas for these actors are mainly related to requirements or preconditions for financial support or development assistance in many of the developing countries. The effects of the actors include pressure on national policies to adopt 'recommendations' such as education finance, widening access, quality assurance, horizontal or vertical diversification, and differentiation in expansion. Elsewhere, and particularly in Europe, the USA tends to be seen as an international competitor: it is the adoption of and compliance with regional agreements such as the establishment of the European Higher Education Area which affect policies and their implementation.

The agendas of European countries are largely driven by the competitiveness imperative with a focus on student and research outputs. The need for harmonisation of procedures and degree structures, the focus on quality assurance and accreditation, and the mobility of students are the mechanisms by which national policies are effected. It is notable that English as a globalised medium of instruction and communication has affected national policies and strategic thinking in both Europe and worldwide.

An important effect of globalisation is the facilitation of the movement of students and professionals, and the promotion of the connectedness and networking of the international community of scholars. Mobility has negative consequences in terms of brain drain and positive consequences in terms of brain gain and the transfer and exchange of knowledge, skills and technology. These have had a marked impact on access and equity in national systems.

The effects of globalisation are continual and dynamic: plans are already being drawn up for a South East Asia grouping which would have a similar agenda to that of the EHEA. Other countries watch these developments with interest as evidenced by the US interest in the Bologna process. The cross-fertilisation of ideas and policies is constant.

Patrick Clancy, in his chapter on measuring access and equity in a comparative context, emphasises the necessity for research findings on which policy decisions are based to be as contemporary as possible. Much of the published research is, in effect, 'historical', based on cohorts of students who finished their studies a number of years ago. As governments strive to reduce social inequalities, they need reliable up-to-date data to inform them of whether their policies are proving effective. Policy borrowing, an aspect of globalisation, is pervasive: policy initiatives need to be carefully evaluated before being copied. Clancy argues that there is an urgent need to collect data on access and equity from those currently in the HE system and to compare these data with those from earlier enrolment cohorts. There is good comparative data on access for women to higher education, and also on the extent of persisting generational inequalities, but little is known about the changes in social group inequalities and about changing inequalities in terms of ethnic groups and of those with disabilities. Clancy examines measures of equity, and looks at the relationship between expansion and equity, using data from the EUROSTUDENT surveys and a limited selection of findings from national surveys to assess changing levels of inequality. A precondition for the analysis of equity in higher education is the availability of reliable comparative measures of participation. Thus an important feature of Clancy's article is his detailed analysis of the OECD data base on higher education statistics to develop an overall index of participation.

The following chapter, also by Patrick Clancy, examines structural diversification in higher education and in second level education systems and explores empirically how these structures are related to levels of participation and equality of access in higher education. The performance of unified, binary, and diversified systems of higher education are examined. He points out that differentiated systems can arguably extend the benefits of higher education to previously underrepresented groups. However, the new forms of higher education providing access to new social groups may offer only limited opportunities.

The ease of transfer from one part of the higher education system to another becomes crucial. Likewise the structure of secondary school systems are of importance in providing opportunities for as high a percentage of pupils as possible to qualify for entry to higher education. Thus school structures are important determinants of both quality and equity. The author draws on the PISA project to categorise second level systems in terms of the level of differentiation/stratification. This structure, he argues, is clearly important in its effects on the pipeline of potential higher education students. To what extent there is an optimum structure for higher education systems, and what exactly it might be, is still not established. The analytical challenge, as he points out, is 'to conceptualise and measure the nature of the diversification which characterises higher education systems and to explore the linkages between such characteristics and their consequences whether this is in terms of levels of expansion and inequality or other outcomes'.

Given that policies to widen participation and improve access for disadvantaged groups are a dominant feature of much government thinking, it is unsurprising that a range of intervention strategies have been developed. Chapter seven, by Heather

Eggins, examines the types and aims of such strategies. Apart from restructuring the higher education system, which Vietnam is undertaking currently, governments continue to make use of a number of types of strategies: the introduction of new programmes to provide the skills needed for the twenty-first century labour market; initiatives to raise aspiration and improve attainment, motivation and self-esteem; and financial interventions. The latter include targeted funding, such as the provision of grants, scholarships and loans to widen participation: a recent example is the rise in the value of the Pell grants in the US. However, in view of the burgeoning demand for higher education, and the rising cost, there is a tension between what can be afforded, and the drive to widen participation.

The recent financial crisis has exacerbated this problem. The British government, for instance, is facing difficult choices across the whole of the public sector, and is calling upon the higher education sector to bear down on costs while protecting quality and access. Despite major financial difficulties the commitment to widen access to the UK higher education system remains: 'our ambition is wide-ranging; from more local vocational study opportunities for those with little recent educational experience, to more help for our most talented young people to go to highly selective universities, whatever their background.' (Grant announcement for higher education 22 December 2009). Recent efforts to widen participation for disadvantaged groups have been having some effect in the UK, but it is evident that those from lower socio-economic groups still find it difficult to access the highly selective institutions.

However, university funding in many countries is being adversely affected by the financial crisis. A number of European countries have already given notice of large cuts. UK universities, for instance, will have to make another £153m of cuts in 2010–11, on top of £180m savings they had already been informed of. Overall, the higher education grant will have fallen by £500m, from £7.8 billion to £7.3 billion, in three years.

The tension between demand for higher education and the supply of places is likely to be found in many countries. In the UK, in October 2009, about 130,000 university applicants failed to find a place: in 2010 it could well be 200,000. Government funding per student is also falling in real terms. The amount per student for 2007–8 was £4,140: in 2010 it will be £3,950 per year. Added to that is a review of tuition fees. Currently fees are set at £3,225 a year: a review is likely to recommend a rise to at least £5000 a year. The concern is whether higher education can remain affordable, and whether the current numbers attending (43%) can be maintained and/or expanded.

The final chapter, by Phuong Nga Nguyen, considers the mechanisms used to support students. These are provided We have combined our brief review of the literature on the diversification of higher education systems and the interface with second level systems with an empirical analysis of how system structure relates by a range of sources: governments, NGOs and Foundations, and higher education institutions. Support is often financial in nature, and includes, from governmental and non-governmental sources, grants, scholarships, bursaries and tuition discounts. Some schemes in developing countries cover accommodation and food.

Another means of support is that supplied by the institution to help with studying: tutoring, language support, revision classes in subjects such as maths, skills training and academic advice. Personal support is also often available, with students being assigned to a personal tutor with whom the student can discuss any welfare or personal problem. Counselling can be offered, with doctors and psychiatrists linked to the university. This range of support can be particularly important for students whose families know nothing of higher education: the alien culture of a higher education institution can be problematic for those totally unused to it.

Student retention is also briefly touched on. It is, in its own right, an important topic which is inextricably linked to access: those from disadvantaged groups often need to be supported in order to achieve success. Reasons for low rates of retention are considered; some of the difficulties are addressed by targeting the improvement of entry grades, by making information about higher education easily accessible, by improving communication between staff and students, and by making sure of the suitability of the course for the individual student. Even so, retention and how to improve it remains an intractable problem.

CONCLUSION

The unique focus of this book is to bring together an analysis of the theoretical literature on equity, to focus on the methodological problems of measuring access and equity from a comparative perspective, and to review the current literature on measuring equity, which points to the need for the development of a comparative research programme. The book also provides a comparative analysis of trends and policy developments and offers a comparative analysis of targeted initiatives, together with support mechanisms, which are currently in place in different societies.

The need for comparative research on access and equity is vital in a context of the further expansion of higher education, and the continuing policy by governments to broaden the social base. The OECD Report (2008) noted that 'attitudes and policies relating to access as well as the consciousness among disadvantaged groups will change and become more central to national debates'. Without question, the future of higher education worldwide will continue to be affected by inequities, and by concerns to achieve, as far as possible, a student population replicating the composition of society as a whole.

BIBLIOGRAPHY

Altbach, P. G., Reisberg, L., & Rumbley, L. E. (2009). *Trends in global higher education: Tracking an academic revolution.* Chestnut Hill, MA: Boston College Center for International Higher Education.

Castells, M. (2000). *The information age: Economy, society and culture* (2nd ed.). Oxford: Blackwell Publishers.

Clancy, P., et al. (2007). Comparative perspectives on access and equity. In P. G. Altbach & P. M. Peterson (Eds.), *Higher education in the new century: Global challenges and innovative ideas.* Rotterdam: Sense.

Department for Business Innovation and Skills. (2009, December 22). *Grant announcement for higher education.* London: BIS.

EUROSTUDENT. (2005). *Social and economic conditions of student life in Europe 2005: Synopsis of indicators*. Hannover: HIS Hochshul-Unformations-System.

Koucký, J., Bartušek, A., & Kovařovic, J. (2009). *Who is more equal? Access to tertiary education in Europe*. Prague: Education Policy Centre, Charles University.

OECD. (2008). *Tertiary education for the knowledge society – OECD thematic review of tertiary education*. Paris: OECD.

United Nations Development Program. (1999). *Human Development Report 1999*. New York: Oxford University Press.

ACCESS AND EQUITY IN HIGHER EDUCATION: HISTORICAL AND CULTURAL CONTEXTS

Introduction

Higher education institutions worldwide operate within national settings, in which various variables shape their historical and cultural contexts. Most meaningful and important differences do exist between different higher education systems. Some higher education systems are very old and their history can be traced back to the first medieval universities, while most higher education systems are relatively young and have been established in the last century. Several higher education systems are composed mainly of public institutions, whereas many others have a strong and influential private sector. The nature of the private sector differs markedly from one nation to another. The private prestigious universities in the USA, like Harvard and Stanford, have nothing in common with the private for-profit institutions that have been established in many countries in the last decade. Many higher education systems are highly diversified and contain various types of institutions, while some others are quite monolithic in their composition. Comprehensive universities reflect the nature of most higher education institutions in some national settings, while specialised institutions are the leading models in other countries. Liberal education and the cultivation of human nature constitute the supreme goals of some leading higher education institutions, while professional training and the response to market demands shape the nature of other higher education institutes. This chapter is divided into two parts. The first part describes briefly how the historical background of several higher education systems has shaped their external and internal boundaries. The second part depicts some unique features of academic cultures that affect the formation of access and equity policies in various national settings.

HISTORICAL BACKGROUND

The historical background of each higher education system shapes to a large extent its external and internal boundaries and as such affects its access and equity policies. External boundaries define which institutions are included in or excluded from any given higher education system. In some countries, like Israel, tertiary level professional institutes are not considered part of higher education because they do not award academic degrees. In other countries, all post-secondary institutions are considered as part of the higher education system, as in the USA, where two-year community colleges constitute an integral part of the higher education system.

The external boundaries have a direct impact on the statistics of access in each country. Hence, it is extremely important to be knowledgeable as to the external boundaries of different higher education systems when comparing their access rates. From time to time, external boundaries change when, for instance, non-academic institutions are upgraded to academic status, or a new higher education law alters the status of tertiary-level institutions or research institutes.

Internal boundaries reflect the structure of each higher education system. They relate to a variety of variables: the overall structure (unified, binary or segmented into several sectors), the hierarchy of different institutions, the focus of the study programmes, budgeting profiles, research and teaching policies, evaluation and accreditation practices, etc. Internal boundaries explain differential access policies for different types of higher education institutions. We examine below the impact of the historical background on shaping the external and internal boundaries of higher education systems in several countries.

United Kingdom and Ireland

Several models of universities have been developed in the islands of Britain and Ireland since the 12th century. The formation of new types of higher education institutions in order to widen access to higher education and cater to the needs of diverse student clienteles has characterised the historical development of the UK higher education system since the 15th century (mainly in Scotland), and most particularly since the 19th century throughout the United Kingdom.

England

England has a very old university tradition. Oxford University has its beginnings in the early 12th century, in groups of young scholars who gathered around the teachers of the town. The exact date of the University's foundation is unknown, and indeed it may not have been a single event that led to the foundation of the University. When Henry II of England forbade English students to study at the University of Paris in 1167, Oxford began to grow very quickly. The University of Cambridge was established as a result of a struggle between Oxford townsmen and the university in 1209. Oxford and Cambridge introduced the idea of a 'collegiate' and a 'residential' university. Both universities are composed of many colleges, and each college enjoys great autonomy in teaching. The system of the residential colleges began with Merton College in 1264. Apart from a short-lived medieval university in Northampton, Oxford and Cambridge were the only universities in England until the 19th century (Guri-Rosenblit, 2006a).

There seems to be a most interesting pattern in the expansion of the English higher education system since the 19th century. Rather than duplicating existing models of universities, new university models have been founded in order to cater to the needs of different clienteles and fulfil diverse national and societal needs. England can be regarded as an inventor and exporter of a variety of university models that have been influential in shaping higher education institutions in many different countries.

When the University of London was established and received its first Charter in 1836 as a state examining body, the external and internal boundaries of the English higher education system changed. The University of London was a totally different type of university in comparison with the Oxbridge model. It was focussed on different student clienteles, and it was more attentive to teaching practical subject matter (Guri-Rosenblit, 2006a; Rothblatt, 1997). Given its nature, it did not regard itself as being a 'residential educating body'. Its buildings were scattered in a large city, and it did not purport to protect its students within closed and guarded walls. Many of its students were able to work and study concurrently. The external boundaries extended greatly when the University of London was given in 1858 a new Charter, which enabled it to enrol students from all over the world (except for medical studies). The University was no longer concerned whether its students had pursued a course of study at a recognised institution, or had studied with a recognised tutor, or had gained their knowledge purely by self-study. Henceforth, all were allowed to enter the examination system on equal terms if they possessed the needed entry qualifications.

Since 1898 the University of London got an additional Charter entitling it also to become a teaching institution. It was decided that the teaching and the examining functions of the university should be split between two separate operations within the one institution. In other words, the University would internal students in its own colleges and institutes, and at the same time would continue to operate as an examining body for students studying in various colleges and institutions all over the world, conferring upon them degrees and diplomas, if they have completed successfully the final degree examinations in relevant study areas. To this date, the external students constitute about one third of the total student body of the University of London. Its external student system has entitled it, in the view of some scholars, to be the first 'open university' in the world (Bell & Tight, 1993).

The University of London is composed of many colleges, academies, institutes and professional schools teaching specialised fields of study, which are autonomous in shaping their academic curricula, and interconnected to each other as a federation. This federal model was subsequently adopted as the basis for universities not only in England, but also in Ireland, Wales, South Africa, Australia and New Zealand. In the USA the idea of a federal university has been transformed into the different entity of a multi-campus system.

Until the 20th century, England constituted one of the most selective higher education systems in the world. The first decade of the 20th century was remarkable for the transformation of six civic colleges, some of which were associated with the University of London, into independent universities (Eggins, 2006). These universities are commonly referred to as the 'red brick universities'. The term 'red brick' was inspired by the fact that The Victoria Building at the University of Liverpool is built from a distinctive red pressed brick. The 'red brick' civic universities were founded in the industrial cities of England in the Victorian era and achieved university status before World War II. The civic university movement started in 1851 with Owens College in Manchester (now the University of Manchester), which became the founding college of the federal Victoria University in 1880 and attained university status when the federal university was dissolved in 1903. The civic universities were distinguished by being non-collegiate institutions that admitted men without reference to religion and concentrated on imparting to their students 'real-world' skills, often linked to engineering. They owed their heritage mainly to University College of London University. The focus on technological subjects distinguished these universities from Oxford and Cambridge and from the newer University of Durham (which was established in 1832) that were collegiate institutions which concentrated on the liberal arts and imposed religious tests on staff and students.

The most significant expansion of higher education in England, and in the United Kingdom in general, took place after the Robbins Report in 1963. The Robbins Report offered a model of a significant broadening of access to higher education. As a result of this report seven new universities were founded during the 1960s (ibid) and a group of Colleges of Advanced Technology were given university status. The seven new universities were variously described as the 'plate glass universities' or the 'green field universities' denoting their modern architectural design and their location in open countryside.

By the mid-1960s, however, a further development took place. Anthony Crosland, the Secretary of State for Education in the Labour government of that time, made a seminal speech at Woolwich in the Spring of 1965 in which he set out his policy that the growth of higher education should be concentrated in the technical college system under direct public control. The 1966 White Paper, 'A Plan for Polytechnics and other Colleges', proposed the incorporation of some 60 colleges of technology, building, art and commerce into 30 polytechnics whose degrees would be validated by the Council for National Academic Awards, a body that had been proposed by Robbins. The courses offered particularly emphasised professional and vocational subjects. Within a decade the CNAA would become the largest degree awarding body in the country. This expansion created the binary system of universities and polytechnics in the United Kingdom which existed until 1992. Interestingly, the pattern of establishing new types of higher education institutions rather than duplicating the existing ones, continued to characterise the great widening of access in England in the 1960s and 1970s.

A totally new concept of a university was manifested in establishing the Open University in 1969. The Open University was based on an open access policy designed to absorb thousands of part-time students, with particular appeal to candidates from a blue collar background. Until the establishment of the Open University, there were almost no opportunities for part-time working adults to enrol for academic study at the existing universities apart from Birkbeck College, University of London which had been founded specifically to meet this need. The British Open University has become a role model for establishing about thirty large-scale distance teaching universities in many countries (Guri-Rosenblit, 1999).

As a result of the Further and Higher Education Act of 1992, the binary system separating universities and polytechnics in England was abolished and polytechnics were given university status. But there still remain differences of mission and subject mix between institutions commonly referred today as 'old' or 'pre-1992' universities, and the 'modern' 'post-1992' universities. In general, the emphasis of the 'old' ones is on providing traditional academic studies rather than professional training, but the line is by no means clear as many of the 'old' universities offer degrees in engineering, accountancy, teacher training, business studies, sports studies, etc. Likewise the 'post-1992' universities tend to place greater emphasis on professional training, like business studies, legal studies, education, but also offer a wide range of academic studies. Since the Robbins Report, the English higher education system has expanded from a 5% participation rate in the 1960s to a mass system with a participation rate of about 43% in 2003 (Eggins, 2006).

A common feature of all universities in England that were established before 2005 is that they are expected to carry out research to a high level and can be described as research universities. In 2005 five higher education institutions were granted university status in England with a different remit. They offer their own undergraduate degrees, but do not have research awarding powers, and are not expected to be research-based universities (ibid).

Furthermore, one of the recent instruments in expanding tertiary education in England and Wales since 2000 has been through the Foundation Degree (Kaiser & O'Heron, 2005). The degree is offered in vocational subjects and is equivalent to two years of full-time study, rather than the three year traditional Honours Degree. It is normally delivered through partnerships between Further Education Colleges and Higher Education institutions. It has employability objectives that require the sustained involvement of employers, and defines a core role for work-based learning. The Foundation Degree is distinctive not least because it gives credit for learning through engagement with employers and for work placements , in addition to learning through more conventional academic study. Again, the Foundation Degree constitutes an example of an innovative degree that has been introduced in England as a major vehicle for expansion. The intention of the government is that it should play a key role in modernising both private and public sector work forces by addressing skill shortages at the associate professional level. In addition, it aims to address low rates of participation by students from lower socio-economic groups, low participation neighbourhoods and by those with disabilities (Eggins, 2006). This new degree is supported by the creation of a new national body, Foundation Degree Forward, whose task is to encourage the creation of close partnerships between employers and further and higher education providers. Scotland and Ireland have not adopted the Foundation Degrees, since their overall tertiary and higher education structures differ in several respects from the English one.

Scotland

The first Scottish university, St. Andrews University, was established in 1411. It resembled in its ethos and mode of operation the Oxbridge model, but the universities of Glasgow (1451), Aberdeen (1495) and Edinburgh (1582) were created on a very different model of how a university should operate. They were established in large cities, and were partially sponsored by the municipal authorities. They have shaped the idea of a 'comprehensive university' that combines together professional schools, practical subjects and the classical liberal arts curriculum (Guri-Rosenblit, 2006a).

The Scottish universities from their very outset admitted everyone who wished to study any taught subject, and were attentive to market demands for offering new fields of study. The Scottish universities, unlike their English counterparts, had shown a willingness to launch almost any new and relatively respectable subject that seemed likely to draw an audience. They were entrepreneurial from their very early days. In the 1830s, for instance, one professor from Edinburgh University dispatched to a rich London patron a proposal for a Chair of business studies that, it was hoped, would attract a wide and varied new student body of all ages from every part of the town (Bell & Tight, 1993). In this case, the private sponsor remained unconvinced. It was, however, his legacy that 40 years later, in 1876, enabled Edinburgh and St. Andrews universities to establish the first university Chairs in Education, specifically to serve the market that they hoped would result from the creation of the new school system established by the Education Act of 1872. The comprehensive university model of the Scottish universities has influenced the formation of many universities in the USA, and in many other national jurisdictions.

The size of the Scottish professor's salary was entirely dependent on the number of students whom he could attract. The fee was placed directly in the professor's hand by the student at the beginning of the session, and those with bulging pockets attracted even more demand because this was evidence to the new students of a particular professor's worth (McPherson, 1973).

A number of Institutes of Technology and 'Central Institutions' underwent a similar status change to that of English technology colleges in the 1960s by being able to offer CNAA degrees. These institutions, like their English counterparts, were awarded university status in 1992.

There are some structural differences between the English and Scottish degrees. First, degree programmes in Scotland are four years in length, whereas they are three years in England. However, the standard age of entry to university studies in Scotland is one year younger than in England. First degree graduates in Scotland get an MA degree. In England most of the 'other undergraduate' or associate degrees are provided by universities (or awarded by universities and provided by Further Education Colleges). In Scotland, the bulk of 'other undergraduate' and associate programmes are offered and awarded by the Further Education Colleges (Kaiser & O'Heron, 2005). Currently the Scottish higher education system is composed of 14 universities and 48 Further Education and Higher Education Colleges. The access rate in Scotland is higher than in England and it exceeds 50%. Historically, participation rates in higher education have been higher in Scotland than in England (Eggins, 2006).

Ireland

The formation of the Irish higher education system reflects its unique history, and the tensions between the Catholic and Protestant religions. Ireland's oldest university, the University of Dublin (Trinity College), received its royal charter in 1592. While some Catholic students were admitted to Trinity in the early years, the operation of religious tests in the seventeenth and eighteenth centuries meant that only members of the Established Church could avail themselves of university education in Ireland (Clancy, 2005). The first concession to allow higher education for Catholics was the granting of direct funding for the establishment in 1795 of a Catholic college at Maynooth. This college was founded to educate Catholic priests, the view being that it was preferable to provide this education at home rather than risk Irish students being 'exposed' to revolutionary thought and fervour which was sweeping Continental Europe in the wake of the French revolution. The problem still remained of providing university education for lay Catholics, as the atmosphere and control of Trinity College remained essentially Protestant. During the course of the nineteenth century several attempts were made to provide a form of university education which would be acceptable to Catholics (ibid).

In 1845 the Queen's College Act established three colleges: Queen's College Cork, Queen's College Galway and Queen's College Belfast. In 1850 these three colleges were linked together under the umbrella of the Queen's University of Ireland established by a Royal Charter.

A papal prescript issued in 1847 condemned the Queen's colleges as 'detrimental to religion', and proposed that the Irish bishops found a Catholic University modelled on Louvain. The Catholic University was established in 1851 and opened in 1854, and John Henry Newman was appointed as its first Rector. The Catholic University was founded and funded independently of the State. While Newman's stewardship was short-lived, the Catholic University, as well as a number of other institutions, evolved to become University College, Dublin.

The University Education Act of 1879 provided for the formation of the Royal University of Ireland, whose examinations were open to all candidates whether they had attended college lectures or not (basically it followed the model pioneered by the external student system of the University of London). In the context of Ireland, the Charter of the Royal University that was granted in 1880 gave an opportunity to improve the position of the Catholic University students to whom recognised university degrees had not hitherto been available. As a result of the establishment of the Royal University, Queen's University was dissolved in 1882. The University College in Dublin took over, under the control of the Jesuit Fathers, all of the work of the Catholic University, except the teaching of medicine which continued under the aegis of the Catholic University Medical School.

The foundation of the Royal University of Ireland portrays British policy towards Ireland throughout the 19th century. This policy attempted to provide an educational system that would satisfy the needs and aspirations of the Catholic majority without offending Protestant susceptibilities, not just in Ireland but in the United Kingdom as a whole (Bell & Tight, 1993). One of the clearest benefits of establishing the Royal University was the educational opportunity that the university gave to Irish women, who until then were denied access to the Queen's University and to the male colleges of the Catholic University. Women, including nuns in enclosed orders, enrolled at the Royal University.

The Irish University Act of 1908 established two new universities – the National University of Ireland and the Queen's University of Belfast and dissolved the Royal University in 1909. Under this act the National University of Ireland became a federal university with its seat in Dublin, and with three constituent colleges established by Charter – University College Dublin, University College Cork, and University College Galway. The Jesuit University College Dublin was given a new constitution and the Catholic University Medical School was merged into it. Power was granted by the 1908 Act to the National University of Ireland to recognise courses of study in other institutions for the purposes of a degree, such as studies at St. Patrick's College in Maynooth (from 1910) or Our Lady of Mercy College in Dublin (from 1975). The Universities Act of 1997 redefined the nature and role of the National University of Ireland. It reconstituted its three constituent colleges as constituent universities. There are currently altogether seven state funded universities in Ireland.

Although the Irish university sector was shaped on the basis of English universities, its interesting history of establishing, reconstructing and dissolving universities in the 19th century and the start of the 20th century reflects the unique historical background of Ireland and the religious tension that constitutes an integral part of the Irish society.

There are several structural differences between the English and Irish higher education systems. Unlike the situation in England where the binary system was abolished in 1992, the Irish higher education system is still structured as a binary system composed of seven universities, and 16 technological colleges, plus a few religious colleges. The rapid expansion in enrolment which started in the 1960s was accompanied by a diversification of the Irish higher education with the development of a large technological sector through the establishment of a network of Regional Technical Colleges and the expansion of a few pre-existing technical colleges (Clancy, 2006). Currently the access rate in Ireland is 55%, significantly higher than in England.

France

France also has a very old higher education tradition, but its development followed a very different path as compared to the British higher education system. The University of Paris emerged from the schools of priests controlled by the Notre Dame Cathedral in the 12th century. The king, Phillip Augustus, conferred a charter on the masters and scholars of the University of Paris in 1200, thus protecting them in relation to the townsmen. The Pope, by a bull of 1231, often called the *Magna Charta Universitatum*, ensured their right to control examinations and licensing of teachers. Many students were enrolled at the medieval University of Paris. There is documentation indicating that in the 13th century it had over 7,000 students (Burns et al., 1980). Many of them were young and poor. However, the original University of Paris, as well as all other French universities, were abolished during the French revolution and the Napoleonic times.

The French higher education system was reconstructed totally anew at the end of the 18th century. The abolition of the 'old' universities and the foundation of totally new higher education institutions fitted the leading spirit of the French revolution that purported to get rid of all of the social institutions of the old regime, and start everything anew. In the new reconstructed system of French higher education, a clear distinction was established between elite institutions (the *grandes écoles*) and the universities.

The first *grandes écoles* were already established at the middle of the 18th century, but they gained their unique status mainly since Napoleonic times. In 1794 the *École Polytechnique* that aimed at preparing artillery officers was founded. A year later was established the *École Normale Superieure* that has served since then as a leading institution in training the political and intellectual elites of French society. The *grandes écoles* enjoy a high and privileged status in the French higher education system, and admission to them is highly competitive and selective, whereas the universities are open to all graduates of high school who possess a *baccalauréat* diploma. In 2006, 5.6% of the 1,357,000 higher education students in France were studying in the two-year preparatory classes for admission to the *grandes écoles* (Goastellec, 2006).

Interestingly, the French medieval universities enjoyed a greater autonomy in conducting their academic affairs, in comparison with the new higher education institutions in France. The French higher education system is considered to be one of the most centralised systems in the world, controlled by governmental and bureaucratic procedures (Rothblatt, 1997).The public universities in France are named after the city where they are found, followed by a number if there are several. Paris, for instance, has 13 universities, labelled Paris I to XIII. All of the universities and specialised higher education institutions are expected to follow the same curriculum in any given subject area. The degree diplomas are national and all of the French universities are considered to be of equal status (Goastellec, 2006). Much of the research is conducted outside the universities in special designated research centres, such as CNRS or INSERM, sponsored by the government, a fact that diminishes the research function of the universities. Nevertheless, a large proportion of the academics are teaching in the universities and are conducting research in mixed research units (*UMR - Unité Mixte de Recherche*) belonging both to the universities and the CNRS.

Studies are divided into several cycles at the French universities. Students can study academic studies in a first two-year cycle, through a three-year programme that leads to a *licence*, and a four-year programme that leads to a *maitrise* (equivalent to a master degree), a 5 year diploma (equivalent to a two-year master degree), and 8 year diploma (Doctorate). Since the 1960s a new middle range selective sector has been initiated in the French higher education system, consisting of two-year University Institutes of Technology (IUT) and Superior Technicians Section (STS). The overall structure of the two-year institutions in France is currently in the course of change in line with the framework of the Bologna Process, which will be discussed later. More than 50% from the relevant age cohorts enter higher education institutions in France (including the two-year institutions), but there is a very high drop-out rate from the French universities, a theme that will be discussed further on.

Vietnam

The historical background of the Vietnamese higher education reflects the impact of its various political rulers on the ethos and practices of its higher learning institutions. In the period of Chinese Imperial domination (from 111 BC to 938 AD) the

Vietnamese system imitated the Chinese education structure, and was composed of primary education lasting about 15 years, and higher education lasting also about 15 years (Nguyen, 2006). The higher learning institutes served mainly for preparing the administrative elite. From 938 to 1850, the period of Vietnamese national independence, higher education was provided by public and private Buddhist schools. The higher education system was still highly selective and aimed only at the privileged classes. The overall system was heavily dependent on competitive examinations. Students had to take the inter-provincial competitive examination to get a bachelor degree. Bachelor holders were eligible to take the Pre-court competitive examination held at the Capital Thang Long to get the degree of a Junior Doctor. Junior doctoral holders could take the prestigious court competitive examination for the first rank of the doctorate degree (ibid).

During the first stage of French Colonialism, the feudal system of Confucian education was maintained, but from the beginning of the 20th century, many professional education colleges were established (such as the College of Medicine and Pharmacy in 1902; the College of Teacher Training in 1917; the College of Experimental Sciences in 1923, etc.) on the basis of French professional education. Although some of these colleges were termed as 'universities', they were basically two-year vocational colleges. From 1924 to 1939, the college system underwent some changes toward establishing a university system. All the colleges were combined to form the University of Indo-China (following the monolithic structure of the national French University) enrolling in total a relatively small number of students - 600 in the academic year of 1939/40 (ibid).

During the period of revolution from 1945 to 1975 the higher education system in Vietnam changed and was divided into two parts. One was under the control of the North Vietnamese government, and the other under French rule, and later on under American domination. The system in North Vietnam adopted the former Soviet Union system, based mainly on specialised institutions focussing mainly on one subject and a few comprehensive universities. In 1974/75 there were in all 41 universities and colleges with 55,700 students in North Vietnam. The South of Vietnam has changed and adopted some of the American higher education features, based mainly on large comprehensive universities. In 1974/5 there were four large public universities enrolling around 130,000 students, and in addition some small community colleges, enrolling only 2,600 students, and 12 private institutions, enrolling about 30,000 students. After the reunification of Vietnam in 1975, for more than two decades all the higher education institutes were organised on the basis of the Soviet model, but from 1991 onwards postgraduate studies were constructed on the basis of the American model. The number of students grew dramatically from 99,807 in 1974/75 to 1,319,754 in 2004/5, enrolled in 137 universities and 127 colleges. The case of Vietnam provides a most illuminating example of how historical developments have a clear impact on the structure of the higher education system, its access policies and academic curricula.

South Africa

South Africa provides another interesting example of a unique higher education system that for many decades reflected the government apartheid policies of the time.

Until 1994, the South African higher education system was segregated into different segments for different racial groups. Its first colleges were created in the midst of the 19th century for its white population, based very much on the model of the federal University of London. In 1873 was established, for instance, the University of the Cape of Good Hope, as a federal university. After all of its eleven constituent colleges developed into autonomous degree-granting institutions, the university was reconstituted in 1951 as the University of South Africa (UNISA) to provide courses for external students only. In 1962 it was established officially as a distance teaching university, and is considered to be the first fully-fledged distance teaching university in the world (Guri-Rosenblit, 1999).

In 1953, the Bantu Education Act called for the creation of new universities for non-white racial groups. The Education Act of 1959 prompted the establishment of four new universities for non-white ethnic groups, and two new universities for Afrikaans. Only a few universities, like the University of Cape Town and the University of Witwatersrand had admitted a small number of black students, in fields of study that were not offered in the non-white universities. In the 1970s more universities opened their gates to small numbers of black and coloured students. As a result the percentage of black students increased significantly, and they constituted 47% of the overall student population in South Africa in 1976, as compared to only 15% in 1960 (ibid).

When the ANC started governing South Africa in 1994, the access rate to higher education of the relevant age cohort was just 15%. However, drastic differences existed between the participation rates of different categories. Among the 'whites', 39% of the relevant age were enrolled in higher education institutions, as compared to 17% of the 'Indians', 12% of the 'blacks' and 9% of the 'coloured'.

The end of apartheid has drastically changed the structure and policies of the South African higher education system. In 1992 a National Education Coordination Committee was established in order to reconsider all the education policies. In 1996 a National Committee on Higher Education was established by Mandela to define how to promote equity in access to higher education. In 1998 the Committee on Higher Education replaced the National Committee on Higher Education (Goastellec, 2006). Very little has been implemented and changed until 2001. Based on the National Plan for Higher Education from 2001 following mergers aimed at abolishing apartheid gaps, higher education institutions in South Africa are mainly required to improve the retention of the existing students and to make their programmes more efficient and effective, rather than to widen participation. Unquestionably, South African higher education operates currently in stormy waters, and it will take a long time to stabilise it and improve its access policies and graduation patterns.

Israel

Young higher education systems have the privilege of choosing the academic structures and models that have evolved over the centuries in different national settings and that best suit their national, social and economic needs. The unique cultural context of each setting defines to a great extent how the higher education system is structured. Israel has a relatively young higher education system. Its first higher education institutions were established in the 1920s, a quarter of a century before the foundation of the State of Israel. Interestingly, though, it was then under the British Mandate, its first higher education institutions were formed on the basis of the German *Humboldtian* university. Since the founding professors of the Technion in Haifa (which was established in 1924) and the Hebrew University in Jerusalem (which was established in 1925) came from Germany, they zealously implemented the idea of the *Humboldtian* research university in the Israeli context. For 50 years this was the only university model in Israel. The other five university-level institutions that were established between 1934 and 1965 (the Weizmann Institute, Tel-Aviv University, Bar-Ilan University, Haifa University, and Ben-Gurion University) have all followed the model of the two veteran institutions. However, the establishment of the Council for Higher Education in 1958 as a buffer body between the universities and the government was influenced by the British University Grants Committee. In 1976 the Budgeting and Planning Committee, which was also based on the British model, was created.

The composition of the Israeli higher education system changed drastically from the mid 1970s. Since then higher education in Israel has moved gradually from a highly selective, elite and research-oriented system to a mass higher education system, in which academic education is perceived by many as a right rather than as a privilege; from a relatively homogeneous student body to a most heterogeneous student body; from a higher education system based predominantly on research universities to a very diversified system, in which the non-university sector is expanding at a tremendous pace and volume, both as a result of several bottom-up initiatives side by side with governmental top-down planning. Indeed, the most conspicuous development of the last two decades is the growth of various types of colleges outside the university sector. No new university has been established in Israel since that of the Open University in 1974.

Upgrading post-secondary institutions to academic status has been one of the main strategies of the Council for Higher Education in expanding the higher education system in recent years. The academic accreditation of post-secondary professional schools can be seen as a response to the growing demand for career-oriented higher education. In the framework of this policy 27 teacher training colleges, as well as 7 of the schools preparing practical engineers, were upgraded to academic status.

Since the late 1980s new colleges were established, both public and private. The new public colleges were established mainly in the periphery, absorbing many students from lower status groups. The private colleges mainly offered studies which were highly in demand in the labour market. Until 1986 there was no private sector in Israeli higher education. In April 1991 the Law of Higher Education was amended and it confirmed the eligibility of founding privately-funded higher education institutions that were not sponsored by the Planning and Budgeting Committee. At the same time it authorised the Council for Higher Education to supervise the programmes in these externally-funded institutions, if the latter wished to get permission to grant academic degrees. In other words, the Council of Higher Education has remained the only body authorised to confer academic recognition on higher education institutes in Israel.

In reality, the private colleges opened the doors to mainly privileged and well-to-do populations, since their tuition fees are much higher in comparison with those in the publicly sponsored universities and colleges (sometimes three-fold or more). Nevertheless, even the private colleges offered special fellowships to qualified applicants from low socio-economic backgrounds.

Altogether there were, in 2006, 67 higher education institutions in Israel: 8 universities (including the Open University), 27 teacher training colleges and 32 other colleges (Guri-Rosenblit, 2006). The proclaimed aim of the Council for Higher Education is to reach in the coming decade a participation rate of at least 50% of the relevant age cohort in higher education institutions.

Ethiopia

The Ethiopian higher education system is also relatively young. Throughout its development it has been influenced by higher education models from various countries. Some of its higher education institutions were established in collaboration with the USA, the former Soviet Union, and several European countries as well as with international bodies, like UNESCO. The major focus of its tertiary level institutions has been on professional education, which is relevant to the societal and economic needs of Ethiopia.

Post-secondary education in Ethiopia started a little over 60 years ago with middle level training in Agriculture. Ambo was the first post-secondary education institution established in 1946. In 1950, higher level education and training in Chemistry and Biology were started in the then University College at Addis Ababa (now Addis Ababa University). Housed in the old Palace compound, this University College grew to become Haileselassie I University in 1961 by including Alemaya and Gondar Colleges. In the early fifties Alemaya Agricultural College and Addis Ababa Commercial College were established. Alemaya was established by technical cooperation between the Imperial Ethiopian Government and the government of the USA. Jimma and Gondar colleges were established in the late 1950s. Gondar started as an institute training public health officers and mid-level health professionals (Yizengaw, 2006).

The early sixties saw the establishment of Bahir Dar Polytechnic Institute and Kotebe College of Teacher Education while in the late sixties Awassa, Bahir Dar Teachers College as well as several faculties and schools of Addis Ababa University were founded. These institutions were under the Addis Ababa University for a long time. Bahir Dar Polytechnic Institute was established with the cooperation of the former Soviet Union and the Imperial Ethiopian government in 1963. The Bahirdar Teachers College was established with the cooperation of UNESCO, UNDP and the Imperial Ethiopian government in 1972. Since the 1970s many more professional colleges were established throughout the country.

Graduate level training started in Addis Ababa University in 1978, immediately followed by Alemaya University (then Alemaya College of Agriculture under Addis Ababa University) in 1983. Later on the Wondo Genet College of forestry started graduate programmes in forestry in collaboration with a Swedish University in 1994 after the faculty was moved out of Alemaya to Wondo Genet.

Higher Education in Ethiopia is organised by types of institution, qualification level and ownership. With respect to type, institutions are designated as University, University College, College or Institute. University status could be granted only by the government. Institutions are also organised as those conferring diploma or/and degrees as well as graduate level (Master and doctorate) degrees. Currently most private higher education institutions offer diplomas. Addis Ababa University, Alemaya University, Debub, Jima, Gonder, Arbaminch, Bahirdar and Mekele universities are all public institutions offering graduate level degree programmes, in addition to undergraduate degree level programmes (ibid).

In 2000, institutions in different regions of the country were amalgamated to form Universities. As such four new universities, namely Debub, Bahir Dar, Jimma and Mekelle, were established. In 2004, Gonder and Arbaminch were upgraded to University level by a Council of Ministers' Charter. Ethiopian higher education is composed currently of nine higher education institutions under the direct auspices of the Ministry of Education. In addition to these, there are three institutions under different Federal government entities, eight teacher-training colleges under Regional Governments and over 64 accredited private higher education institutions.

As the system's geographical spread extended, enrolments also grew. In the 10 years between 1991 and 2005 the annual intake of students has grown from a bare 6,000 to over 36,000 in Ministry of Education sponsored institutions alone. The number of graduates has also increased from 17,579 in 2000/1 to about 28,455 in 2004/5. At the graduate level the enrolment has increased from 1,286 in 2000/1 to over 3,600 in 2004/5. However, Ethiopia has still a very low access rate to higher education. For a population of over 70 million, the enrolment in higher education remains low. In 2004 there were 220–240 students per 100,000 inhabitants (as compared to 62–70 in 1995).

DOMINANT FEATURES OF ACADEMIC CULTURES

This section examines several dominant features of academic cultures that also influence access and graduation policies in different national settings. The discussion refers to the degree of diversification, massification and flexibility of the higher education systems, the interrelations between access and exit (retention) policies, the nature of the coexistence of public and private higher education institutions, and the role of language, particularly the English language, in promoting globalisation trends in higher education.

Diversification, Massification and Flexibility

There seems to be a close interrelation between the patterns of diversification and the flexibility of higher education systems and their access policies. The more diversified and flexible a higher education system is, the more likely it is to exercise a mass-oriented or even universal access policy. For hundreds of years, higher education has been considered as a privilege for the few and well-to-do, and its main purpose was to educate and train the elites. Since the end of World War II, a huge expansion of higher education systems has taken place. Recent decades have seen an accelerated widening of access to higher education worldwide. This has been accompanied in many countries by an extensive diversification of their higher education systems, through the foundation of new types of higher education institutions, both public and private, and a significant expansion of the existing institutions. However, diversification by itself does not suffice. As aforementioned, England has invented new types of higher education institutions since the 19th century, but until the 1960s it was a very elitist system, enrolling only 5% of the relevant age cohort. American higher education, on the other hand, has provided an illuminating example of a diversified, flexible and mass-oriented system from its very start.

The history of American higher education is characterised by the growth of multi-purpose institutions which continue to add functions and responsibilities without discarding older commitments (Rothblatt, 1997). The American higher education system is the most pluralistic and diverse system in the world. It has inherited most of the existing university ideas from Europe, and it has adopted them in a very flexible way. It has also invented new types of higher education institutions, such as the community colleges, land-grant universities and corporate universities. American higher education institutions have been expansion-minded since the War for Independence and have generally shown a willingness to stretch existing resources to support new ventures. By the 19th century, the United States had laid the basis for a highly diversified and stratified system that provided opportunities of universal access to higher education to all of its citizens, at a time when all higher education systems in Europe were extremely selective and based on meritocracy (Trow, 2000).

The United States has the leading research universities in the world, side by side with community colleges open to all who wish to pursue post-secondary education. It has large-scale multi-campus universities that teach many thousands of students side by side with small-scale colleges. It operates broad comprehensive universities concurrently with specialised institutes. It has created what Clark Kerr called a "multiversity model" (Kerr, 1963).

American higher education has always been characterised by the confluence of different educational practices. The early colonial colleges followed the curricular practice of Oxford and Cambridge, and the Scottish universities have had a significant impact in shaping comprehensive universities, which include faculties of arts, science and social science and professional schools. The modular system was also adopted from Scotland. The Americans have defined an acceptable 'academic currency' from the outset (Trow, 2000). The currency of a 'unit' is used in all American higher education institutions, and it enables ease of transfer of academic studies from one institution to another. The European Credit Transfer System introduced by the Bologna Process aims at achieving a comparable academic currency in Europe (Bolag, 2003). In the late 19th century, the land-grant colleges and universities added a strong practical dimension of training and service to society to the more familiar traditions, and the new *Humboldtian* idea of a research university has been most successfully implemented in the leading research universities of the USA (Guri-Rosenblit, 2006a). The idea of the federal university of London was adopted in the Unites States in the form of multi-campus universities, such as the reputable University of California system that is composed nowadays of ten high status universities, or the network of the State University of New York (SUNY) that is composed of different types of higher education institutions.

One of the most unique features of the American higher education system is not merely its diversity, but most specifically its flexibility, which can hardly be found elsewhere. Even students at community colleges can transfer eventually to leading research universities if they excel in their studies. In the three-tier California system, there is a written agreement between the community colleges, the state universities and the University of California systems, that defines exactly the percentage of students from community colleges that can be admitted each year even to a prestigious university like UCBerkeley, and continue there their third and fourth year of studies towards an undergraduate degree from the renowned research university.

European higher education has evolved in a different way. Particularly after the foundation of the nation states in the 19th century, the national higher education systems were perceived mainly as training the political, intellectual and professional elites of each state. Each nation shaped the structure of its higher education system on unique underlying premises that seemed to fit best its political and societal needs. Multiple academic cultures flourished within the different states, manifested through diverse access policies, many study tracks leading to a wide range of diplomas and degrees of different lengths and reputation, and a wide spectrum of different types of tertiary and higher education institutions.

As aforementioned, some of the systems, which, as in England, were quite diversified, in the sense that they contained many types of universities and other higher education institutions, have not necessarily turned into mass-access oriented systems. Countries with a socialist ideology have stayed quite elitist in their access policies to higher education. The fact that all of the former communist countries have provided higher education free of charge, has not turned them into systems that adopted a mass access policy. Most of the Eastern European countries had a very low access rate until the 1990s, ranging from 11% to 23% (Neave, 2003; Kovac et al., 2006; UNESCO, 2003). Even in the communist countries higher education was perceived for decades as a privilege based on meritocracy rather than as a civil right.

The flexibility of the American system, enabling students to move from one type of higher education institution to another has been nearly non-existent in most countries. It is almost unthinkable to this date to move in the midst of academic studies from Paris University to a *grand école*, from a college in Israel to the Hebrew University, from a 'new' English university to Oxford and Cambridge. Even the most diversified higher education systems in Europe portray inflexible patterns of mobility between different types of higher education institutions.

The last decade has witnessed far-reaching reform in Europe, aimed at consolidating and integrating the various national higher education systems into a harmonised and balanced continental system. On June 19, 1999 representatives of twenty nine countries signed the Bologna Declaration and set in train an intensive process which aims at establishing a harmonised and/or unified Higher Education Area of Europe by 2010. By the Berlin meeting of the Ministers of Education in 2003, there were already forty countries that had signed the Bologna Declaration (Commission of the European Communities, 2003).

It appears that European higher education systems, under the Bologna Process, are currently becoming more flexible. The Bologna Declaration specified the means to achieve its goal: the use of a common three-tier degree structure (BA, MA and doctorate), the Diploma Supplement, the European Credit Transfer System, quality evaluation and the Europeanisation of academic curricula. Many higher education systems in Central and Eastern Europe had been based for centuries on a five-year first degree structure (which is equivalent to an MA degree). No bachelor level studies were available. The lengthy degree resulted, among other things, in a high drop-out rate during the study period.

Each stage in advancing the Bologna Process requires greater commitment to the commonality of purpose and action in the field of higher education, so that, by this year (2010), higher education services can flow freely from one side of the continent to the other, as material goods do today (Commission of the European Communities, 2003; UNESCO, 2003). Students of all ages will draw on the most convenient services, relevant in the terms of their intellectual interests, career development or social commitments. For learners, and administrators, the freedom of movement in a common European intellectual space will offer equal conditions of access to many providers and users of higher education, equal conditions of assessment and recognition of services, of skills and competencies, and equal conditions of work and employment. The tools given by the Bologna Declaration are intended to invent a European model of higher education sufficiently strong to establish its attractiveness *vis-á-vis* the rest of the world, and particularly *vis-á-vis* the American model.

Concurrently with decreasing the diversity between higher education systems at the macro-level, the architects of the Bologna Process have stressed from the outset that it is of tremendous importance to acknowledge the legitimacy of institutional diversity and heterogeneity of academic cultures. They emphasised that diversity must be preserved, even if convergence and common issues of concern should be implemented and pushed forward (UNESCO, 2003). In other words, the trend of convergence does not remove the inherent diversity of higher education institutions in European countries. Various types of higher education institutions will continue to operate in all national settings, and they will portray both vertical differences (based on various hierarchical and ranking criteria) and horizontal differences (targeted to different student clienteles) (Guri-Rosenblit, 2005; Neave, 2003). However, it is most likely that institutes of the same kind, such as 'world-class' research universities will exhibit in the future a greater resemblance (Altbach, 2004; European Commission, 2004).

In the long run, the Bologna Process is likely to influence access policies and practices in many other higher education systems in other continents. Many countries in Africa, Asia and Latin America are in close relations with European countries through the processes of globalisation and internationalisation, and the changes of higher education structures, diplomas and accreditation are likely to affect their policies and practices. It is most likely that the broadening of access in many third world countries will be characterised by greater diversity of their higher education institutions and by a greater flexibility of movement between higher education institutions within national borders and beyond them.

Access-Exit Policies

Access policies have changed drastically in the last thirty years all over the world. Many higher education systems have moved to a mass-oriented and even a universal access policy (Trow, 2000). The target of reaching at least a 50% participation rate of the relevant age cohort in higher or more broadly tertiary education is echoed in policy documents of dozens of countries in the last decade (Kaiser & O'Heron, 2005). However, access policies do not automatically reflect exit policies. Drop-out rates in some higher education systems are very high, and are a result of different dominant cultures in various national settings that perceive totally differently the role of the state in providing adequate infrastructures and support systems to assure high retention rates. In countries like Germany, France and Italy, the democratisation of higher education has been manifested through providing higher education to all high school graduates free of charge, but it is up to the students to prove their capabilities and to cope with the study requirements and the poor infrastructure of many overcrowded universities. In some universities, classes are crowded with hundreds of students who can hardly see the lecturing professors, not to speak of being able to communicate with them.

The English higher education system has been very concerned with the importance of the exit/graduation phase from its outset. The Oxbridge model makes a clear distinction between the role of the residential colleges that teach small numbers of students under the close supervision of caring tutors, and the role of the university that examines the students at the end of three years. To this date, Oxford and Cambridge universities have refused to adopt the modular system that was adopted by all other universities in England in 1992. Their students do not get grades throughout their studies. Their degree and its level (the Honours degree is divided into first, upper second, lower second and third levels) is totally dependent on the comprehensive exams that the students take at the end of their studies apart from certain groups of subjects which also have a block of examinations at the end of the year. London University, which was initially established as an examining body for studies conducted in colleges outside the university, still has to this date a third of its students registered as external students from all over the world. They do not study in the Institutes of the University of London, but do take its final examinations.

The emphasis of the English academic culture on the exit phase is also manifested through the unique external examiners' system. The external examiners' system seeks to ensure the comparability of standards across higher education institutions, by appointing external academics to evaluate, and even modify the content and the structure of the final examinations in any given university (except Oxford and Cambridge, whose professors serve as external examiners, but are not examined by others). Even the examinations that are given in international locations in various countries by UK universities are monitored through external examiners.

Such an emphasis on the crucial importance of the final phase of academic studies in the UK higher education system from its very early start may explain to a great extent the fact that the UK higher education has one of the highest retention rates in the world – 83% in 2005 (Clancy, 2006; Eggins, 2006).

In some countries in the Far East, like Japan and Vietnam, the graduation rates are also very high. In Japan it was 85% in 2003 (OECD, 2004), and in Vietnam it was nearly 95% in 2002 (Nguyen, 2006). It seems that the unique feature of the Chinese and Japanese cultures which emphasises the importance of working hard and succeeding after the individual is given the opportunity in any given field, be it sports, education, or work, is manifested also in higher education. In Vietnam, for instance, students have to pass very demanding entrance examinations. After they are admitted, they try their best to fulfil all the requirements in order to get the degree they enrolled for. However, there are differences between different types of higher education institutions. It is less competitive to get into a non-public university than into a public university in Vietnam. Nearly 7% drop out from non-public universities as compared to only 3.5% from public universities (ibid). In any case, the attrition rates in Vietnam are very low.

In the former Communist countries, the retention rates were also very high until the 1990s, since the participation rates were also very low. Those who got admitted were expected to complete their studies, and the majority of students did so. The situation changed after the reconstruction of the former Soviet Block. The higher education systems expanded dramatically, without providing necessary infra-structures for high retention, and by enabling many outside private providers to operate within the national jurisdictions of these countries. As a result, the attrition rates in some of the former Eastern European countries are currently very high. Poland, for instance, which expanded its higher education system hugely, enables nearly 70% of its relevant age cohort to study in various higher education institutions, but it has a drop-out rate of 41% (OECD, 2004), and the Czech Republic, which currently admits only 30% of the relevant age cohort to higher education, still experiences a drop-out rate of over 50% (ibid).

As mentioned previously, many European countries have very high drop-out rates ranging from 62% in Switzerland, 55% in Italy, 45% in Germany, 42% in Austria to 34% in France (ibid). However, theretention/drop-out statistics should also handled with care. Some of the statistics include the completion of two-year studies, as in France, which are not included in many other countries. In France, for instance, 45% complete the first two-year cycle, and 21% complete the three-year cycle (Goastellec, 2006), which are combined together in a completion rate of 66% – definitely problematic statistics. Unquestionably, the Bologna Process will contribute in the future to the creation of various measures that will assist in improving the retention rates in many European countries.

Public-Private Sectors

The interrelation between public and private higher education institutions portraysdifferent academic cultures and an impact on access policies in different countries. In some countries, there is almost no private sector in the higher education system. In England, for example, apart from Buckingham University which is private small-scale university, there are no private universities and colleges, and in Scotland and Ireland the proportion of private institutions is very low (Clancy, 2006, OECD, 2004).

The United States, on the other hand, has a very strong component of private higher education institutions, and it is particularly proud of its private research universities, that have established themselves as leading world class universities, and are the envy of and models for imitation by many nations. Japan, China, India and Germany have all proclaimed in the last decade that they are intending to establish world-class universities comparable to the American ones. However, the unique interrelation between the academic institutions and the corporate world in the USA non-existent in any other country (Levy, 2008). The generous donations and endowments of the business world and private alumni to American universities are the envy of all other countries, and are hard to imitate, because they are built on strong cultural roots that have been cultivated for centuries in American society.

Private higher education is far from being uniform. Only a few private institutions provide elite or semi-elite options. The rising bulk of private higher education institutions throughout the world accommodate mainly the exploding demand for higher education. Beyond the few leading private research universities in the US, there are other types of private institutions, like Phoenix University, that constitutes the largest for-profit distance teaching university in the USA, many non-profit and for-profit consortia, and corporate universities that cater to various clienteles and expand access opportunities in American higher education.

Quite evidently, privatisation constitutes one of the most striking global changes in higher education systems in the 21st century (Altbach et al., 2009; Douglass et al., 2009; Dogramaci, 2008; Levy, 2008). Privatisation has spread in recent years to Asia, Latin America, Africa, Central and Eastern Europe and the Middle East. In some countries, the percentage of private higher education institutions is striking. In Indonesia, 96% of the higher education institutions are private; in South Korea they constitute 87%; and in Japan 86% (Tilak, 2008).

The widening of access to higher education in Europe has also been linked to the development of many private higher education institutions. In some of the countries of Central and Eastern Europe, which experienced enormous increases of students, the proportion of private institutions in the overall number of higher education institutions is remarkably high. For instance, in Slovenia the private institutions constitute 82% of the total number of higher education institutes; in Poland - 63%; in Romania - 60%, and in Hungary - 52% (UNESCO, 2003, p. 5). But the prevailing number of these private universities and colleges is small, and provides mainly high demand subjects of study in business administration, economics and some other social science subjects.

The flourishing of these private enterprises has drastically changed the external and internal boundaries of many higher education systems, and affected the horizontal and vertical patterns of diversity in each national milieu (Guri-Rosenblit, 2005). Unlike the well-established leading private universities in the USA, most of the private providers in European countries, as well as in many other countries worldwide, have weak infrastructure, relatively unstable full-time academic faculty, and they operate mainly for profit.

The emergence of a plethora of new providers of higher education, particularly private providers, has created an acute problem. In order to ensure the harmonisation of higher education at the system level, it is of tremendous importance to set stringent quality assurance measures. Nowadays, the Bologna Process in Europe aims at establishing accreditation agencies, both as state agencies and self-regulatory bodies of academic institutions, in order to enhance a quality assurance culture, setting clear criteria for the evaluation of the quality of higher education provided by both old and new higher education institutions. The introduction of the 'European Credit Transfer System' is viewed as a principle instrument in achieving transparency of the quality of academic programmes. Quality assurance mechanisms, the definition of clear "academic currencies" and diploma supplements will provide a more homogeneous and articulated degree system, which will enable easy comparison of diverse degree requirements and structures (Bolag, 2003, UNESCO, 2003). Quality assurance mechanisms have also been established in the last decade in many Latin American and Asian countries.

Language and Globalisation

Universities in different national settings are entrusted with cultivating the national language/s as an important cultural asset. In Ireland, for instance, prior to the war of independence between 1916–1921, higher education institutions were pivotal in the revival and spread of the Irish language as a spoken and literary medium which became a major political objective linked to the development of a sense of national identity (Clancy, 2006). Such was the case in Israel with the Hebrew language. When the Technion was established in 1924, its professors wanted to teach in the German language. A "war of languages" took place, and the final decision was that all studies in educational institutions, including higher education, would be conducted only in Hebrew. National languages will continue to develop and thrive in the future. However, in the globalised world we live in, it is quite obvious that English has become the lingua franca of the academic world, and this trend will intensify in the future. In China alone, there is evidence that in recent years five million Chinese are added each year to the number who are "English speaking". It is not merely the major language of conferences, academic publications and research journals, but it also has an important impact on increasing the number of transnational students. It is not by accident that the English speaking countries are the main advocates of transnational education and support the finalisation of the GATS (General Agreement on Trade in Services).

The UK is currently one of the leading exporters of higher education. According to the Shanghai Ranking of Higher Education Institutions, the UK has the second largest global market share, (behind the US), which is worth up to £11 billion directly and £12 billion indirectly to the UK economy each year (Eggins, 2006). UK universities are international organisations with long-established links with universities and other organisations around the world. They have been consistently successful in welcoming international students and researchers attracted by the wide range of high quality courses and educational support, and a world class research base. In 2003/04 there were 213,000 international students and 104,000 students from other EU countries in UK higher education institutions. There were also many more international and EU students on exchange (Socrates-Erasmus) and study-abroad programmes in UK universities (ibid).

The UK is committed to a strategy of international competitiveness through the Prime Minister's Initiative (PMI). Launched in 1999 by Tony Blair, the then Prime Minister, the initiative aimed to increase the number of international students in UK higher education, recognising their importance in fostering international relations and bringing long-term political and economic benefits. Targets were set to attract an additional 50,000 international students into higher education and an additional 25,000 students into further education by 2004/05. This target was achieved ahead of time. China was the largest supplier of overseas students to UK. The UK Government has funded the British Council (with offices in 110 countries) to launch a major five-year world-wide marketing initiative to encourage international students to study in the UK. This campaign includes the branding initiative, Education UK, designed to help UK higher education institutions promote themselves (ibid).

The Australian government has also greatly increased its numbers of transnational students in the last decade. It aims to have one million transnational students in 2025, a seventh of the total numbers (Guri-Rosenblit, 2005).

Transnational education is a potent manifestation of the impact of globalisation upon higher education, and is potentially the most significant one (Altbach et al., 2009; Douglass et al., 2009; Deem, 2001; Enders & Fulton, 2002). The positive aspects of transnational education include: widening of learning opportunities at various higher education levels by providing more choice for citizens in any given national jurisdiction; challenging traditional education systems by introducing more competition and innovative programmes and delivery methods; helping make higher education more competitive; assisting in diversifying the budgeting of higher education; and benefiting through links with prestigious institutions, mainly in developing countries. For instance, several prestigious American universities are operating currently in Qatar through the funding of the 'Qatar Foundation for Education, Science and Community Development', a non-profit organisation founded in 1995 by the Emir of Qatar (ibid). Cornell University opened there a branch of its medical school; Texas A&M University operates an engineering programme; Virginia Commonwealth University operates a programme in design arts; and Carnegie Mellon University has opened a campus for undergraduate studies in computer science and business. These respected universities provide high-level higher education studies in their field of expertise.

However, there are also negative aspects of transnational education. Currently many unregulated providers of higher education operate for-profit in many countries. They are not subject to external or internal audit/monitoring processes, and their operation remains outside official national quality assurance regimes. Many of these institutions constitute 'degree mills' that provide low level education. Furthermore, some claim that there is unfair advantage enjoyed by some transnational providers in comparison to the strictly regulated national providers, that might cause loss of income to the latter. Unquestionably, the intricacy of relationships between different types of transnational providers, delivery methods and programmes, creates a highly complicated situation, which affects the horizontal and vertical patterns of higher education structures at the national and international levels.

It is most likely that transnational education will grow in the future, and it will accelerate competition between various types of higher education providers. At the same time, much greater attention will be devoted by national higher education authorities and international organisations to monitoring and defining appropriate quality assurance regulations to ensure the quality of the higher education provided by transnational providers, as well as to secure and preserve the traditional values of higher education.

CONCLUDING REMARKS

This chapter has highlighted the importance of the historical background in order to understand how the external and internal boundaries of higher education systems are defined, and how these boundaries, as well as the unique features of academic cultures, affect the formation of access policies and retention patterns in various national settings. External boundaries define which institutions are included in or excluded from any given higher education system, and the internal boundaries relate to the overall structure and hierarchy of a higher education system. There are unique patterns in the historical development of higher education systems. In the UK, for instance, since the 15th century, there seems to have been a pattern of inventing new university models in order to cater to the needs of different clienteles and to be attentive to new societal and national needs. In France, on the other hand, since Napoleonic times, a rigid system, which distinguishes between a small elitist sector and equal status multiple universities, has been established, and this structure, with little amendment, exists to this date.

Political rule has an important impact on shaping the ethos and operating practices of various higher education systems. The case of Vietnam clearly reflects the impact of the Chinese rulers, the domination of the former Soviet Union, and the influence of France and the USA on shaping the nature of its higher education institutions throughout its history. However, the direct ruler does not always have a say in the local higher education system. In the case of Israel, its first higher education institutions were established during the British Mandate, but they were based on the academic tradition of the founding professors who came mainly from Germany, and thus were founded on the tradition of the Humboldtian research universities.

Many countries have a unique historical background that greatly affects the dominant culture of their higher education systems. The development of the Irish higher education reflects from the outset the tension between the Catholics and Protestants. South Africa, as an Apartheid state, had built its higher education system on the underlying premises of segregation and partition, and in the last fifteen years is in the process of totally restructuring its higher education. Ethiopia, as a developing country, has built its higher education system in line with its economic and social needs, and has been assisted by many outside superpowers, ranging from the USA, the former Soviet Union, other European countries, to international bodies, like UNESCO and the World Bank.

Most higher education systems expanded extensively in recent decades. Diversification constitutes a common feature of widening access to higher education. But diversification itself does not suffice to turn a higher education system into a mass-oriented one. Flexibility turns out to be a significant feature in ensuring greater access, and greater equity in higher education. In this sense, the American higher education system is the most pluralistic and flexible system in the world, and it provides an illuminating example of how it is possible to nurture the leading world class universities, and at the same time to provide opportunities to all to study in community colleges, and for those who excel to move to elitist research universities. The Bologna Process in Europe is currently aiming at increasing flexibility, mainly between various higher education systems, and establishing a European higher education system that will be on a par with the USA.

Academic cultures also affect policies of retention. In some countries, like Germany, Italy and France, the democratisation of higher education has been manifested mainly through access policies, but the drop-out rates are very high. In the UK, Japan, Vietnam, and the former communist countries, the retention rates have been very high due to different features built into their academic cultures. It seems that concern about retention rates will remain high on the agendas of higher education systems worldwide.

The nature of private higher education is also related to national academic cultures. It is tremendously difficult, if not impossible, to imitate the unique nature and status of the leading private research universities in the USA. Most of the new private higher education ventures are operating mainly for-profit, and some are considered to provide a low level of study. Differential quality assurance agencies and mechanisms have been established in the last decade in order to monitor the quality of higher education institutions, with a particular emphasis on the new private providers.

Last, but not least, in the globalised and internationalised world we live in, the English language constitutes a very important vehicle for promoting and widening transnational education, which means that in the near future millions of students will either study outside their national jurisdictions, or study towards degrees offered by external bodies, or through distance education. The English speaking countries have a significant advantage in transnational education. Already, several countries in Europe and elsewhere have started providing some of their academic courses in English, in order to be part of this huge competitive venture.

Altogether, the various historical and cultural variables that were briefly examined in this chapter, demonstrate that any comparative study on access, equity and retention policies has to relate to many more facets than the descriptive statistics.

BIBLIOGRAPHY

Altbach, P. G. (2004). The costs and benefits of world-class universities. *Academe, 90*(1), 1–5.

Altbach, P. G., Reisberg, L., & Rumbley, L. E. (2009). *Trends in global higher education: Tracking an academic revolution.* A report prepared for the UNESCO 2009 World Conference on Higher Education. Paris: UNESCO.

Bell, R., & Tight, M. (1993). *Open Universities: A British tradition?* Buckingham: The Society of Research into Higher Education & The Open University Press.

Bolag, B. (2003, September 26). European higher education seeks a common currency. *Chronicle of Higher Education,* 52.

Burns, E. M., Lerner, R., & Meacham, S. (1980). *Western civilizations: Their history and their culture* (Vol. 1). New York: W.W. Norton Co.

Clancy, P. (2005). Education policy. In S. Quin, P. Kennedy, A. Matthews, & G. Kiely (Eds.), *Contemporary Irish social policy* (pp. 85–86). Dublin: University College Dublin Press.

Clancy, P. (2006). *Access and equity: National report of Ireland.* An internal paper, New Century Scholars Program of Fulbright.

Commission of the European Communities. (2003). *The role of the Universities in the Europe of knowledge.* Brussels: European Commission.

Deem, R. (2001). Globalisation, new managerialism, academic capitalism and entrepreunerialism in universities: Is the local dimension still important? *Comparative Education Review, 37*(1), 7–20.

Dogramaci, A. (2008). *Private University initiatives in Turkey: The Bilkent experience.* A paper presented at the conference on Privatization in Higher Education, Samuel Neeman Institute, The Technion, Haifa.

Douglass, J. A., King, C. J., & Feller, E. (Eds.). (2009). *Globalization's muse: Universities and higher education systems in a changing world.* UC Berkeley, CA: Berkeley Public Policy Press.

Eggins, H. (2006). *Access and equity: National report of United Kingdom.* An internal paper, New Century Scholars Program of Fulbright.

Enders, J., & Fulton, O. (Eds.). (2002). *Higher education in a globalizing world: International trends and mutual observations.* Dordrecht: Kluwer.

European Commission. (2004, April 23). The ingredients for building a world-class university. *ORDIS News.*

Goastellec, G. (2006). *Access and equity: National report of France.* An internal paper, New Century Scholars Program of Fulbright.

Guri-Rosenblit, S. (1999). *Distance and campus Universities: Tension and interactions. A comparative study of five countries.* Oxford: Pergamon & International Association of Universities.

Guri-Rosenblit, S. (2005). Higher education in transition: Horizontal and vertical patterns of diversity. In R. Nata (Ed.), *New directions in higher education* (pp. 23–45). New York: Nova Science Publishers.

Guri-Rosenblit, S. (2006a, June 19). *The many ideas of a 'University' and their diverse manifestations.* An invited presentation at the Lower Silesia University, Wroclaw.

Guri-Rosenblit, S. (2006b). *Access and equity: National report of Israel.* An internal paper, New Century Scholars Program of Fulbright.

Kaiser, F., & O'Heron, O. (2005). *Myths and methods on access and participation in higher education.* Enschede: CHEPS, University of Twente.

Kerr, C. (1963). *The uses of University.* Cambridge, MA: Harvard University Press.

Kovac, V., Ledic, J., & Rafajac, B. (2006). *Understanding University organizational culture: The Croatian example.* Frankfurt: Peter Lang.

Levy, D. (2008). *Private higher education's global surge: Emulating US patterns?* A paper presented at the conference on Privatization in Higher Education, Samuel Neeman Institute, The Technion, Haifa.

McPherson, A. (1973). Selections and survivals: A sociology of the ancient Scottish universities. In R. Brown (Ed.), *Knowledge, education and cultural change*. London: Tavistock.

Neave, G. (2003). On the return from Babylon: A long voyage around history, ideology and systems change. In J. File & L. Goedegebuure (Eds.), *Real-time systems: Reflections on higher education in the Czech Republic, Hungary, Poland and Slovenia* (pp. 15–40). Enschede: CHEPS, University of Twente.

Nguyen, P. N. (2006). *Access and equity: National report of Vietnam*. An internal paper, New Century Scholars Program of Fulbright.

OECD. (2004). *Education at a glance: OECD indicators 2004*. Paris: Organisation for Economic Co-Operation and Development.

Rothblatt, S. (1997). The idea of a university and its antithesis. In S. Rothblatt (Ed.), *The modern University and its discontents: the fate of Newman's legacies in Britain and America* (pp. 1–49). Cambridge: Cambridge University Press.

Tilak, J. B. G. (2008). *Current trends in private higher education in Asia*. A paper presented at the conference on Privatization in Higher Education, Samuel Neeman Institute, The Technion, Haifa.

Trow, M. (2000). *From mass higher education to Universal access: The American advantage*. Research and Occasional Paper Series, Center for Studies in Higher Education, UC Berkeley.

UNESCO. (2003). *Report on trends and developments in higher education in Europe: 1998–2003*. Paris: European Centre for Higher Education (UNESCO-CEPES).

Yizengaw, T. (2006). *Access and equity: National report of Ethiopia*. An internal paper, New Century Scholars Program of Fulbright.

MERIT AND EQUALITY:
INTERNATIONAL TRENDS AND LOCAL RESPONSES

Introduction: Access and Equity

When one compares the development of different societies, the tension between meritocratic access to higher education and equity in access reveals distinctive histories of access and plural definitions of equity. The comparison also underlines the internationally accepted fact that increasing access to higher education constitutes a pre-requisite for the development of any given society, and that higher education, in order to be equitable, should offer access to students regardless of their social origin. Thus, the definition of equity means that equality of opportunity should be offered to all the citizens of any given society.

The concept of equity is recent. It appears during the 20th century with the slow recognition of women having equal rights with men. Before this period, inequalities between individuals were perceived as legitimate and have characterised the social structure and organisation of societies. Merit was by its nature "inherited". It was linked to the belief that merit was not evenly spread in society but located within a group, a class, a race, etc. Both concepts of merit and equality have been redefined and transformed throughout the last century. The definition of merit has shifted to one of the recognition of individual accomplishment while equity has been perceived as the even distribution of rights and, later on, of opportunities. The policies relating to access to higher education mirror these transformations of meanings. This chapter describes the evolution of a process that moves from a notion of inherited merit through equality of rights to equality of opportunities to positive discrimination for disadvantaged groups.

The first section of the chapter deals with the history of "inherited" merit. The second section is dedicated to the identification and analysis of four developments that have redefined the historical meaning of inherited merit, while the third section presents evolving norms of equality, accompanied by a commentary on the diversification of higher education structures and institutions. A fourth section gives an account of another determinant in the implementation of equity policies: statistical databases and their relationship to an intrinsic understanding of any society's legitimate identities and national priorities. Building from all these dimensions, a fifth section analyses how the continuing tension between "merit" and "equality" is handled, specifically in elite institutions through the diffusion of admission tools.

The ultimate goal of this comparison is to identify international trends and local realities related to access policies in higher education, putting in perspective the diffusion of norms within the configurations of higher education systems. Based on an analysis of a number of countries represented in our Fulbright research group (Ethiopia, France, Ireland, Israel, South Africa, the United Kingdom, the United States, Vietnam), and drawing from selective examples taken from these countries, this chapter reveals that higher education systems are becoming more closely aligned in the way they deal with merit and equality in their admission policies.

INHERITED MERIT: THE DOMINANT NORM IN THE PAST[1]

In earlier periods higher education systems have always been organised around the principle of merit, commonly defined in a restrictive manner. Merit was considered to be inherited, or, to borrow from Roemer's theory (1998), to draw upon circumstances. This norm evolved during three historical periods each characterized by the organisation of universities in different ways.

In the Middle Ages, no academic requirements limited access to universities, not even the necessity to be literate or to have previously attended school. European universities were not yet formalised organisations: they could be defined as "communal corporate organisations" (Schwinges, 1992). The various institutions of the education sector did not carry out a particular role in society. In the early modern period, universities were more socially selective than previously, and dedicated to the education of an elite. The preparation of the students was predominantly concerned with the arts faculties, which, as a consequence, were characterised by the highest level of attendance but also by a lower level of prestige (Di Simone, 1996).

From the 19th century, academic qualifications became pre-requisites to access higher education. This development went hand in hand with the development of separate tracks within secondary school systems, thus enhancing class differences in access to higher education (Rüegg, 2004).

During these three periods, although to a varying extent and modified by specific national or institutional processes, three main "circumstances" can be seen to characterise "inherited merit", which influence access: being a man, belonging to a broad social group, and, within that, being a member of a particular social group.

Being a man

Being a man has long been a condition of access to higher education. The first exceptions to this rule appeared in the 17th century: a woman in Utrecht was allowed to follow university classes on condition that she remain hidden behind a curtain. In Padua, in 1678, Elena Lucrezia Cornaro Piscopia was the first woman to be awarded a doctorate in philosophy. This distinction can be viewed as a social exception in that she belonged to the old Venetian aristocracy, which was highly powerful and influential (Di Simone, 1996). But these exceptions did not presage the opening of higher education to women. Fifty years passed before such an exception occurred again and then only for women coming from very powerful upper class families. One must wait until the end of the 19th and beginning of the 20th century for women's education to take hold, for example with the creation of women's colleges in Cambridge and Oxford. In 1901, only 3% of French students were women. At that time, the record was probably held by a Swiss university: in

1903–1904, 35% of students at the University of Bern were women. However, this example did not indicate a particular progressiveness within Swiss society: nine out of every ten of these students were not Swiss but foreign upper class students (Ringer, 2004), and mainly Russian aristocrats.

Indeed, until at least the beginning of the 20th century, this situation illustrated an international norm that went beyond the sole context of higher education: the whole organisation of society reflected a patriarchal organisation which simultaneously indicated the superiority of men and the "inferiority" of women, as formalised in national laws[2]. Men's exclusive access to higher education pointed up the link between a restrictive conception of equality held by society and the norms and principles used in organising access to higher education. More importantly, the slowness in making higher education available to women was conditioned by another "circumstance" restricting access: that of social status.

Belonging to a social group

Indeed, in terms of the norm of "inherited merit", social standing is a determinant in access to higher education, as revealed by the fact that, from the Middle Ages, one of the very few formal requirements to be admitted to university consisted in being able to provide a proof of one's legitimate birth and of one's Christian baptism (Schwinges, 1992). Other criteria indicated that attendance at university was largely an urban affair. All European universities apart from the two English ones were located in mediaeval towns of more than 10,000 inhabitants.

However, depending on the countries and the historical period, the most important element in accessing university (even more important in the model of the Parisian University than in the Bologna model) consisted in being admitted as a scholar to the circle of a 'magister'[3]. And this depended on the prevailing social norms: "the student upon entrance to the university selected his magister in accordance with the rules of local provenance, friendship, acquaintance, introductions and patronage (…) (Schwinges, 1992, p.174). The student must thus be able to identify himself and to make his social connections explicit.

At another level, the ability to identify oneself was also central when it came to exemption from fees, receiving financial aid or getting community support: for example, if in the Middle Ages and early modern period, admission fees were *de jure* applicable to all students, they were *de facto* primarily applied to middle class students, also called "divites" (the rich). Selection thus operated on two criteria: social status (i.e. being part of the aristocracy) and economic status (i.e. being part of the rich middle class) (Schwinges, 1992).

It was therefore necessary not only to belong to a general social group, but, depending on the places and periods, to belong to certain specific social groups.

Belonging to the Right Church and the Right Social Group

Besides the necessity for each student to be identified as part of a social group, the necessary conditions for access also included ascribed socio-cultural groups and religious affiliation. In the Middle Ages, it was about being Christian, living in an urban area and belonging to the aristocracy or the middle class. In early modern Europe, in the 16th century, a shift towards an 'aristocratisation' of the universities can generally be observed although in some countries (in England for example) the number of "commoners'" sons increased. In the 18th century, the University of the Enlightenment tended to become more socially selective, increasingly excluding the less well-to-do.

In the early Modern Age, religious affiliation became even more crucial as, for example, many Protestant universities made the profession of the reformed faith compulsory, while in 1564, Pope Pius IV made it compulsory to be of Catholic faith to graduate (Ridder-Symoens, 2003). At institutional levels, those restrictions were adapted to local rationales, for example, in favouring the foreign students, which in some places accounted for a large part of the student body. Confessional restrictions had a strong impact on Jews, who were not allowed to graduate. Once again, local variations of this constraint could be found, mainly in Italian universities, which registered Jewish students. Padua, for example, charged registration fees three times higher for Jewish students. In the 17th century, Dutch universities adopted the Italian example, followed by German universities at the beginning of the 18th century (with an exception made for the Doctorate). But it is only in the 18th century that these religious restrictions were abandoned (Di Simone, 1996), although not everywhere: in Oxford and Cambridge, one must wait until 1850's for Catholics and dissenters to be allowed to matriculate, and 1871 to be entitled to graduate (Ringer, 2004).

Thus, the structure of society informed access to university, and also access to degrees. In the 15th century, the high costs linked to student life for the middle classes made it very difficult for them to pursue their studies to the completion of a degree. As a result, degrees played an important role when it came to competition for ecclesiastical and secular positions (Rüegg, 1992). Family background was an important determinant: in Europe at the end of the Middle Ages, students were mainly part of the so-called "middle or upper classes". The beginnings of higher education systems, independently of structure, developed in terms of the double principle of a certain social mobility (mainly between bourgeoisie and noblesse) and the domination of specific professions: "studying had become a common practice in some royal officers', lawyers' or doctors' families" (Charle, Verger, 2004).

University matriculation had progressively been introduced as a requirement: this prerogative of Rectors was aimed at controlling the devolution of privileges and registering the names of those entitled to benefit (Schwinges, 1992).

Of course, the situation varied depending on the countries. At the end of the 18th century, the question of the education of the aristocracy was handled in different ways. For example, while most of the systems tended to be socially highly elitist, in Austria, Joseph II decided in 1783 to close two academies in Vienna and use their resources to finance scholarships for public school students. Every country has developed a higher education system with its own specific approach to access. However, the general trend found in European universities from their inception to at least the end of the 18th century is characterised by selection based on social status.

Preparing Leaders for Church and Society

Indeed, the various means of access are linked to the functions carried out by higher education institutions. During the Middle Ages, churches, monarchs and cities expected universities to educate individuals that could afterwards provide services for them. Popes expected universities not only to provide them with scholars to be recruited for their offices (and, to some extent, with potential cardinals), but also to strengthen the power of the Church. The same rationale was pursued by the European monarchies who wanted to use university graduates to consolidate their administrations and counterbalance the power of the aristocracy (Rüegg, 1992).

The transformation of European universities that occurred between the 16th and the 18th centuries transformed them from "corporate and independent bodies into public institutions aimed at creating a ruling class" (Di Simone, 1996). During the 19th century in the United States, the children of the White, Anglo-Saxon, and Protestant social group of the East Coast were the first to gain access to the private Colleges that were being created. In South Africa, the first Colleges, were built in Cape Province (1830–1870) for, initially, the children of British migrants. In Indonesia, the first colleges, (transformed after independence into universities) were created by the Dutch in the former Batavia to provide access to their offspring and those of the *Priyayi*, the Indonesian elite who worked for the colonisers.

Thus, the concept of "inherited merit" can be traced back to the domination of a particular group and the necessity for the ruling class to reproduce itself through higher education. This seems to characterise the inception of all higher education systems independent of their origins.

SHIFT IN INTERNATIONAL RATIONALES

This norm of inherited merit has progressively been challenged by the development of a new understanding of the role of the higher education sector. In the context of the shift towards industrialised societies and, later, to information societies, four main rationales can be identified that have had a strong influence on access norms and policies: human capital theories, democratisation, the importance of science and the knowledge society.

Human Capital Theories

Human capital theories probably find their roots in Adam Smith's 18th century examination of the link between instruction and productivity. But it is in the 1960's that American researchers (Clark, 1962, Schultz, 1963, Becker, 1964, Drucker, 1969, etc.) developed the concept by establishing a relationship between the level of education of the workforce and economic growth. Consequently, education has been considered as an investment aimed at improving productivity, economic growth, and social stability. Thus an increase in access to higher education was called for.

Besides legitimising the necessity to improve the level of education for everyone in society, human capital theories and their alternatives have been highly debated. They assume two underlying principles, each one of which is open to question, and both are disputed.

The first underlying principle concerns the collective effect of educational investment in education: investing in higher education is supposed to produce a collective improvement in the level of development of the whole society, and in economic growth. Fitzgerald and Delaney (cited in Heller, 2002), for example, have analysed data showing that "eliminating income-related gaps in access to post-secondary education would add hundreds of billions of dollars to national income annually". However, other researchers have argued that the relation between the level of education of a society and economic growth was complex and dependant upon other variables. Aghion and Cohen (2003), for instance, have associated the effect of education on economic growth with the degree of economic development of a country, and other research (Jaoul Grammare, 2007) has pointed out that higher education and economic growth were linked in the American and Japanese cases but not in the French one.

The second underlying principle deals with the individual economic return on investment in education and thus with individual benefits. Individuals who have invested in education are supposed to have a more advantageous position in the marketplace and better earnings. This is exemplified in Hungary, Indonesia, Portugal and the US, where 30–40 year old graduates have an income on average 80% higher than the income of high school graduates (OECD, UNESCO, 2002, OECD, 2004).

Higher education degrees have thus become the main route to social mobility. Indeed, the higher education sector is recognised at international level as a vector of economic and social benefits for individuals and their families (as university graduates usually earn more than their high school counterparts), and also for society as a whole (Imenda et al, 2004). Nevertheless, degrees do not always lead to social mobility, as the most valuable and costly degrees are gained by the offspring of high income families. In massified higher education systems, such as the French one, social specialization following different tracks creates "segregated democratization" (Duru-Bellat, 2006). When a large proportion of one age group enters higher education, degrees become positional goods, engendering diploma races between students and social groups. This analysis echoes that of other researchers (Raftery and Hout, 1993; Shavit and Blossfeld, 1993), showing that inequalities between individuals are maintained until the advantaged class reaches a point of saturation, a process characterised as Maximally Maintained Inequality.

The analytical distinction between societal/collective and individual benefits from higher education has caused economists to examine the relative strengths of private versus social rates of return to investment in higher education. While the dominant view may be that the private rates of return exceeds the social return (Psacharopoulos & Patrinos, 2004) this has not questioned the international consensus that investment in post-compulsory education enhances the welfare of nations (OECD, 2001).

Democratisation

The human capital rationale thus calls for the democratisation of higher education systems. This second rationale has two dimensions: the outcomes associated with the opening up of access to higher education and the continuously expanding expectations of what mass higher education should offer. Indeed, the expected outcomes of mass higher education are intertwined with economic expectations: improving the level of society's education should improve its economic development. However, the positive effects of mass higher education are also expected to be non-monetary and to be played out at collective and individual levels. This will be exemplified, first, at a collective level through the improvement of developmental and democratic organisations: civic institutions, political involvement, human rights, etc. (Appiah & McMahon, 2002).

Second, the widening of access is also expected to improve social cohesion, individual well-being and individual opportunities (and to some extent provide more social mobility). Two reports from the OECD (2001 and 2007) have particularly developed these perspectives, focussing on the role of education in collective and individual well-being as well as on other social outcomes. Recommendations made by the European Ministers of Higher Education also develop this objective: the Bologna Process is associated with the goal of improving social cohesion, reducing social inequalities and gender inequalities (Ministres en charge de l'Enseignement Supérieur en Europe, 2005). Increasing access is thus expected to enhance societal democratic organisation and equality.

In view of these expectations, higher education systems have undergone during the 20th century a marked growth in numbers from 13 million students worldwide in 1960 to more than 80 million in 1995 (UNESCO, 1998) and about 100 million in 2000 (Gradstein and Nikitin, 2004). This increase is partly linked to population expansion. Still, the access rate testifies to the growth of mass higher education. For example, in Europe, at the very beginning of the 20th century, European higher education systems registered around 1% of the age group (Ringer, 2004). At the beginning of the 21st century, an average of 51% of the corresponding age group entered higher education in the OECD countries (OECD, 2004). Thus in one century higher education has been transformed from an elitist good to a nearly universal one.

The focus on expanding access has shifted to considering qualitative aspects (Prost, 1986), i.e. reducing social inequalities in schools. Studying the French case, P. Merle (2000) has proposed a typology of the different forms of democratisation. He describes democratisation in access to the Baccalauréat as 'equalising democtatisation'. He characterises the process whereby the social group differences previously evident at second level completion are simply transferred into higher education as 'uniform democratisation'. Thirdly, 'segretative democratisation' refers to the process whereby inequalities work their way into the differentiation by types of study and speciality. This research on the qualitative aspects of mass higher education also includes a shift from focussing on access to focussing on graduation and access to the labour market. It suggests a complex picture of understanding inequalities, and an increased need to link higher education research to higher education policies: Knowledge Production or 'Scientification' is the third rationale involved in the changing norms of access.

Knowledge Production

'Scientification' has been identified by Habermas (1973) as a trend characterised by the development of research based on State demands and by the increasing role of research consultants in public services. Studying the relationship between Politics and Knowledge, he underlines the existence of interdependency between the values engendered by specific interests and research techniques that are themselves oriented toward certain values.

The use of research findings to influence policies regarding access to higher education can be traced back as far as the 1930's when J. B. Conant, in the US, developed the Scholastic Aptitude Test (SAT) to use as a tool for access to universities. The aim of this technique was to measure "pure intelligence", disconnected from culture (Goastellec, 2003). It illustrates the development of tools to measure and scientifically define the criteria for access to higher education, and, more broadly, prefigures a shift in the status attributed to science after World War 2 when scientific information and methods came to the fore in political thinking (Alestalo, 1989) and increasingly informed higher education policies. Research Knowledge can thus be seen as contributing to the use and diffusion of scientific-based knowledge, linking it to a phenomenon which appeared later on in the century: the knowledge society.

The Knowledge Society

The rationale of the knowledge society was developed at the end of the 1990's: knowledge and its diffusion became central. This rationale was linked to that of the Information Society, as expressed by Manuel Castells when he stated that the knowledge society "has to do with a society in which the conditions for generating knowledge and processing information have been substantially changed by a technological revolution focused on information processing, knowledge generation and information technologies." (Castells, 1996) The knowledge society produces commodities of high knowledge value. Knowledge and expertise constitute the crucial elements in production, with information and communication technologies comprehensively supporting the interaction, dissemination and exploitation of knowledge, plus the provision and accessibility of services. In view of this, the role of education becomes even more crucial. This notion has been adopted by UNESCO (2003):" the concept of "knowledge societies" includes a dimension of social, cultural, economic, political and institutional transformation, and a more pluralistic and developmental perspective ... The knowledge in question is important not only for economic growth but also for empowering and developing all sectors of society".

The emergence of "knowledge societies" and of globalisation increasingly put higher education systems in perspective and, as a consequence, stimulated competition. On the one hand international organisations (OECD, UNESCO, the European Community) have built up comparisons of access rates between countries. On the other hand, the development of comparative research has provided typologies which characterise societies regarding their access rates, such as the one proposed by Martin Trow (1973) which distinguishes between elitist, massified and universal higher education systems. These dynamics have the effect of placing a symbolic pressure on public bodies to increase access. This rationale, in effect, acts as a worldwide reference point used in most policy papers at the level of international organisations (OECD, UNESCO, World Bank, European Union...) and found in national ones (Ministries of Education, national research centres...). It is commonly used in research papers: a Google search associating "knowledge society" and "higher education" provides nearly four million hits which is reduced to two million when using Google Scholar. This underlines the fact that the rationale of the knowledge society enhances the role attributed to higher education.

These four rationales give both an account of and develop our understanding of the role of higher education, and shed light on the norm of equality which is now prevailing in relation to access to higher education.

EVOLVING NORMS OF EQUALITY

Defining Equality

These four rationales not only affect the organisation of higher education but also bring about the affirmation of a new norm. Higher Education, considered as a public good impacting on the individual, should be accessible to the largest possible number, regardless of background. It should be representative of national diversity, and, in effect, testify to the democratic dimension and to the legitimacy of the State. Thus emerges a second norm of admission that evolves out of the principle of allowing women equal access: equality as a political principle of admission to higher education. Two main conceptions of equality have developed from two different responses to the nature of equality (Sen, 2000). On the one hand, those who promote a formal equality of rights defend identical treatment for all (Barber, 1995, D'Souza, 1993, Bloom, 1987, Barry, 2002). There is thus no consideration of social identities which might bring about inequality. As a consequence those disadvantaged social identities have no legitimacy in the public sphere. On the other hand, those who declare themselves in favour of the equality principle, consider with John Rawls (1987) that inequalities are acceptable if they produce advantages for the less favoured members of the society. Recognising the problems which bring about inequalities constitutes a prerequisite to improving equality of opportunity. These different perceptions of equality characterised the debate on access during the last two decades of the 20th Century, while higher education systems underwent a phase of internal differentiation which had direct bearing on the principle of equality by expanding participation as well as widening the range of courses offered.

Diversification of Structures and Institutions

In order to improve equality of access, governments developed, at diverse levels, the same strategy: the expansion and internal diversification of the higher education system. This was seen most markedly during the second half of the 20th century, when new universities were created to address geographical inequalities. For example, in France, new universities were created in areas which were until then deprived of higher education institutions. The number of university towns doubled between 1945 and 1970. Expansion continued in middle-size towns between 1980 and 2000 (Filâtre & Grossetti, 2003). In South Africa, new universities were established in the 1960's and 1970's in line with the policy of apartheid, with institutions dedicated to Black, Indian and Coloured communities and others for the Afrikaaner community, such as Rand Afrikaans University or Port Elizabeth University (Waast, Gaillard, 2001). In Indonesia, also, the Javanese university monopoly came to an end with the creation between 1956 and 1963 of one state university for each province. In England, following the Robbins Report in 1963, higher education expanded from a small number of elite institutions to a broad and more geographically dispersed group of universities and colleges. In Ethiopia, the last decade saw the establishment of new regional universities which balanced those around Addis Ababa, the capital. In Vietnam, the extension of the higher education system is currently on the government agenda, with the aim of ensuring the spread of higher education institutions across all areas of the country.

In order to cope with the increasing demand for access and the wide social mix of the student body, governments have diversified the higher education systems, introducing new types of institutions and/or new curricula.

In the US, as early as the beginning of the 20th century, the decision was taken to create public institutions, in parallel with universities, which offered two year professional curricula, with the aim of developing local access to higher education. These Community Colleges (or Junior Colleges) absorbed the demand for access and constituted, at the end of the 20th century, 40% of the student body. These Colleges therefore diversified academic trajectories, academic levels and students' social origin: in 1999, the students coming from the highest income families were proportionately four times more numerous in these colleges than those coming from low income families (39% versus 10%, Heller, 2002). In France, the creation of Brevet de Technicien Supérieur (1959) and Institut Universitaire de Technologie (1967) was part of the same dynamic: these met the needs of the academically less gifted and less prosperous students and provided short and professional curricula. In Israel, public undergraduate colleges were established in the 1980's in outlying areas in order to reach students from disadvantaged backgrounds. In Indonesia, this demand was met by private institutions which registered in 1999 71% of new entrants to higher education (Depdiknas, 2000). Many governments have chosen to externalise the costs generated by the relative opening up of access by providing a framework for the development of private institutions. These institutions tend to register exclusively students from middle and upper class families whose academic background does not allow them to access public universities. At the opposite end of the spectrum, short and professional curricula offered at public universities (Diploma) favour a relative social diversification of the student body as well as requiring the qualitative management of access.

In Ireland, the rapid expansion in enrolment which commenced in the 1960's was accompanied by a diversification of the system with the development of a large technological sector, mainly through the establishment of a network of Regional Technical Colleges in the 1970's and the expansion of the few pre-existing technical colleges, principally in Dublin. The student enrolment at these institutions which offer mainly vocationally oriented two year certificate programmes in applied sciences, engineering, business studies and art and design today accounts for 38% of all enrolments, compared with 54% for the seven state-funded universities. In Israel, universities were created between 1925 and 1965 on the model of the Humboldtian University system, and formed an elitist system. The expansion of the higher education system has been diversified, mainly with the development of a non-university sector as a result of bottom-up initiatives side by side with governmental top-down planning. The 1980's saw the creation of new colleges, both public and private, with the new public colleges being established mainly in outlying communities, to absorb students from lower status groups. As a result, massification has been partially fulfilled outside the universities: in 2005, 54% of all undergraduates were enrolled in colleges, compared to 46% in the universities. In Ethiopia, where only 1.5% of the age group enters higher education, and massification is still a long way off, the extension of the higher education sector has been partly provided for by the private sector. Ten years after the creation of the first private institution, the sector registered 23% of the students nationwide. In Vietnam, the higher education system is diversified, and the expansion of the system has also been organised outside the universities, through the introduction of semi-public universities[4], those established by public authorities[5] and private[6] higher education institutions (after 1993). This latter trend has been encouraged since 2001 by the cooperation of foreign higher education institutions to deliver degree courses using sandwich modes. The MOET Strategic Plan also foresees the creation of new universities and colleges before 2010, and calls for the consolidation of community colleges as well as expanding the university network in order to increase their size and provide more opportunities for those coming from low socio-economic backgrounds.

The creation of new public universities has transformed the geography of higher education systems and institutional diversification has modified their organisation. However, while some democratisation of access to higher education has affected the system as a whole, it is not necessarily the case for the prestigious and selective institutions. Higher education massification has principally affected less or non-selective institutions: diversification has allowed the expansion of numbers. In order to evaluate more qualitatively the principle of equality, local and/or national statistical databases have been introduced. These aim to apply specific criteria to the student body and thus measure at the institutional level as well as at the system level how far the principle of equality has been realised.

While the establishment of new institutions testifies to the quantitative development of higher education an understanding of qualitative development calls for an
examination of databases which take account of social categories and national
priorities.

DATABASES REFLECTING SOCIAL CATEGORIES AND
NATIONAL PRIORITIES

Higher education authorities as well as institutions regularly produce statistical
databases which are more or less comprehensive, more or less complex, and whose
aim is to be democratically transparent, presenting proof of their efficiency, and
providing an evidence base for future policy development. A comparison of these
databases reveals specific national priorities.

First, the development of the Internet as a tool for providing information throws
light on different traditions. For example, the American Federal site concerned
with quantitative data on education (the National Council for Education Statistics)
offers on-line access to quantitative information on higher education and students.
Changes in students' registration patterns are accessible from 1947. Ethno-racial
diversity has been measured since 1967. In the same way, the South African
Department of Education has given information on the shape of the student body
for each institution since 1986, including the ethno-racial groupings and the
language used. In Israel, the Council for Higher Education provides no data, but
the central Bureau of Statistics offers an insight into the composition of the student
body from 1990 to 1994. The French Ministry of Education only offers access
to a restricted amount of quantitative data covering the years 2001 to 2006. These
approaches, which are related to a specific relationship between the State and its
citizens, are also present at the institutional level. Thus, American and South
African authorities and universities make their student data widely available, while
the availability of this kind of information remains more constrained when it comes
to the French or Israeli higher education system.

Thus, an analysis of the organisation of universities in societies with different
cultures reveals highly differentiated databases. They are arguably representative
of the way higher education institutions are legitimated by citizens and users, and
testify to the democratic functioning of universities. These statistical systems, built
up to classify the population, illustrate the link between original conceptions of the
national state and institutional practices.

Whatever the criteria and the national categories (race, social group, etc.) used
to describe the student body and map the social inequalities of access, all share
at least a pretension to be indicators of democratisation. These categories are
symptomatic of the countries: each country defines criteria which make sense in
terms of its history. In Indonesia, geographical provincial origin is one of the tools
used to classify the population. This statistical construction goes back to a specific
understanding of identities, linked to the model of national integration. Based on
the model of the unification of a heterogeneous geographic area, the Indonesian
state uses the provincial origin to map social inequalities: racial, ethnic and social

identities are taboo, and strictly restricted to the private sphere. In the US, which has been called a melting-pot of races, it is the ethno-racial dimension which is the main criterion to delineate social inequalities. In France, the republican model defines the human being as a universal category: the measurement of social injustice relies on socio-professional categories, a euphemism for social class. In Ireland, social diversity is traditionally related to socio-economic groups, as well as information in the national census. In Israel, students' data provide information on religion, geographic origin and school district, but the socio-economic background is missing.

Far from being fixed, the information systems evolve in line with changes in social composition, depending on negotiations between the State and civil society. Changes in the ethno-racial categories of the American census together with those of admission regulations for entry into higher education underline this process. In the US, until 1980, the statistical categories gave a perspective of society based on two categories (Black-American/White-American). This construction, inherited from past segregation, was inherent in the need to compensate the injustices faced by the black population and make it possible to implement affirmative action for black students. In 1980, three categories were added (Native-American, Hispano-American, and Asian-American). This more detailed categorisation acknowledged the diversity of the American population and enabled authorities to use affirmative action for other ethnic groups. Indeed, the period of segregation ended in 1954, and in 1980 there were no special measures to favour access specifically for the Black-American student. Affirmative Action concerned all the under-represented groups in higher education. In 2000, a new distinction was introduced: categories were developed which took into account national origin. Ethno-racial groups were therefore no longer homogeneous. For example, the "Asian-American" category includes a highly heterogeneous group of those of varied geographic origin, arriving in the US in different and successive immigration waves. Meanwhile Asian-American students have not benefited from the Affirmative Action policies owing to their over-representation in Higher Education; as a result some of this broad group have suffered from discrimination. Finally, changes in the classification used in the US census testify to a shift in the conception of otherness, a change that can also be traced in the admission process. Increasingly, students are evaluated in a holistic way which takes into account their individual life history and all aspects of their identity. Merit thus becomes the measure for assessing the academic results which are obtained taking account of the social, economic, cultural and academic handicaps of each student. The notion of inherited merit thus disappears, to be replaced by that of academic merit.

CONTINUING TENSION BETWEEN MERIT AND EQUALITY

While the analysis of the differentiation of higher education systems and the development of information systems allow for an elaboration of the issue of social inequalities it does not eradicate the tension between merit and equality. On the one hand, the measurement of academic merit is always influenced by circumstances. On the other hand, equality of opportunity is not a given situation but depends on the specific organisation of access arrangements. A good example of this tension is illustrated by the American attempt to build a national test examination (the SAT, Scholastic Aptitude Test) during the first half of the 21st Century. This test was initially supposed to select the best academic students, independently of their social origins. Based on the idea of a random assessment of intelligence, this test was devoted to measuring pure intelligence, disconnected from culture. History soon revealed that circumstances (ethno-racial and geographic) had a major effect on the results obtained in this test.

The way this tension is handled is, at a national level, constrained by the interpretation of the founding principles of the nation, the organisation of the particular university and the institution's degree of autonomy. The organisation of the whole higher education system and the organisation of access reveal how this tension is handled. An analysis of the French higher education system shows how, in the republican model, merit is supposedly distinct from equality, the first one being officially used only by the "Grandes Ecoles". The academic selection they operate is supposed to be purely meritocratic, and produces a socially determined recruitment: about 80% of the students come from high income families. At the opposite end, the universities' admission process, which is formally non-selective, is expected not to distinguish between individuals in regard to their academic origin. The weak degree of autonomy of the universities means that they must respect the legal framework imposed by government and thus, under the constraint of equality, absorb the undifferentiated massification of the student body. Nevertheless, some differentiation in terms of the students' social background remains. The widening of access to higher education is concomitant with an "increasing social hierarchy of the different tracks" (Duru-Bellat, 2006, p. 21). Thus, in this higher education system, the 'equality of man' in the national ideology, is being gainsaid by what is known of the students' background, broadly influenced by their social origin (Bourdieu, 1985, 1989, Erlich, 1998, Euriat et Thélot, 1995).

On the other hand, in the US, merit and equality are not dissociated. Universities are characterised by a strong democratic tradition which is responsive to social demand. The ability of students to contribute to university decisions is important due to their participation in the governing bodies and various university committees of the institution. As a result, depending upon the policies higher education institutions implement and the results they obtain, their position is permanently re-evaluated by the users, the students and their families.

Higher education systems and the way in which access is organised inform the national management of the tension between merit and equality. How an institution handles this tension depends on its position in the overall national higher education market and also on its relationship with the government and with its stakeholders. The tension between merit and equality reaches its apogee at the most prestigious institutions because they expect to recruit the best students and these are expected to be representative of national diversity. Conferring the most valuable professional degrees, they also need to prove their ability to deliver these degrees fairly, regardless of the students' social background. Initiatives such as Affirmative Action have been mainly implemented in the most prestigious institutions of higher education. Although higher education institutions play an important role in establishing fair admission processes, government and states increasingly provide incentives to encourage equity in access.

Elitist Institutions at the Centre of the Controversy

The statistical categories used to map the student body correspond to different ways of interpreting social inequalities in access. These inequalities always exist, whatever institution is considered, but it is particularly noticeable when it comes to the more selective institutions. Examples can be found in most countries: some 146 colleges in the US – about 10% of the institutions, which include the small circle of Ivy League[7] institutions and the big public universities; the historically white institutions in South Africa; the "Grandes Ecoles" in France; the most ancient Javanese universities in Indonesia; the eight historical universities in Israel; and the Universities of Addis Ababa in Ethiopia. In these institutions, the tension between merit and equality is marked: they are simultaneously expected to provide high quality graduates drawn from socially diverse backgrounds (and thus to turn equality of opportunity into reality), and to provide a fair range of degrees based on merit.

The South African context illustrates this problem. Since the integration of the distinctive higher education systems that formerly served different ethno-racial communities, the institutions that have faced the strongest increase in demand for access are those that used to admit exclusively white Afrikaans-speaking students. *De facto*, the recruitment pattern of the most elitist institutions was, and tends to be, socially unequal. This tendency is all the more problematic as global access to higher education increases: it is, however, understandable when the burden of social, economic, cultural and academic factors on individuals is taken into account.

In the US, considerable progress has been made in eradicating gross social inequalities of access but the search for a socially fair admission process was initiated at the beginning of the 20th century. With the end of racial segregation, selective institutions such as the University of California at Berkeley developed admission processes aimed at integrating merit and equality. These procedures have slowly diffused to other higher education systems. Institutions' international networking has helped to spread the knowledge of admission tools.

In Vietnam, the arrangements for access to higher education are being reorganised in order to achieve social fairness and offer more opportunities to people from every walk of life to obtain a continuing education. This aim, established by the government, is based on the national higher education entrance examination set up in 2002 in order to ensure social equity in admission criteria and process. The centralised admission process, organised by the government, provides students with a straightforward procedure for access to higher education. As this examination is highly selective (about 15% of the examinees are accepted), the benchmark differs in relation to the geographic origin of the students (mountainous areas; remote areas with disadvantaged social backgrounds; country areas; provincial cities and their suburbs; and large conurbations such as Hochiminh and Hanoi). This arrangement acknowledges the differences in high school levels and educational facilities with respect to the students' location, and thus tends to equalize the opportunity for access. In addition, foundation courses for ethnic minority groups are provided by some universities under the supervision of the government, which has set up a special policy allowing these students to enrol in universities without an entrance examination.

The Introduction of Tools to Regulate Admission

The history of the regulation of access illustrates the fact that tools for selection were introduced when policy makers considered that too many graduates were produced for the number of professional positions available (Rüegg, 2004).

The first attempt to introduce tools to regulate admission probably dates from the 16th century, when the lecturers of the University of Jena asked for a limitation on the numbers admitted from those graduating from high schools. Their aim was to increase the level of homogeneity of the student body but the proposal was refused by the local rulers who were afraid that a student exodus would weaken their university. Indeed, it was only at the end of the 18th century that the prerequisite to graduate from secondary school in order to enter university emerged (Di Simone, 1996). One must wait until the first half of the 20th century to find the introduction of admission tests and the implementation of admission rules.

Although, as stated earlier, the information used for the measurement of inequalities of access differs according to the particular society, the international diffusion of "university knowledge" (modes of organisation, tools, techniques) favours a shared transformation of admission norms and organisation. For example, the National Institute for Testing and Evaluation (NITE) established by the Israeli universities in 1981, whose aim was to construct a Psychometric Entrance Test that would be valid for applicants to all the Israeli Universities, shares similarities with the American SAT. The NITE was to provide standardised tests accepted by all the universities, and is in addition to the *Bagrut*, a high school leaving certificate quite similar to the French *Baccalauréat,* created by Napoleon in 1808, or the German *Abitur*, introduced in Prussia in 1788. As in the US, some kind of Affirmative Action practices exist at the institutional level, aimed at providing access to disadvantaged students on the basis of their socio-economic background or ethnic group.

The adoption of a national entrance examination to enter public universities in Indonesia illustrates the same trend. This might not have taken place if the Indonesian elite had not traditionally studied at the University of California, Berkeley. By chance, an Indonesian graduate student in computer sciences underwent a training period in the company which commercialised the SAT (Scholastic Aptitude Test). Later on, he developed a similar entrance examination in Indonesia, solving the problem of the management of access to Indonesian higher education. Following the establishment of this test, a second route was developed which allowed universities to promote the diversity of the student body by favouring minority students. Elsewhere, the adoption in France by the Parisian Institute of Political Sciences of a second route to entry was clearly inspired by those methods used in the United States[8]. In South Africa, the reform of the Higher Education sector drew on a consultation with the international community of researchers. The introduction of Affirmative Action practices, as well as the reorganisation of the admission process, involved the potential use of a national entrance examination developed by the University of Cape Town, which testifies to the international diffusion of admission tools, and, more discretely, to a norm of qualitative equalisation of access.

In Ireland, in response to the statutory requirement set out in the Universities Act (1997) and other legislation, most third level colleges have introduced their own direct admission procedures to deal with non-standard admissions outside the framework of the CAO (Central Applications Office) which allocates places nationally to almost all higher education institutions on the basis of academic achievement. This pool of reserved places represents a form of affirmative action designed to facilitate access by students with disabilities, mature students and students from socio-economically disadvantaged backgrounds who would not meet the standard academic requirements for admission. In many cases Affirmative Action is taken in respect of school leavers from socially disadvantaged families by admitting students with levels of achievement which fall short of the Leaving Certificate points' requirements for traditional students. It is widely accepted that where access is regulated by competition, this favours those who enter the competition with superior economic, social and cultural resources. The absence of a "level playing field" provides a rationale for some affirmative action (Clancy, 2006). In the same vein, the national higher education entrance examination used to admit students to Ethiopian universities incorporates an affirmative action dimension by enabling female students, disabled students and students from disadvantaged regions to enter with a lower level of achievement.

CONCLUDING REMARKS

Access to higher education worldwide is characterised not only by shared change processes, but also by local interpretation of these global trends. At a normative level, the organisation of access is characterised by a shift from being organised according to the norm of inherited merit to that of the norm of equality of rights to enter higher education, and finally to the norm of equality of opportunity. This change in norms is supported by new policy rationales calling for a new under-standing of the economic and societal role of higher education.

At the organisational level, the norm of equality of rights is sustained by a diver-sification of institutions and degrees, while the equality of opportunity norm is supported at institutional level by a wide range of admission policies and by the development of detailed statistical databases. Most public scrutiny has centred on the selection processes operated by the most elitist and prestigious institutions which are increasingly required to defend their selection of a ruling class.

At another level, international comparison also reveals the evolution of higher education systems. Today, governments not only try to set up their higher education systems to attract international elites but also increasingly try to devolve the responsibility of access to the higher education institutions. This involves a double process: at the national level, the systems become more differentiated by setting up specific programmes of study and by aiming to attract a specific student body. More broadly, the challenge for these institutions consists in building up a specific identity which can be advertised in the media. The increasing number of rankings, newspapers or books advertising higher education institutions testifies to this. However, at the international level, networking has become essential. Networking, often driven by elitist institutions, has progressively diffused throughout the whole global system and increased the internationalisation of practice, especially affecting those concerned with diversifying student recruitment. This has been achieved through setting up alternative routes to admission and providing information regarding access to higher education, as well as offering additional tutoring for high school students coming from disadvantaged backgrounds.

Thus the comparison of national systems underlines the increasing alignment of higher education configurations. Henceforth, in a context of globalisation, the management of the tension between merit and equality will become much more the responsibility of the institutions. At the same time, public authorities will require those institutions to develop a more entrepreneurial management, which, in the future, will probably strongly influence the resolution of this tension.

NOTES

[1] For a more detailed analysis of access norms see Clancy, Goastellec, 2007 and Goastellec 2008.

[2] See for example the codes of nationality analysed by P. Weil, in Kastoryano, 2005.

[3] Magister is the title then given to a person having a licence from a university to teach philosophy or liberal arts. University teachers are thus generically called magister.

[4] In the case of semi-public universities, the facility is owned by the state and managed by a public authority at the central or provincial level, but all operating costs are covered mainly by student tuition fees and financial sources raised by the institution.

[5] Universities owned and managed by a public authority at the central and provincial level, but all operating costs are covered mainly by student tuition fees.

[6] Private universities are owned and managed by private individuals with costs covered by student tuition fees.

[7] This prestigious private university association includes the universities of Brown, Columbia, Cornell, Dartmouth, Harvard, Pennsylvania, Princeton and Yale.

[8] In 2001, the governing body of this institution adopted conventions allowing specific student admission (dossiers and interviews instead of the usual entrance examination) with 7 high schools which are part of the Priority Education Zones (ZEP). If this second route of admission does not directly promote student access on the basis of ethno-racial or social group, then positive discriminatory targets would come into play for groups that, in the US, would without doubt be considered as ethnic or racial minorities" (Calvès, 2005, p.31). Simultaneously, it answered a socio-economic need in that decisions were taken on the basis of the students' socio-economic background.

BIBLIOGRAPHY

Aghion, P., & Cohen, E. (2003). *Education et Croissance*. Rapport pour le Conseil d'Analyse Economique, 143 p.

Alestalo, M. (1989). On the conditions for the scientification of politics. *Science Studies, 2,* 11–18.

Appiah, E. N., McMahon, W. W. (2002). The social outcomes of education and feedbacks on growth in Africa. *The Journal of Development Studies, 38*(4), 27–68.

Barber, B. (1995). Face à la retribalisation du monde. In *Esprit* (pp. 132–144). Le spectre du multiculturalisme américain.

Barry B. (2002). *Culture and equality: An egalitarian critique of multiculturalism.* Cambridge: Harvard University Press.

Becker, G. S. (1964, 1975, 1993). *Human capital. A theoretical and empirical analysis, with special reference to education.* Chicago: The University of Chicago Press.

Bloom, A. (1987). *The closing of the American mind.* New York: Simon and Schuster.

Bourdieu P., & Passeron, J.-C. (1985). *Les héritiers, les étudiants et la culture.* Paris: Minuit.

Bourdieu, P. (1989). *La noblesse d'Etat, grandes écoles et esprit de Corps.* Paris: Minuit.

Calvès, G. (2005). Les politiques de discrimination positive. In *Pouvoirs* (Vol. 111, pp. 5–18). Paris: Seuil.

Castells, M. (1996). *La société en réseau.* Paris: Fayard.

Charle, C., & Verger, J. (2004). *Histoire des Universités.* Paris: PUF.

Clancy, P. (2006). *Access and equity: National report of Ireland.* An internal paper, New Century Scholars Program of Fulbright.

Clancy, P., & Goastellec, G. (2007). Questioning access and equity in higher education: Policy and performance in a comparative perspective. *Higher Education Quarterly, 61*(2). Oxford: Blackwell Publishing.

Clark, B. R. (1962). *Educating the expert society.* San Francisco: Chandler Publishing Company.

D'Souza, D. (1993). *L'éducation contre les libertés, politique de la race et du sexe sur les campus américains.* Paris: Gallimard.

Depdiknas. (2000). *Indonesian education statistics 1999/2000, facts and figures.* Jakarta: Ministry of National Education, Office of Research and Development.

Di Simone, M. R. (1996). Admission. In W. Rüegg (Ed.), *A history of the University in Europe, Vol. 2, Universities in early modern Europe (1500–1800).* Cambridge: Cambridge University Press.

Drucker, P. F. (1969). The educational revolution. In dans A. H. Harsey, J. Floud et C. A. Anderson (dir.), *Education, economy and society* (pp. 15–21). Toronto: Collier – Macmillam Canada.

Duru-Bellat, M. (2006). *L'inflation scolaire. Les désillusions de la méritocratie.* Paris: Seuil.

Eggins, H. (2006). *Access and equity: National report of United Kingdom.* An internal paper, New Century Scholars Program of Fulbright.

Erlich, V. (1998). *Les nouveaux étudiants, un groupe social en mutation.* Paris: A. Colin.

Euriat, M., & Thélot, C. (1995). Le recrutement social de l'élite scolaire en France, évolution des inégalités de 1950 à 1990. *Revue Française de Sociologie, XXXVI*, 403–438.

Filâtre, D., & Grossetti, M. (2003). La carte scientifique française. In M. Grossetti & P. Losego (Eds.), *La territorialisation de l'enseignement supérieur et de la recherche, France, Espagne, Portugal.* Paris: L'Harmattan.

Goastellec, G. (2003). Le SAT et l'accès aux études supérieures: le recrutement des élites américaines en question. *Sociologie du Travail, 45*, 473–490.

Goastellec, G. (2006a). *Access and equity: National report of France.* An internal paper, New Century Scholars Program of Fulbright.

Goastellec, G. (2006b). *Access and equity: National report of South Africa.* An internal paper, New Century Scholars Program of Fulbright.

Goastellec, G. (2008). Globalization and implementation of an equity norm in higher education. *Peabody Journal of Education.*

Gradstein, M., & Nikitin, D. (2004). *Education expansion: Evidence and interpretation.* Washington, DC: World Bank Research Working Paper.

Guri-Rosenblit, S. (2006). *Access and equity: National report of Israel.* An internal paper, New Century Scholars Program of Fulbright.

Habermas, J. (1973). Scientifisation de la politique et opinion publique. In *La technique et la science comme idéologie* (pp. 97–132). Paris: Gallimard.

Heller, D. E. (2002). *Conditions of access, higher education for low income students.* Westport, CT: American Council on Education/Praeger series on higher education.

Imenda, S. N., Kongolo, M., & Grewal, A. S. (2004). Factors underlying technikon and university enrolment trends in South Africa. *Educational Management Administration and Leadership, 32*(2), 195–215.

Jaoul Grammare, M. (2007). *Enseignement supérieur et croissance économique: analyse économétrique de l'hypothèse d'Aghion et Cohen.* AFC, Working Paper N° 10.

Kastoryano, R. (2005). *Les codes de la différence. Race, Origine, Religion. France, Allemagne, Etats-Unis.* Paris: Presses de Sciences Po.

Merle, P. (2000). Le concept de démocratisation de l'institution scolaire: une typologie et sa mise à l'épreuve. *Population, 1,* 15–50.

Ministres en charge de l'enseignement supérieur en Europe. (2005). *la dimension sociale de l'espace européen de l'enseignement supérieur et la compétition mondiale.* Recommandations issues du Séminaire de Paris, 28/01.

Nguyen, P. N. (2006). *Access and equity: National report of Vietnam.* An internal paper, New Century Scholars Program of Fulbright.

OECD. (2001). *Du bien-être des nations: le rôle du capital humain et social.* Paris: OCDE editions.

OECD. (2004). Rapport sur l'éducation.

OECD. (2004). Education at a glance.

OECD. (2007). *Understanding the social outcomes of learning.* Paris: OCDE.

OECD & UNESCO. (2002). *Financing education, investments and returns, analysis of the world education indicators.* Paris: UNESCO/OCDE.

Prost, A. (1986). *L'enseignement s'est-il démocratisé?* Paris: PUF.

Psacharopoulos, G., & Patrinos, H. A. (2004). Returns to investment in education: A further update. *Education Economics, 12*(2).

Raftery, A. E., & Hout, M. (1993). Maximally maintained inequalities: Expansion, reform and opportunity in Irish education, 1921–1975. *Sociology of Edication, 66,* 41–62.

Rawls, J. (1987). *Théories de la justice.* Paris: Seuil.

Ridder-Symoens, H. (2003, avril 30–mai 3). Living together: Catholics and Protestants at early modern Universities. In FIUC (Ed.), *L'Université Catholique à l'Epoque Moderne. De la Réforme à la Révolution. XVIème – XVIIIème siècles.* Actes du Troisième Symposium, Mexico.

Ringer, F. (2004). Admission. In W. Rüegg (Ed.), *A history of the University in, Europe, Vol. III, Universities in the nineteenth and early twentieth centuries (1800–1945).* Cambridge: Cambridge University Press.

Roemer, J. E. (1998). *Equality of opportunity.* Cambridge: Harvard University Press.

Rüegg, W. (1992). Themes. In H. De Ridder Symoens (Ed.), *A history of the university in Europe. Vol. 1, Universities in the Middle Ages.* Cambridge: Cambridge University Press.

Rüegg, W. (2004). *A history of the University in, Europe, Vol. III, Universities in the nineteenth and early twentieth centuries (1800–1945).* Cambridge: Cambridge University Press.

Schultz, T. W. (1963). *The economic value of education.* New York/London: Columbia University.

Schwinges, R. C. (1992). Admission. In H. De Ridder Symoens (Ed.), *A history of the university in Europe, Vol. 1, Universities in the Middle Ages.* Cambridge: Cambridge University Press.

Sen, A. (2000). *Repenser l'inégalité.* Paris: Seuil.

Shavit, Y., & Blossfeld, H.-P. (Eds.). (1993). *Persistent inequalities: A comparative study of educational attainment in thirteen countries.* Boulder, CO: Westview.

Trow, M. (1973). *Problems in the transition from Elite to mass higher education.* Berkeley, CA: Carnegie Commission on Higher Education.

UNESCO. (2003). Towards knowledge societies. An interview with Abdul Waheed Khan. *A World of Science, 1*(4).

UNESCO. (1998). *Conférence mondiale sur l'enseignement supérieur. "Déclaration Mondiale sur l'Enseignement Supérieur".* Paris: UNESCO.

Waast, R., & Gaillard, J. (2001). *"Science in Africa". Country Report.* IRD, University of Stallenbosch.

World Bank. (2000). *Higher education in developing countries: Peril and promise.* Washington, DC.

Yizengaw, T. (2006). *Access and equity: National report of Ethiopia.* An internal paper, New Century Scholars Program of Fulbright.

THE IMPACT OF GLOBALISATION ON ACCESS

Globalisation is a complex concept used by different people with increasing frequency but often with different meanings. It is generally considered to mean the process of the growing integration of capital, and technological information across national boundaries in such a way as to create an increasingly integrated world market. Generally globalisation is described as a set of processes, which in various ways make supranational connections, international networks, integration of economies, and connection of cultures. Accounts of globalisation, therefore, mainly focus on economic, cultural and political perspectives.

Education is central in almost all strategies for national development, both in developing and developed countries of the world. It produces and supplies skilled human resource/capital to economies and nations. It generates important knowledge and serves the community through its outreach activities, improving livelihoods and overall national development. Furthermore, it employs a large workforce, which must be managed effectively and efficiently. Higher education has an economic aspect in the advancement of resource development through public and private investment, a political aspect in raising the overall level of education capacity and competitiveness, and a socio-cultural aspect in the provision of access, equity and opportunity. Furthermore, it has to respond to the demands of society, of commerce and industry and of the economy to ensure national development and sustainability.

Common elements of the way in which globalisation impacts on higher education are manifested through:
- Government or public budget reductions while institutions are required to do more with less.
- A significant push to diversify income by increasing non-governmental alternative revenues and resources.
- Increased commodification of knowledge, as intellectual property and the need to diversify are becoming increasingly important.
- Reorganisation promoted by national governments to relate higher education more closely to national economic and social agendas.
- Pressures for new forms of accountability by governments and public requiring more reporting, performance reviews and assessment.
- Quality requirements intended to monitor processes and outcomes, and usually tied to budgeting.
- Concerns for social justice and equity in access.
- Increased international mobility of capital, information and productive capacity.

Globalisation has thus affected positively or negatively, directly or indirectly, higher education and university systems in both developed and developing countries. The global process has intensified competition within the global economy. The World scenario, at regional and global levels, and the policies and practices of donors and development partners have influenced the policy thinking, directions and implementation of higher education in many countries. Although there was earlier a general neglect in investing in higher education particularly by developing countries, there has been, since the 1990's, some reconsideration and revival in the support for the sector in many countries.

The directions and actions taken by governments worldwide had huge support and encouragement from international organisations such as the World Bank (2000, 2002, 2004), OECD (1998), UNESCO (1998, 2008, 2009) and other initiatives such as the Partnership for African Higher Education, and the Commission for Africa (2005)).

The World Conference on Higher Education (UNESCO, 1998) was unanimous in considering that "a renewal of higher education is essential for the whole society to be able to face up to the challenges of the twenty-first century, to ensure its intellectual independence, to create and advance knowledge, and to educate and train responsible, enlightened citizens and qualified specialists, without whom no nation can progress economically, socially, culturally or politically." The Declaration of the Conference emphasised that since society is becoming "increasingly knowledge-based ..., higher education and research now act as essential components of culture, socio-economic and environmentally sustainable development of individuals, communities and nations." Thus, even in the twenty first century, the development of higher education figures among the highest national priorities across nations, and is emphasised in the conclusions of the World Conference of UNESCO in 2009. The OECD publication (OECD, 1998) speaks of a 'fundamental shift' and a 'new paradigm' of tertiary education for all, as well as referring to a "historic shift" and a "cultural change". The publication stresses: "it is an era of searching, questioning and at times of profound uncertainty, of numerous reforms and essays in the renewal of tertiary education".

The Human Development Report (UNDP, 1999) sets out the mission of higher education, resolving that "beyond its traditional functions of teaching, training, research and study, all of which remain fundamental", higher education must "promote development of the whole person and train responsible, informed citizens, committed to working for a better society in the future".

The Task Force report (World Bank and UNESCO, 2000), presents a powerful message that "higher education is no longer a luxury; it is essential for survival". The Task Force concluded that, without more and better education, developing countries would find it increasingly difficult to benefit from the global knowledge-based economy. The report emphasised economic growth and better living standards; development of enlightened leaders; expansion of choices, facilitation of social mobility and helping the talented to fulfil their potential; and the capacity to address local problems with appropriate solutions in such vital areas as environmental protection, prevention and management of illness, industrial expansion, and development of infrastructure. The broader social, economic and political systems within which they are situated had a major effect on whether higher education institutions could deliver the above stated benefits or not. The report advocated that developing countries needed to invest in good education that gives graduates the necessary versatile skills of lifelong learning, rather than focusing narrowly on specific disciplines. This advice is consistent with the other non-economic goals of higher education: the inculcation of values of tolerance, responsibility, enterprise, creativity, and public duty. These require an open and non-hierarchical learning environment and an emphasis on practicality and relevance.

A further policy paper (World Bank, 2004) has contributed to the shift in the long standing neglect of the higher education sector by the Bank, emphasising the contribution of higher education to building a country's capacity for participation in an increasingly knowledge-based world economy, enhancing economic develop-ment and reduction of poverty.

The unfortunate side-effect of the long years of emphasis on primary education in Africa has been the neglect of secondary and tertiary education from which are produced the doctors, teachers, nurses, police officers, lawyers and government workers of tomorrow (Commission for Africa, 2005). Africa needs higher education institutions that attract students, researchers and teachers to study and work in Africa - at present there are more African scientists and engineers working in the USA than in Africa. Skilled professionals are key to building improvements in the administration and in the technical ability which Africa so gravely lacks. The international community is called upon to commit some US$500 million a year, over ten years, to revitalize Africa's institutions of higher education and up to US$3 billion over ten years to develop centres of excellence in science and technology, including African institutes of technology (Commission for Africa, 2005). Higher education institutions can improve the accountability of governments and build participation in society and citizenship. They also generate independent research and analysis that supports the vibrant debate that can greatly improve the effectiveness of government policies in the whole of Africa.

ACCESS AND EQUITY IN THE CONTEXT OF GLOBALISATION

Globalisation, it can be argued, is the backcloth against which all the issues relating to access and equity in higher education are played out. It affects "the broad economic, technological, and scientific trends that directly affect high education and are largely inevitable in the contemporary world" (Altbach 2006). This has a number of effects.

The Knowledge Society

The desire by governments to take part successfully in the market-driven competition to prosper in the world economy has brought about the 'knowledge society'. A new social hierarchy has been established, based on knowledge and access to knowledge. In order to maximise a country's ability to participate in the knowledge society, governments have recognised the necessity to train as many young people as possible in the skills that are needed. This, in turn, places pressure on governments to produce as many skilled graduates as possible, and thus expand access to their higher education institutions. The gateway to the knowledge society can arguably be seen as the holding of degrees. Thus the efforts by countries to expand the percentages of their population who are graduates can be directly linked to the belief that this will provide the basis for prosperity. It is common to find countries setting targets for participation in higher education e.g. the UK set a target of 50% participation by 2010 (Eggins 2003).

Competition

Economic forces driven by globalisation also produce fierce global competition, in which the expansion of access to higher education plays a part. As countries expand their higher education systems, they seek to deliver the graduates at the best possible price. As a result institutions are encouraged to diversify their income streams, and students are expected to share the cost of their education by contributing to it themselves. Since the global financial crisis, and the resultant recession, countries have found their budgets under pressure, with inevitable cutbacks in overall higher education funding. This has heightened the need for institutions to attract funds from other sources.

Higher Education for Profit

One major source of income for many countries is international students, who will often pay higher fees than home students. The demand is enormous, and unlikely to be halted. UNESCO data indicate that there were over 2.8 million international students worldwide in 2007, a rise of a million in seven years. Forecasts by an Australian research company (Altbach 2009) indicate that by 2025 the could well be some 7.2 million international students.

Realised in these terms, the expansion of access is already a major source of income to countries that can attract good numbers of students from overseas. The Australian government set a policy of expanding this market, and have been markedly successful: Andreas Schleicher, of the OECD (2007), commented that "Australia and New Zealand have been really smart: they have invested in good provision and good quality programmes. They charge high fees but it is a comercially viable service". Education has thus become a highly successful business in Australia which now contributes about A$15.5 billion to the economy, making it the country's third largest export industry.

However, the dependence on international students to boost the economy has its own dangers. The global financial downturn has not only stemmed the flow in some countries of the numbers of such students, but has also threatened the viability of private higher education institutions. On November 5 2009 four private institutions run by the Global Campus Management Group in Sydney and Melbourne were closed after the group failed to repay debts of A$20 million. This has caused much difficulty for the hundreds of Chinese students enrolled in these colleges, who were told their tuition fees were unlikely to be refunded.

What is instructive, however, is the response of the Chinese commentators. One senior manager at the Australia-China Educational and Cultural Development Center, a Beijing overseas education agency, predicted that there would be a 30% reduction in Chinese students studying in Australia in 2010, due to the collapse of some private education institutions. The website for the Chinese Embassy in Australia noted that ten private institutions had closed since May 2009. In July 2009 there were 130,000 Chinese students enrolled in education institutions across Australia; an expected decrease in Chinese students translates into a measurable loss of revenue for a major government enterprise (China Daily, Nov 10 2009). Not only this: such problems can cause difficulties in relations between countries – the Chinese consulate in Sydney went as far as to caution Chinese students from studying in Australia (China Daily Nov 9 2009). The effects of globalisation on access can be rapid and unsettling.

It is clear that private higher education worldwide has been caught up by the financial crisis in a number of countries. In Brazil the effects on private education have been somewhat different. Small local private institutions which have sprung from local communities and were tailored to their needs have also found themselves in a weak financial position and have been bought out by large companies, thus putting their ability to serve the local populace at risk.

Quality

The concern for quality is a direct result of the effects of globalisation. Its definition is interpreted somewhat differently in different national contexts. However, the 1998 UNESCO World Conference's definition remains sound:

> "Quality in higher education is a multidimensional concept, which should embrace all its functions, and activities: teaching and academic programmes, research and scholarship, staffing, students, buildings, facilities, equipment, services to the community, and academic environment." UNESCO 1998. The UNESCO World Conference of 2009 further expanded in its Communique on the importance of quality assurance: "quality assurance is a vital function in contemporary higher education and must involve all stakeholders. Quality requires both establishing quality assurance systems and patterns of evaluation as well as promoting a quality culture within institutions."

High quality of provision attracts students: loss of quality is soon noised abroad, with consequent loss of international students, and the revenue that accompanies them. Quality is therefore an aid to marketing and provides a safeguard for the standards of courses. A countrywide system of quality assurance provides a kitemark which has much appeal for students considering a choice of countries to which they might apply. The whole of UK higher education comes under the aegis of the Quality Assurance Agency. Their reports are freely available on the web and comments on particular courses can be easily accessed, giving detailed information on the last assessment in terms of the standards of teaching and delivery of the curriculum. The establishment of a framework for quality assurance for the whole of the EU is now being pursued by signatories of the Bologna Agreement, with the establishment of ENQA, the European Association for Quality Assurance in Higher Education.

The desire to establish and advertise global comparisons of quality in higher education is one of the drivers behind the recent phenomenon of global league tables of universities, and the aspiration by a number of countries to have one or more 'world class' universities. This is arguable a direct response to the pressures of globalisation. A listing at a high level in the international league tables has a proven effect on the number of international applications and their quality. One can argue that such league tables – the two best known are those of the *Times Higher Education* World University Rankings and the Shanghai Jiao Tong Academic Ranking of World Universities – provide useful which facilitates access and can bring about structural improvements in the higher education system. The reaction to the Shanghai Ranking of Higher Education institutions by French universities, for instance, is a clear response to international competition. Four universities of Bordeaux have merged and taken the name of University of Bordeaux in order to ne more visible and better ranked. However, countries who pour valuable resources into attempting to establish 'world class universities' may be running the risk of draining much needed funds from other institutions, and thereby having a deleterious effect on the access opportunities available to the bulk of their citizens. The Indian government had, in 1998, a policy aim of establishing four world class universities: in 2009 the policy priority is to expand higher education capacity overall, thus enabling greater numbers of their citizens to become graduates. Recently the OECD has expressed unhappiness at the influence of league tables: they can distort the global higher education system in an unhelpful way, with the consequent loss of valuable economic wealth.

One effect of globalisation, however, has proved very positive. The concern for social justice and democratisation, driven by the United Nations agenda for the fair treatment of human beings, and the UN convention of human rights, has helped to open up access to education as a right for all individuals. On the one hand, this has fuelled the demand worldwide for access to higher education, and has become a policy concern for governments. The expansion of access opportunities and the establishment of equity has both educational and social goals: skilled workers for the labour force to move a country forward in the knowledge economy, and equal opportunities for all citizens, with the avoidance of discontents that have a capacity to cause civil unrest. Thus governments also have a policy concern for global social justice.

Supranational Actors and Donors

The part played by supranational actors and donors in influencing access opportunities in higher education has been considerable. The pressures of globalisation have intensified the effects on individual countries. The structures of the international agencies themselves (UNESCO, OECD, World Bank) are concerned to promote social justice alongside economic development. Indeed, the principle of access and equity is specified in the foundation documents of those bodies, as it also is in the Bologna Agreement. The fact that major actors have a direct or indirect influence on higher education policies can be seen in both national and global contexts. At national levels, the context of the specific country and region defines the major actors. The national policies of most developing countries are influenced by locally active non-governmental, bilateral and multilateral organisations. In many cases diplomatic missions that manage and process bilateral agreements and support have direct influences on policy, strategic issues and implementation related to higher education and the larger education sector.

Historically, the Ethiopian higher education system has been significantly influenced by the British and American systems. The language of instruction, the curricula, methodology of teaching, assessment and marketing, of students and faculty, etc. are imported from these systems. Similarly, Vietnamese higher education has been influenced by a number of "international actors" which included Chinese, French, the Soviet Union, American, World Bank and other international donors. Beginning in the early 1990's, with the policy shift of the World Bank and the increased support by European Union/Commission, UNDP and bilateral governments (Sweden, Norway, Netherlands, Ireland, etc.) have been major actors in policy developments and their implementation related to higher education in Ethiopia.

Examples of the influence of one country on another are legion. Both the United Kingdom and the United States have had important influences on the development of the Irish higher education. The higher education framework, which existed at the time of Independence, was principally a variant on the UK model. For a long period after Irish independence the US was an important role model for higher education policy makers, influenced by the strong cultural ties between the two countries and by the significant number of teaching staff at Irish universities who earned their doctorates in US universities. More recently the emerging European Higher Education Area has provided a context for the development of policy. However, it is probable that the OECD has been the most significant international agency in respect of the development of Irish education. The relationship is a long one dating back to 1961 when the OECD held its first major conference in Ireland on the role of education in economic growth and development.

Two kinds of globalisation forces are at play regarding the French higher education system: the European Higher Education Area (EHEA) and international competition. The European Higher Education Area (EHEA) is largely used as an argument to reform the national higher education system, which is otherwise very difficult to reform due to the strong power of the academic professions (and even moreso, the disciplines). The creation of the EHEA and the process of building a common framework is able, long-term, to bring about the reform of national systems.

Two levels of globalisation forces are at play in South African Higher Education: the South African Democratic Community (SADC) and the international competition. The historically white South African universities have long played in the same field as "western" institutions, and the question now is how to maintain this recognition and to enlarge it to include the historically disadvantaged institutions, or, at least, some of them. The politics of mergers that takes place is thus helping to bridge this historical divide although at some risk of losing the original identities.

The many policy initiatives of the government and higher education institutions in Ethiopia have been informed by the developments elsewhere in the World. Furthermore, they are usually commented upon and indirectly influenced by studies provided by or technical assistance given by donors and development partners. The specific requirements of different actors, mainly donors and development partners, have had some influence. Though the major influences relate to the way policies and strategies are implemented, there are also some roles played in the initiation and development of policies and strategies. These refer to, in some cases, setting priorities for policy and action, recommending ways in which they should be addressed, and the manner and framework by which they are to be implemented. Such studies as those conducted by the World Bank (2004) and many technical reports by international experts have had their influence in shaping some policy or strategic considerations, particularly in terms of implementation. There are much so-called 'policy conditionality' associated with external assistance that strongly needs to be reduced.

The influence of the EU, and the Bologna Process, as well as the OECD, has had marked effects on European countries. In addition, research such as PISA that mostly deals with secondary education has put some pressure on national governments to improve the level of achievement of their students by comparing the results of various countries. Most actors influencing French higher education are European- such as the European Association for Quality Insurance in Higher Education (ENQA). The ENQA sets up standards and guidelines for quality assurance in the European Higher Education Area. In France, three agencies are part of this association: The National Committee of Evaluation (CNE), a government organisation and independent body which has under its authority all the institutions of Higher Education in France; The Commission for Engineering degrees (CTI); and the General Inspectorate of Education of Research (IGAENR), an organisation under the aegis of the Ministry of Youth, Education and Research.

Impetus is also given at the national and local level to put some emphasis on specific dimensions (quality, mobility...) and to participate in the international movement of increasing the level of universities' autonomy. The three main goals already in play are the harmonisation of the degree structure, the focus and development of tools for the assurance of quality, and students' mobility. So both the definition of the common goals and the way there are afterwards defined at the national and institutional levels are generated by the overarching bodies. One advantage is that the national government can use the European process to legitimise reforms that would not have been possible otherwise. Some mechanisms, for instance, have been built into the career ladders of the senior academic faculty that encourage them strongly to go on sabbaticals, initiate cooperative research projects, participate in international forums and symposia, and publish their work in international journals.

Where different external forces are attempting to bring about different reforms, one after the other, the results can cause difficulties of adjustment. In some countries tensions develop between the bodies influencing policy and the individual governments who are carrying out the policy. Vietnamese higher education was first influenced by the Chinese system for some decades; then it came under the domination of the French, and imitated the French education system. After the country was divided into two parts, the South of Vietnam followed the American model of education, whereas in the North, higher education was similar to that in the former Soviet Union. Since the launch of the Renovation in Vietnam in 1987 by the government, the international agencies that have had a profound influence on higher education in Vietnam are the World Bank, UNESCO, and American, Australian and other Western higher education systems. In relation to access and equity, the World Bank Higher Education Project which started in 2000, had the aim of increasing the average size of higher education institutions; and expanding the proportion of scholarships allocated to students from the three lowest income quintiles; improving the average length of study of students and their graduate rates.

Since the re-unification of Vietnam in 1977, the agenda of the international actors (World Bank, Asian Development Bank, and other donors from Japan, Europe and America) would be hard to categorise. But the main purposes could arguably be for mutual benefit, or political considerations to lessen the dominating influence of a particular actor, to introduce external culture to Vietnam and/or to influence the country's higher education in a particular direction.

In the case of Ethiopia, the internal regulations and working processes of the major actors (particularly the development partners) are visible in directly or indirectly influencing higher education policy and strategy.

The general notion of priority for primary education and neglect of the higher levels of education has had a direct influence on policy and strategy. The influence could be on the availability of loans and grants or other support, or on other development partners or donor groups etc. The major agenda that drives the influence is related largely to the provision of support for national development and the reduction of poverty. While some influence is positive, some influence carries negative tones and tends to be in contradiction to the principle of country ownership of the initiatives and development agendas.

A very important principle usually neglected by development partners is the need to focus efforts around a clear set of country-owned and defined objectives and expected results, and then following through with viable stages of implement-tation strategies. Development partners need to make sure that their efforts are fully aligned with the strategies of the recipient country rather than with their own competing priorities and procedures. The reporting requirements of donors and development partners which are hardly harmonised with national systems, the insistence in the use of most of the funding for technical assistance, and lack of understanding and willingness to support sustainable and long-term capacity building efforts are a few of the most critical influences. Most, if not all, donors will have their specific requirements for reporting which are different from the national system and which create poor performance in the disbursement and utilisation of funds for future intended use. Many insist that a large part of the fund be used for the employment of technical assistance from the countries or elsewhere without addressing the real issue of local capacity building. Many focus on short programmes rather than on long-term staff development, local institutional strengthening and capacity building. This is largely the case in Ethiopia and Vietnam and possibly to some extent in South Africa.

Developed countries display different forms of influence. The European Higher Education and Research Area, which has an influence on countries such as Ireland and France and to some extent Israel, is largely a reaction to the "domination" of the American higher education. Its attraction for foreign students is that it plays an important role in the setting up of a single framework of studies that facilitates student mobility within the European higher education structure. And the same dynamic is at play when research is considered. Collaboration between universities for both teaching and research is encouraged.

The last decade has witnessed a growing tendency in Israeli universities and colleges to initiate collaborative study programmes with universities abroad. Many colleges have engaged in collaborative programmes with external universities, in order to enable their students to move directly towards a master degree, after completing their first degree in an Israeli college. This policy was one of the background factors that prompted the entrance of British and American universities into the market of Israeli higher education. Israeli academics also participate in various European Union research projects. Though Israel is not part of the Bologna Process, the Council of Higher Education has initiated in recent years an Accreditation and Quality Evaluation Scheme, which might enable Israeli students in the future to take part in the European Credit Transfer System.

An OECD study of the education system in Ireland, Investment in Education (1955), acted as the foundation document for modern Irish education, setting the tone for a reorientation of educational policy focused on the development of human capital. It also identified the equity agenda as an important feature of education policy. Both new policy directions were signalled by an impressive data gathering exercise, which demonstrated the importance of empirical research, providing an early paradigmatic example of evidence based-policy making. It is evident that the policy consensus, which emerged from the OECD, has been a major factor in setting the direction of the Irish educational agenda. Reviews influencing Irish policy makers include one on the international literature on access and equity (Skilbeck, 2000) and an overview of international trends in higher education policy (Skilbeck, 2001). Some critics of the latter study suggest that the neo-liberal agenda, which pervades the OECD policy agenda, has been used to legitimate a growing instrumentalism in Irish higher education policy. Thus the effect of globalisation can be charted in the interaction of global organisations, and external forces, with individual higher education systems, in a continual process of ebb and flow.

International Mobility

The international mobility of students, and of staff, can be seen as a major response to the pressures of globalisation. As the awareness of the opportunities to study elsewhere grows, and the information becomes more available as to where might be appropriate, so the demand expands. Although the GATS (General Agreement on Trade and Services of the World Trade Organisation (WTO) has not been finally signed into law with respect to considering higher education as a tradeable, service commodity, the ability of students to move at will to any country they choose in order to study is in keeping with this approach. As mentioned elsewhere, the growth in international students has been phenomenal, with an estimation of 7.2 million by 2025. What is interesting in examining the flows of students is that the presumption of South-North and North-North continental flows are no longer the only factors. South-South flows are growing. Considerable numbers of foreign students can now be found in China, Singapore, Qatar, Abu Dhabi and Egypt. In South Africa in 2004 there were 52,579 international students of whom 86.6% came from the South or from the developing world (Altbach 2009). Pawan Agarwal (2008) noted 'a growing South-South movement which indicates the emergence of regional hubs'.

The US remains in the forefront as the place of choice for transnational students, and figures reported for autumn 2008 showed a rise of 8% to almost 672,000 on the 2007–8 academic year (World University News Nov 2009). India is the leading country of origin with 103,000 students, a growth of 9%. China also shows a massive rise of 21%, to 99,000. Another large group comes from South Korea, with over 75,000. Sending countries showing huge percentage rises were Vietnam (+45%) – 12,823, Saudi Arabia (+28%) – 12,661 and Nepal (+30%) – 11581. Although the economic downturn is slowing down the flows, students are still enrolling from abroad. Some 50% of campuses reported that numbers were continuing to increase; 24% reported a decrease, and 26% noted static numbers.

Interestingly President Obama has recently put out a US-China Joint Statement (November 2009) which will enable 100,000 US students to study in China over the next four years (a figure which will equal those from China in the US). The statement also announces an agreement to create a 'new bilateral mechanism' to facilitate people and cultural exchanges. Such an initiative is indicative of the pressure of globalisation to bring about cooperation between governments and, by modern electronic means, facilitate its happening.

The movement of students is paralleled by the movement of top academics globally, and the choice of places is somewhat similar to those of students. However, North-North movements (e.g. Europe to the States) and South-North movements still predominate but there are examples of South-South travel, as in the placing of Nigerian academics in Ethiopia to aid the development of that system (Semela and Ayalew 2008). The expansion of private education has been rapid in many countries, with a consequent rise in demand for qualified staff. Advertisements for positions in the Far East, Asia and the Middle East appear weekly in the UK *Times Higher Education.*

Doctoral students frequently undertake or complete their doctoral studies abroad. Pakistan, for instance, pays for 250 doctoral students per year to study in Germany, France, Austria and China. Brazil sends around 20% of its students to train abroad, mainly in the US. China expects its high achieving students to have some period of study abroad, often at Masters' or Doctoral level. Such experience will be seen as very advantageous if the individual applies for a post in the top Chinese universities.

In recent years governments have put effort into attracting back those students, particularly doctoral candidates, who have been studying abroad. Latin America has a number of examples of good initiatives: countries that can offer stability, government support, sound professional standing, incentives, international collaboration and institutional capacity building appear to be the most successful. There is some evidence that erstwhile students are returning to their home countries, but this is more often found in emerging nations, such as Brazil, China and India, where the possibilities of a good future career are attractive to the individual.

One other phenomenon brought about as a result of the pressures of globalisation is the development of professional and academic curricula to facilitate access. As governments seek to expand the numbers entering and graduating from higher education, the institutions have developed 'access' curricula. In the UK there are one year 'access' courses for those with very few credentials to bring them up to the necessary level to enter higher education. Examples are 'access' courses in Nursing and Physiotherapy. On entry to universities there are also short in-house training sessions on such topics as essay writing, how to use a library, and basic mathematics. Such an approach can facilitate access for both domestic and international students.

One other facet of globalisation should be mentioned – that of the growing availability on the web of open source material. Although online education and e-learning enterprises have suffered some spectacular failures, there is now a steady growth in courses offered by universities which combine web delivery with some face-to-face interaction. MIT (Massachusetts Institute of Technology) has led the way with making its course material freely available. This can be viewed as a new tool to expand access which enables students disadvantaged by location and personal circumstances to take part in academic study. The English language, to this point, is supreme but other languages, such as Chinese, may well be used at a future time. There are inherent problems with making huge archives of course material available for free on the web: chiefly the tension between intellectual philanthropy and intellectual property. These matters are not resolved: they relate back to questions of the perception of universities and their role in society. Are they essentially an instrument for public good, or a market trader?

The establishment of overseas campuses points up the conundrum. Are they there to make profits for the university which sets them up, or are they to serve the populace in their location and enable access to knowledge which would otherwise not be available? The growth of overseas campuses has been marked in recent years. In 1999 there were 35: now there are 162, but five have closed. (Observatory on Borderless Higher Education 2009). A quarter of the campuses are in the United

Arab Emirates: international higher education hubs can be found in the Middle East and SE Asia. Institutions from twenty two countries have established overseas campuses, both public and private universities and colleges. The US has 78 such campuses, with Australia having 14, the UK 13 and France and India 11. Other countries are now involved: Lebanon, Malaysia, South Korea, Sri Lanka and Switzerland all have at least one overseas campus. The successful campuses are able to attract students who are unable to gain entry to higher education on their home campus, thus widening access.

CONCLUSION

The impact of globalisation on access and equity is considerable, and its effects are continuing. The global downturn is likely to exacerbate the problems caused by it, but the trends will continue. Inequalities at global level, between different regions, between countries and within countries, are likely to become more marked. However, the combination of governments' awareness of the need to expand access, and the continuing demand for access may give higher education some protection. The OECD report 'Policy Responses to the Economic Crisis' (June 2009) recommended that the population to be the hardest hit should be identified; resources should be targeted to those vulnerable populations; and investment should be made in demand-side financing programmes, such as the provision of scholarships and grants. Thus countries could continue to innovate for long-term growth and make the continuing expansion of access deliverable.

BIBLIOGRAPHY

Agarwal, P. (2008). India in the context of international student circulation: Status and prospects. In Hans de Wit, et al. (Eds.), *The dynamics of international student circulation in a global context*. Rotterdam: Sense.

Altbach, P. G., & Knight, J. (2006). *The internationalization of higher education: Motivations and realities in the NEA 2006 almanac of higher education*. Washington, DC: National Education Association.

Altbach, P. G., Reisberg, L., & Rumbley, L. E. (2009). *Trends in global higher education: Tracking an academic revolution*. Chestnut Hill, MA: Boston College Center for International Higher Education.

Becker, R. (2009). *International branch campuses: Markets and strategies*. London: The Observatory on Borderless Higher Education.

China Daily. (2009, November 9). Beijing.

China Daily. (2009, November 10). Beijing.

Commission for Africa. (2005). *Our common interest: Report of the commission for Africa*. Addis Ababa: United Nations Economic Commission for Africa.

Eggins, H. (Ed.). (2003). *Globalization and reform in higher education*. Maidenhead: Open University Press.

OECD/IMHE. (2009). *The impact and influence of league tables and ranking systems on higher education decision-making and academic behaviour*. Paris: OECD.

OECD. (1965). *Investment in education, report of the survey team appointed by the Minister for education*. Dublin: Stationery Office.

OECD. (2009). *Policy responses to the economic crisis*. Paris: OECD.

Organisation for Economic Co-operation and Development. (1998). *Education at a glance: OECD indicators 1998*. Paris: OECD.

Semela, T., & Ayalew, A. (2008). *Ethiopia in Higher education in Africa: the international dimension* (D. Teferra & J. Knight, Eds.). Boston: Center for International Higher Education, Boston College.

Skilbeck, M., & Connell, H. (2000). *Access and equity in higher education: An international perspective*. Dublin: Higher Education Authority.

Skilbeck, M. (2001). *The university challenged: A review of international trends and issues with particular reference to Ireland*. Dublin: Higher Education Authority.

UNESCO. (1998). *Higher education in the twenty first century: Vision and action: World conference on higher education 1998*. Paris: UNESCO.

UNESCO. (2008). *Declaration of the regional conference on higher education in Latin America and the Caribbean -CRES*. Paris: UNESCO.

UNESCO. (2009). *Communique, 2009 world conference on higher education: the new dynamics of higher education and research for societal change and development*. Paris: UNESCO.

United Nations Development Program. (1999). *Human development report 1999*. New York: Oxford University Press.

The White House, Office of Press Secretary. (2009, November 17). *US-China joint statement*. Beijing.

World Bank. (2002). *Constructing knowledge societies: New challenges for tertiary education*. Washington, DC: The World Bank.

World Bank. (2004). *Higher education development for Ethiopia: Pursuing the vision*. Washington, DC: The World Bank.

World Bank and UNESCO. (2000). *Higher education in developing countries: Peril and promise, the task force on higher education and society*. Washington, DC: The World Bank.

World University News. (2009, November 22). *US: More students go abroad, more arrive*. Issue 0102.

Yizengaw, T. A. (2007). *The Ethiopian higher education: creating space for reform*. Addis Ababa: St. Mary's Publishing.

MEASURING ACCESS AND EQUITY FROM
A COMPARATIVE PERSPECTIVE

Introduction

The massive and continuing expansion of education in recent decades, in almost all societies, points to the centrality of education in the project of modernity. Between 1970 and 2000, globally, average enrolments in secondary education increased by 180 per cent while over the same period enrolments in tertiary education have nearly quadrupled (Gradstein and Nikitin 2004). By the start of this century, a child aged 5 can expect to be enrolled in school for 11 years, on average. This school life expectancy ranges from 8 years for Africa and 10 years for Asia to 14 years in North America and 16 years in Europe (UNESCO 2005). An analysis of this expansion has attracted the attention of several analysts. In a recent review of the worldwide expansion of higher education Schofer and Meyer (2005: 916–7) argue that this expansion reflects global institutional changes linked to the rise of a new model of society: increasing democratisation and human rights, scientisation, the rise of national development logics and the structuration of international organizations. In a review of the consequences of global educational expansion Hannum & Buchmann (2003) have identified six related assumptions which underpin this process. These include a belief that education leads to the following: economic development of societies and enhanced earnings for individuals; improved health and slower population growth; a reduction in social inequalities and enhanced democracy. And while not all of these assumptions are supported by empirical research findings, a widespread belief in these and related propositions has underpinned educational expansion.

A common thread in much of this analysis is the identification of twin objectives both economic and social. Educational expansion is driven by considerations of economic growth. At this level the main concern is with the scale of expansion. With the advent of globalisation and technological change, individuals and governments see educational expansion as the key to personal enhancement and national competitiveness. In more and more countries public policy targets have evolved from that of achieving universal completion of primary education to achieving universal completion of secondary education towards achieving mass enrolment in higher education. Analytically separate from the issue of the scale of expansion, the social agenda is concerned with concerns of social justice and ideals of democratisation. The concern here is less with the issue of expanding participation but with widening access to higher education to previously under-represented groups. This distinction is central to this paper.

Following this brief introduction, the next section of the paper deals with comparative indicators of participation in higher education. We deal separately with measures of entry, enrolment and output of higher education systems. The section on enrolment measures is based primarily on an extensive analysis of the OECD database on higher education statistics. In the light of this analysis we develop an overall index of participation and rank 27 OECD countries on this index. We briefly explore some correlates of differential participation rates. The third section of the paper is concerned with measures of equity. Traditionally this concern related primarily to the representation in post compulsory education by gender and social class but is now extended to a consideration of representation by race and ethnicity, age and disability. Our analysis here is focused almost exclusively on socio-economic disadvantage. We review the comparative literature on the relationship between expansion and equity, drawing especially on some recent work which we argue challenges the long established conventional wisdom in this area. In observing that the most authoritative research is based on cohort analysis, which is necessarily 'historical' and thus is not especially useful for policy makers who wish to evaluate the effect of more recent policy developments, we point to the need to develop comparative measures that assess changing levels of inequality using the most recent enrolment data. This section of the paper includes our analysis of the EUROSTUDENT surveys and a limited selection of findings from national surveys.

COMPARATIVE INDICATORS OF PARTICIPATION IN HIGHER EDUCATION

A recent trend evident in many countries is a heightened interest in comparative data on participation in higher education. This is partly explained by the view that in a knowledge society a country's competitiveness will increasingly be determined by the quality of education and training of the labour force. Many countries are anxious to 'benchmark' their educational achievements against the leading countries, which may be seen as key competitors. This desire for accurate comparisons is not matched by the availability of comparative statistics, which facilitate such a ranking exercise. In spite of the concerted efforts of the OECD and UNESCO and more recently of the EU it is remains hazardous to attempt to make accurate comparisons between countries. This is partly a function of the differences between countries in their higher education systems. There is variation between countries in the definition of what constitutes higher education and how this differs from other forms of post-secondary education. In some countries higher education is mainly focused on the 18–21 age groups, who study full-time while in other countries part-time and mature students make up a very large percentage of higher education enrolments. Some counties classify separately full-time and part-time students while in other countries there is no recognition of the part-time category even though very many students may indeed study part-time. Quite apart from the different forms of participation, higher education systems differ in the duration of study programmes. In addition to the inherent difficulties listed there is also evidence that some countries seem to differentiate between the statistics they produce for internal national purposes and those produced for international agencies such as the OECD. This can be interpreted benignly as a perception that national policy requires a different set of statistics but there is also the possibility that international comparisons are being utilised as part of a political process to bolster national pride by improving a country's standing in the international arena.

Both the OECD and UNESCO (and more recently in cooperation with EUROSTAT) have attempted, both separately and in cooperation, to develop a suite of indicators that capture some of the main features of the variability between countries. Since the range of counties, which fall within the remit of OECD and UNESCO differs significantly it is not surprising that the OECD can aspire to greater detail in their comparative indicators. The work of these supra-national agencies has been supplemented by the work of other researchers, most notably by Kaiser & O'Hearn (2005), and by the Educational Policy Institute. This institute's report on accessibility and affordability provides a good example of the potential for comparative research as well as demonstrating some of the constraints arising from existing data inadequacies (Usher & Cervenan 2004). Among the various indicators that have been developed to quantify access to higher education, it is possible to identify three types of measures which have been used to capture inter-country differences in participation. In combination, an examination of entry rates, enrolment rates and output measures such as graduation rates or measures of the educational levels of the adult population have the potential to provide a robust measure of higher education participation in a country.

Entry Measures

Entry rates into higher education offer the potential for the most unambiguous comparison. Entry rates measure the inflow to higher education at a particular period rather than the total stock of students enrolled, which is measured by enrolment rates. The entry rate seeks to measure the percentage of the population who are afforded the opportunity of availing of higher education. Traditionally, this was measured as the number of new entrants to higher education in a particular year, expressed as a percentage of the population at the typical age of entry – frequently the average size of the 18–19 age-cohort, or the average size of the age cohort from which at least 70% of the entrants belong. This is described as the *gross entry rate*. Although easy to calculate since it does not require very detailed data on the age distribution of entrants this measure lacks precision because of the lack of correspondence between the age distributions of the enumerator and the denominator. More recently the *net entry rate* is more widely used especially in OECD countries. The net entry rate for a specific age is obtained by dividing the number of first-time (new) entrants of that age by the total population in the corresponding age group, multiplied by 100 (OECD, 2004: 143). The overall net entry rate is calculated by summing the rates for each single year of age. While this is a comprehensive measure complications arise from the definition of new entrant. A new entrant to a particular college or university may have previously been enrolled in another college, on a similar or different programme[1]. Furthermore, since most countries identify different sectors of higher education the movement of students between sectors leads to double counting if the same student is classified as a new entrant in each sector. The OECD differentiates between Type A higher education and Type B higher education. The former refers to programmes that are largely theoretically based and designed to provide qualifications for entry into advanced research programmes and professions with high skill requirements while Type B programmes are more occupationally oriented, typically of shorter duration, and lead to direct labour market access. Since some students who enter Type B may enter Type A at a later period and since it is possible that the same student may be enrolled simultaneously on both programmes the two entry rates cannot be added together to obtain overall entry rates. While it is clear from the design of the Data Collection Manuals jointly prepared by UNESCO-UIS, OECD and EUROSTAT that there is a full realisation of the need to differentiate between new entrants to a particular programme and first time entrants into higher education of any type, the quality of the data provided by national statistical agencies does not allow for this kind of precision.

In Table 1 we present some statistics on entry rates to higher education and on a closely related phenomenon, upper secondary graduation rates, for 27 OECD member countries. We present three figures on net entry. The first relates to data from those countries that do not differentiate between programme type (whether A or B). These are described as 'aggregate entry rates'. If we can assume that countries have correctly excluded from these returns those students who are repeat or re-entry students this statistic is a highly useful one for the purposes of comparative analysis of access to higher education. In the next two columns we enter separately figures for entry rates for Type A and Type B higher education. Because we are cautioned against summing these two separate entry rates we do not have any overall figure on entry to higher education for these countries. This is a serious limitation, which greatly inhibits comparative analysis. It is our view that, taking account of the limitations of data at national level, the drive towards greater precision to differentiate between programme types has been premature leaving us with a most unsatisfactory situation whereby we have no summary statistic on access to higher education. The lack of a useable indicator on the rate of entry to higher education is a serious impediment to comparative analysis that needs to be rectified. While we can compare the entry rate for the countries which only report a single rate (Australia, Finland and the US) and those whose enrolments are almost totally confined to Type A higher education (Italy, Mexico, Netherlands, Norway and Poland) we have little guidance on how to interpret the other statistics. For the three countries which report only an aggregate rate, Finland has the highest rate followed by Australia and the US. Looking separately at entry rates to Type A higher education New Zealand and Korea have entry rates in excess of 50% while the rates exceed 30% in the case of France, Belgium, Japan and the UK. While in some cases such as Ireland it is possible to sum the two rates without any significant double counting (author's local knowledge) this is clearly not the case in many other countries. It is evident from Table 1 that the caution against summing entry rates for Type A and Type B would appear to be fully justified.

For example, the sum of the two rates greatly exceeds 100% in the case of New Zealand and amounts to 100% in the case of Korea. Furthermore, the combined figures for many other counties exceed what is generally accepted at nation level to be the higher education entry rate. Our inability to rank countries on the rate of admission to higher education is indeed a serious gap in comparative statistics and an impediment to comparative analysis.

Table 1. Rates of Entry to Higher Education and Upper Secondary Graduation Rates in OECD Countries in 2003

	Net Aggregate Entry Rate	Net Entry Rate (Type A)	Net Entry Rate (Type B)	Upper Secondary Graduation Rate		
				Total (unduplicated)	General Programmes	Pre-vocational/ Vocational programmes
Australia	68	NA	NA	NA	69	47
Austria	NA	35	9	NA	15	54
Belgium	NA	34	33	NA	36	61
Canada	NA	NA	NA	NA	N/A	NA
Czech Rep.	NA	33	9	88	18	71
Denmark	NA	53	11	86	54	56
Finland	73	NA	NA	84	52	69
France	NA	39	34	81	34	70
Germany	NA	36	16	97	35	62
Greece	NA	.NA	.NA	96	58	40
Hungary	NA	69	7	87	33	53
Iceland	NA	83	9	79	59	46
Ireland	NA	41	17	91	66	29
Italy	NA	54	1	81	29	65
Japan	NA	42	31	91	67	24
Korea	NA	49	51	NA	63	30
Luxembourg	NA	NA	NA	71	27	44
Mexico	NA	28	2	36	32	4
Netherlands	NA	52	1	NA	32	62
New Zealand	NA	81	53	NA	125	A
Norway	NA	68	1	92	59	43
Poland	NA	70	1	86	40	56
Portugal	NA	NA	NA	NA	NA	NA
Slovak Rep.	NA	40	3	56	11	55
Spain	NA	46	21	67	46	25
Sweden	NA	80	7	76	38	38
Switzerland	NA	38	17	90	33	59
Turkey	NA	23	24	41	27	15
UK	NA	48	30	M	NA	NA
USA	63	NA	NA	73	73	NA

We have included in Table 1 data on Upper Secondary Graduation rates, differentiating between the total (unduplicated) graduation rate and graduation from general and pre-vocational/ vocational programmes. These rates relate to what is conventionally understood as the most important 'pipeline' for higher education entry. Thus, for example, the stagnation in high school completion rates in recent years has been a major concern of policy makers in the US (Orfield 2004). And while the US system allows multiple opportunities for entry to higher education through the life cycle the failure to increase high school graduation rates is likely to represent a constraint on future expansion of the higher education system. In contrast, Deer (2005) has remarked that the expansion of higher education in France is a 'mechanical phenomenon' stemming from the politically encouraged growth in participation at upper secondary level and from the increased success rates at the baccalaureate level. In the case of Germany, Ertl (2005) notes that the expansion of higher education is restricted by the selective secondary school system which only allows around 40% of young people to achieve the formal qualification needed for higher education. The latter remark underlines the importance of the distinction between general and vocational programmes since it is the general programmes which supply the great bulk of higher education entrants. While in most countries vocational programmes can lead to higher education, especially those designated as pre-vocational or pre-technical, not all such programmes do so. Most vocational programmes prepare students for direct entry into specific occupations without further training. The OECD reports the country means for the upper secondary enrolment patterns, by programme orientation, as 51% for general programmes, 4% for pre-vocational programmes and 45% for vocational programmes; about a third of the latter enrolments are on combined school and work-based programmes. As in the case of higher education entry rates, the quantification of upper secondary graduation rates is not unproblematic. This is well signalled by the failure, over a long period, of OECD analysts and UK officials to agree an appropriate definition for the UK of what constitutes upper secondary graduation. The reader is cautioned that, just as in the case of entry rates to higher education types A and B which we have discussed above, graduation from general programmes and pre-vocational/ vocational programmes as reported in the final columns of Table 1 cannot be added. Six countries report total Upper Secondary graduation rates in excess of 90%. However these countries have in fact very different profiles of secondary education. In the case of Japan and Ireland these overall high graduation rates are mainly accounted for by graduation rates of about two-thirds from general programmes while in case of Germany and Switzerland the overall high rates reflect high graduation rates from pre-vocational/ vocational programmes with only about one third of the cohort graduating from general programmes. The division between general and vocational programmes is more even in the case of Greece and Norway.

Enrolment Measures

In the absence of satisfactory comparative measures of rates of entry to higher education we turn our attention to an analysis of enrolment data. It is of interest to note that while the OECD has accumulated an impressive data-base on higher education enrolment in recent years they have not published any summary indicators using these data. Instead they have preferred to calculate education expectancy, defined as the number of years of full and part-time education in which a 5-year-old can expect to enrol over his or her lifetime, differentiated by level of education. It is estimated that by 2003, on average, a 17-year-old can expect to receive 2.8 years of tertiary education in OECD countries. This calculation is based on a variant of an indicator which we discuss below (sum of age specific enrolment rates) and projects current enrolment levels into the future. While this is a discriminating measure we concur with Kaiser & O'Hearn (2005: 32) that it lacks face validity and that it is difficult to understand what the score means.

The present analysis follows from an intensive interrogation of the valuable OECD data-base of statistics on higher education enrolment for 2003. The most striking feature of this analysis is the differences between countries in the pattern of HE enrolments. This is first evident when we look at the age distribution of higher education students (Table A1[2]). In all countries the highest percentage of HE enrolments relates to those in the 20–24 age group; the percentage of total enrolments in this age group range from 64% for Poland to 33% for the UK. The main differences between countries are reflected in the percentages aged less than 20 and those who are aged 30 or over. In the case of seven countries (Ireland, Mexico, Turkey, Belgium, Greece, France and Korea the percentages aged under 20 exceed 25%. In contrast in the Scandinavian countries (Iceland, Denmark, Sweden, Finland, and Norway) less than 5% of higher education students are aged less than 20 years old. The pattern of representation of older students among higher education enrolments is almost the mirror image of what we find for younger students. All of the Scandinavian countries have a significant percentage of students aged 40 or over. This is also true of the UK, New Zealand, Australia and the United States. These differences are also reflected in the mean ages of HE students which are also shown in Table A1. This Table also includes the standard deviation of these distributions which range from less than 4 for Greece, Turkey and Poland to more than 10 for the UK, New Zealand, Australia and the United States. It is clear that in some countries higher education enrolment is heavily concentrated among a narrow age range, typically the young, while in other countries it spans a very wide age range.

These differences are best illustrated in an analysis of enrolment rates by age. We have calculated and displayed graphically age specific enrolment rates for the 27 OECD countries for which data were available. The graph of age specific enrolments, only a sample of which can be shown here, reflects both the shape of the distribution (how it is distributed by age group) but also the 'enrolment intensity', which reflects the percentage of each age group enrolled. The findings from our analysis replicates those from an earlier analysis of net rates of participation in nine countries which identified three general patterns regarding the age composition of participants in higher education (Kaiser et al 2005). The first pattern is the early peak, followed by a flat tail; the second is also skewed to the left but the peak is less high and participation of the older age-group is more significant; the third pattern is a more even distribution across the age spread.

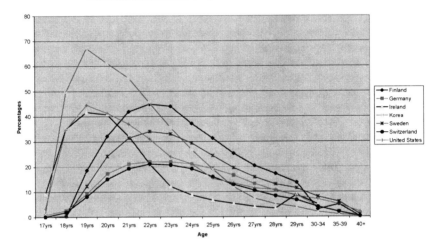

Figure 2. Age Specific Enrolment in Higher Education for Selected Countries 2003

These patterns are clearly evident in Figure 1 which is based on a sample of selected countries drawn from our 27 country analysis. Korea, the United States and Ireland exhibit early peaks; Finland and Sweden demonstrate later peaks while Germany and Switzerland demonstrate lower peaks but a more even spread across the age ranges. Variation in enrolment rates for the older age groups is less easily identified in this graph. They are however more evident in Table A2 (appendix). Here we note that in only 3 countries (Iceland, New Zealand and the US) does the enrolment rate for those aged 40 plus reach 2%; a further 6 countries have a rate of 1%. The enrolment rate for the 30–39 age-group reaches 7% in Finland and Sweden while it reaches 6% in Australia, Iceland, Norway and the United States; in contrast this rate is less than 1% in Greece and Turkey.

Informed by the foregoing analysis of the OECD data-base on higher education statistics and taking account of indicators previously used by other analysts we present in Table 2 four indicators of enrolment. The first of these is still widely used by UNESCO and was previously used by the OECD. The *gross enrolment rate* is based on the number of students enrolled, regardless of age, expressed as 'a percentage of the population … in the five-year age group following on from the secondary school leaving age' (UNESCO, 2005: 149). Finland, Korea, Norway and the US have the highest rates, all in excess of 80% while Sweden, Australia an New Zealand all have rates in excess of 70%. The main limitation of this measure is the somewhat arbitrary nature of the denominator selected. While this may be better suited to those countries with a strong clustering of enrolments in the younger age groups it may be less suitable for those countries with a high percentage of older students. Also the choice of a five-year age span is somewhat arbitrary since many students graduate from higher education programmes in a shorter space of time. The utility of the measure is a function of the limited data requirements since many countries are unable to supply fully comprehensive data on the age of higher education students. The next measure presented in Table 4, the *net enrolment rate aged 18–29*, is based on the total higher education enrolments of all aged 18–29 divided by the population of the same age group. This indicator has been used by the National Centre for Educational Statistics in its comparison of higher education enrolments in the US and other G-8 countries (NCES, 2005). Where higher education is confined to this traditional age-group this is a relatively robust indicator. However as we saw from Table 1 above this excludes about one-third of enrolments in several countries, thus it must be considered a somewhat arbitrary measure.

Table 2. Selected Measures of Participation in Higher Education for OECD Countries in 2003

Countries	Gross Enrolment Rate	Net Enrolment (18–29 Age Group)	Sum of Age Specific Enrolments	Enrolment Intensity
Australia	74	21	280.8	36.6
Austria	49	14	179.5	22.2
Belgium	61	22	267.5	46.8
Canada	58	NA	NA	NA
Czech Republic	36	13	169.5	29.9
Denmark	67	19	235.6	31.5
Finland	86	27	334.9	44.5
France	56	21	253.6	40.5
Germany	51	15	190.2	22
Greece	68	29	362.5	53.9
Hungary	51	18	225.8	31.8
Iceland	55	17	219.5	29.2
Ireland	50	18	233.7	41.2
Italy	57	18	233.1	33.9
Japan	49	NA		
Korea	85	3	392.2	64.1
Luxembourg	NA	NA	NA	NA
Mexico	22	9	104.9	16.8
Netherlands	58	19	235.8	33.1
New Zealand	74	20	247.2	35.3
Norway	81	20	262	34
Poland	60	21	259.7	40.5
Portugal	53	18	229.3	30.6
Slovak Republic	32	13	158.9	24.2
Spain	62	21	268.9	37.1
Sweden	76	21	264	33.5
Switzerland	49	13	166.2	20.7
Turkey	28	7	90.89	15.6
UK	64	16	211.7	35.1
USA	81	25	310.1	42.9

With these reservations in mind we include a new measure which is not currently in use: the *sum of age specific enrolments* is based on the sum of the net rates of enrolment for each year of those aged 17 to 29 and the net rates of enrolment for those aged 30–34, 35–39 and those aged 40+. This measure effectively calculates the total area under the curves that we have graphed in Figure 1 above. While acknowledging Kaiser & O'Hearn's (2005: 19) contention that this measure may have low face validity since it does not meet the conventional expectations of indicating what *percentage* of the population are enrolled in higher education it is clearly the most comprehensive measure since it takes account of variability in the structure of higher education enrolments between countries, giving appropriate weight to all enrolments whether these are highly concentrated among younger students or whether enrolments are dispersed among a much wider age span. Because of its comprehensiveness we are impressed with the value of this indicator which can be used as a stand alone measure or, as we propose, as part of a suite of indicators to measure participation in higher education. Korea, Greece, Finland and the US have the highest score on this indicator with rates in excess of 300. Turkey, Mexico, the Slovak Republic and Switzerland have the lowest rates on this measure. The rates for the Czech Republic, Austria and Germany are also relatively low, being less than 200.

We include a further measure of enrolment, which we describe as 'enrolment intensity'. Enrolment intensity is based on the average enrolment rate for the two years of age with the highest enrolment. This measures the two highest peaks in enrolment rates for each country as demonstrated in Figures 1, above. For 12 countries, enrolment intensity is highest for those aged 19–20; this is the case for Australia, Belgium, France, Greece, Ireland, Italy, Korea, Mexico, Slovak Republic, Turkey, the UK and the US. For 7 countries it is highest for those aged 20–21: this is the case for the Czech Republic, Hungary, Netherlands, New Zealand, Poland, Portugal, and Spain). For Austria and Norway enrolment intensity is highest for those aged 21–22. In the case of 5 countries, Finland, Germany, Hungary, Sweden and Switzerland enrolment intensity is highest for the those aged 22–23, while in the case of Denmark enrolment intensity is highest for the 23–24 age group.

Output Measures

The third set of indicators of participation relates to the output from the higher education system and thus reflects previous enrolments. In Table 3 we show the percentages of the adult population aged 25–64 and separately those aged 25–34, and 35–44 with higher education and also the overall graduation rates and, separately, the graduation rates for Type A higher education. Canada, Israel and the US have the highest percentage of the population (25–64) with higher education with rates of 44%, 43% and 38% respectively. Of the OECD countries Italy, Turkey, Portugal, the Czech Republic and the Slovak Republic have the lowest rates of third level graduates among the population aged 25–64. We show separately the percentages with higher education for the younger adult cohorts, those aged 25–34 and those aged 35–44. In the majority of countries these rates

Table 3. Selected Output Measures on Participation in Higher Education

	Percentage Population Aged 25–64 with Higher Education	Percentage Population Aged 25–34 with Higher Education	Percentage Population Aged 35–44 with Higher Education	Graduation Rates: All Higher Education	Graduation Rate Type A Higher Education
Australia	31	36	32	49	49
Austria	15	15	16	19	19
Belgium	29	39	31	NA	NA
Canada	44	53	NA	NA	NA
Czech Republic	12	12	15	21	17
Denmark	32	35	34	52	42
Finland	33	40	38	50	49
France	23	37	23	45	27
Germany	24	22	26	30	20
Greece	18	24	22	NA	NA
Hungary	15	17	16	38	35
Iceland	26	29	30	50	43
Ireland	26	37	27	56	37
Italy	10	12	11	28	27
Japan	37	52	NA	61	34
Korea	29	47	32	NA	NA
Luxembourg	15	19	16	NA	NA
Mexico	15	19	17	NA	NA
Netherlands	24	28	26	NA	NA
New Zealand	31	32	31	NA	NA
Norway	31	40	33	44	40
Poland	14	20	13	44	NA
Portugal	11	16	11	NA	NA
Slovak Republic	12	13	11	13	12
Spain	25	38	27	38	25
Sweden	33	40	35	40	33
Switzerland	27	29	29	29	27
Turkey	10	11	8	11	10
UK	28	33	28	52	38
USA	38	39	39	42	33

differ significantly from those for the full adult cohort, reflecting the recency of enhanced opportunities for higher education in these countries. This is well illustrated in the case of France, Japan, Korea, Spain, Ireland and Belgium where the percentages with higher education for the youngest adult cohort are significantly greater that that for the total cohort. This situation contrasts with that of the US where the earlier advent of mass higher education leaves little variation between the different adult cohorts in the attainment of higher education. Several other countries also show little variation between cohorts in the percentages with higher education. Austria, Germany, Italy and Switzerland all reveal constant levels of higher education attainment between different adult cohorts; in these instances the output of higher education graduates appears to have stabilised at much lower levels than in the case of the US.

The final two columns in Table 3 present a more immediate indicator of the output of higher education systems, tertiary graduation rates. We present two indicators, one which relates to graduation from all forms of higher education and one which relates to graduation from Type A higher education. Regrettably these data are not available for many countries, thus this indicator is of limited value for the purposes of comparative analysis. There is a particular risk of some double counting where the same student may graduate with different levels of qualifications in successive years. Looking first at total graduation rates, Japan, Ireland, Denmark, the UK, Finland and Iceland all have graduation rates of 50% or over while if we limit our focus to graduation from Type A higher education Australia, Finland, Iceland and Norway all have graduation rates of 40% or over.

Higher Education Participation Index

In the introduction we stated that an optimum indicator of participation in higher education should combine a measure of entry rates, enrolment rates and graduation rates. We have interrogated separately each of these dimensions. Although strongly committed to the superiority of entry rates as an optimum measure, which I have used over a period of more than two decades in my own national research (Clancy, 2001), it is not defensible to use either of these measures that we examined in Table 1 above for the purposes of comparative research. We can of course use the entry rate to Type A or Type B higher education, but we cannot combine these to get an aggregate rate. In relation to output measures the situation is more satisfactory although, as we noted above, the large number of countries that cannot provide graduation rates prevents us from using this measure. We feel that the percentage of the population aged 25–34 with higher education is a good measure that is easily understood and widely available. Perhaps the main caveat is that it may underestimate the qualification level in those countries with a late age of entry and with relatively long programmes. Thus, we also deem it appropriate to take into account the additional indicator of the percentage of the population with higher education aged 35–44. When we look at indicators on enrolment rates we have a number of options. We can use gross enrolment rates, still used by UNESCO but no longer used by the OECD since the age distribution of the denominator (the percentage of the population ... in the five-year age group following on from the secondary school leaving age) does not match the age distribution of the enumerator which includes all enrolments in higher education, irrespective of age. It might be argued that it makes inadequate allowance for those programmes that last more than 5 years, whether because of the 'formal' duration of these programmes or because many students prolong their studies, which they combine with work. In that context we are attracted to the use of the sum of age specific enrolment rates where all enrolled students are included in the calculations irrespective of age. For opposite reasons we are attracted to the measure of 'enrolment intensity', which measures the percentage of enrolments in the two years that have the highest levels of enrolment. This measure which might be thought of as a proxy for entry rates since it takes particular account of the all those who experience some higher education, many perhaps on short cycle programmes. These three measures of enrolment are highly inter-correlated (see Table A3, appendix); similarly the two measures of higher education attainment of the 25–34 and 35–44 age groups are highly correlated (r = .93). Although the inter-correlation of the enrolment indicators and the higher education attainment indicators are more modest averaging .59 we have decided to use all five indicators to provide an overall measure of participation in higher education. The distribution of each of these measures is shown in Table 4.

To arrive at a single summary measure we standardise the scores on each of the five indicators out of 100 before being added; the resultant sum is divided by 5 to give a score out of 100. Korea, Finland and the United States score highest on this index of participation, although as we illustrated in Figure 1 their enrolment profile is rather different. Korea's top position is secured by a very high early peak, highest 'enrolment intensity', highest age specific enrolments and the highest percentage of the population of those aged 25–34 with higher education. In contrast while the US also has an early peak in enrolment rates it is less high than that of Korea. It has, however, significantly higher enrolment rates for the older age groups and has the highest percentage of those aged 35–44 with higher education, reflecting the earlier expansion of higher education. The enrolment peak for Finland is somewhat later than for either of these countries and remains significantly higher for the age range 23–29. Norway and Sweden also show a high score on our index of participation while Australia, Greece and New Zealand also record scores in excess of 70. It is of interest to note that this top one third is drawn from four continents, Asia, Europe, America, and Australia. (It should be remembered that both Canada and Japan are missing from our database.) The middle group of countries on this ranking are all European countries, with the UK occupying the middle position in the ranking, with Denmark, Spain, France and Ireland having slightly higher scores and the Netherlands, Iceland, Poland and Switzerland having slightly lower scores. Of the 27 OECD countries included in our analysis, Turkey and Mexico have the lowest participation rates followed by the Slovak and Czech Republics. Five European countries make up the remainder of the bottom third; these are Austria, Portugal, Italy, Hungary and Germany.

Table 4. Selected Indicators of Participation in Higher Education for 27 OECD Countries (ranking in parenthesis)

Country	Gross Enrolment Rates	Sum of Age Specific Enrolments	Enrolment Intensity	Percentage Aged 25–34 With Higher Education	Percentage Aged 35–44 With Higher Education	Index of Participation in Higher Education*
Korea	85 (2)	392.2 (1)	64.1 (1)	47 (1)	32 (6)	96.2 (1)
Finland	86 (1)	334.9 (3)	44.5 (4)	40 (2)	38 (2)	87.5 (2)
U S	81 (3)	310.1 (4)	42.9 (5)	39 (5)	39 (1)	84.6 (3)
Norway	81 (3)	262 (9)	34 (13)	40 (2)	33 (5)	76.8 (4)
Sweden	76 (5)	264 (8)	33.5 (15)	40 (2)	35 (3)	76.6 (5)
Belgium	61 (12)	267.5 (7)	46.8 (3)	39 (5)	31 (8)	74.9 (6)
Australia	74 (6)	280.8 (5)	36.6 (10)	36 (10)	32 (6)	74.7 (7)
Greece	68 (8)	362.5 (2)	53.9 (2)	24 (17)	22 (18)	72.6 (8)
New Zealand	74 (7)	247.2 (12)	35.3 (11)	32 (13)	31 (8)	70.3 (9)
Denmark	67 (9)	235.6 (14)	31.5 (18)	35 (11)	34 (4)	69.8 (10)
Spain	62 (11)	268.9 (6)	37.1 (9)	38 (7)	27 (13)	69.7 (11)
France	56 (16)	253.3 (11)	40.5 (8)	37 (8)	23 (17)	66.1 (12)
Ireland	50 (21)	233.7 (15)	41.2 (6)	37 (8)	27 (13)	66.0 (13)
U K	64 (10)	211.7 (20)	35.1 (12)	33 (12)	28 (11)	65.0 (14)
Netherlands	58 (14)	235.8 (13)	33.1 (16)	28 (16)	26 (15)	61.1 (15)
Iceland	55 (17)	219.5 (19)	29.2 (21)	29 (14)	30 (10)	60.8 (16)
Poland	60 (13)	259.7 (10)	40.5 (7)	20 (19)	13 (23)	55.0 (17)
Switzerland	49 (23)	166.2 (24)	20.7 (25)	29 (14)	29 (11)	53.5 (18)
Germany	51 (19)	190.2 (21)	22 (24)	22 (18)	26 (15)	51.1 (19)
Hungary	51 (20)	225.8 (18)	31.8 (17)	17 (21)	16 (20)	48.7 (20)
Italy	57 (15)	233.1 (16)	33.9 (14)	12 (25)	11 (24)	46.5 (21)
Portugal	53 (18)	229.3 (17)	30.6 (19)	16 (22)	11 (24)	46.0 (22)
Austria	49 (22)	179.5 (22)	22.2 (23)	15 (23)	16 (20)	42.1 (23)
Czech Rep.	36 (24)	169.5 (23)	29.9 (20)	12 (25)	15 (22)	39.1 (24)
Slovak Rep.	32 (25)	158.9 (25)	24.2 (22)	13 (24)	11 (24)	34.3 (25)
Mexico	22 (27)	104.9 (26)	16.8 (26)	19 (20)	17 (19)	32.5 (26)
Turkey	28 (26)	90.89 (27)	15.6 (27)	11 (27)	8 (27)	24.8 (27)

* *The scores on each of the 5 indicators have been standardized out of 100 before being added to arrive at an overall participation score, which is divided by 5 to give a score out of 100. Countries are listed in accordance with rank on composite score.*

It is of interest to compare the overall ranking on the composite index with the ranking on each of the five separate indicators. To facilitate this comparison we show, in parenthesis, in Table 4 the ranking of each country on each of the separate indicators. In general there is a good deal of consistency in the rankings on the separate indicators. Of greater interest is where we identify significant deviations between a country's ranking on an individual indicator and the ranking on the overall index. These deviations draw attention to particular features of a country's higher education system. The discrepancy between the high scores on the enrolment measures and lower scores on the educational attainment levels of the adult population evident for some countries illustrates the recency of the expansion of higher education. This is especially obvious in the case of Greece. The same discrepancy evident in the case of Italy is more likely to reflect the higher levels of non-completion. Ireland's disproportionately high score on enrolment intensity (relative to its score on the other indicators) illustrates the extent to which higher education is concentrated among young school leavers and contrasts with the situation in Norway and Sweden which have disproportionately lower scores on this measure. In these countries, as we noted, higher education is not the prerogative of school leavers. From a methodological point of view, an important implication of this analysis is that it demonstrates the risks attached to using any single enrolment indicator as a measure of participation. With this caveat in mind the single indicator that appears to be the most robust measure is the gross enrolment rate which has the highest correlation with the composite measure (see Table A3).

Some Correlates of Participation

Moving beyond the consideration of the individual measures which form the composite index of participation it is of interest to examine some of the correlates of the overall index. In Table A4 (appendix) we present data on a limited number of correlates. Two of these variables relate to the nature of the enrolment: we show the percentage part-time, where this distinction is observed (see above), and the percentage enrolled on Type B higher education. We also show the percentage of private expenditure on higher education institutions and the representation of foreign students as a percentage of total enrolments. Finally we show the percentage increase in higher education enrolments over the period 1982/2002 and the GDP per capita in US dollars using PPPs. Having ranked the countries in terms of their score on the higher education participation index, it is of interest to note how these characteristics are linked to the pattern of participation. For example, Korea's leading position in terms of overall participation has been achieved with the highest level of dependence on private expenditure (85%) and the second highest percentage of students on Type B higher education; its growth has been achieved primarily over the past two decades and with a relatively low level of GDP per capita. This pattern is very different from that of the six next highest countries on the participation index. And while all of these have relatively high levels of affluence their high levels of participation have been achieved with different levels of dependence on private funding, high in the case of the US and Australia and very low in the case of Finland and Norway or low in the case of Sweden and Belgium.

A distinguishing feature of Belgium's higher education system is the high level of participation on Type B higher education (51%). Apart from Korea, already mentioned, in only four other countries (Ireland, the UK, Greece and Turkey) does enrolment on these types of programmes reach 30% of over. While there is a modest relationship between levels of enrolment on type B programmes and participation levels (R = .32), this relationship is not statistically significant. Neither is the relationship between private expenditure and enrolment level statistically significant (R = .37). In fact the only statistically significant relationship evident from Table A4 is that between level of participation and GPD per capita (R = .57). In general, countries that have high levels of GDP tend to have higher levels of participation in higher education. But even this is by no means a one-to-one relationship as demonstrated by the relatively low levels of participation of affluent countries such as Austria, Italy, Switzerland and Germany. The identification of the direction of causality is of course a difficult question. High levels of participation may ultimately contribute to economic growth but they may also reflect consumption decisions facilitated by affluence. How these relationships will be in the future is a different question. It is evident from our analysis that high levels of enrolment growth in some countries represent an attempt to catch up with the situation in other countries. Furthermore it should be pointed out that we have not been able to include in this analysis information on the quality of higher education. This may be a more important variable than the quantitative dimension. It is hoped to extend this analysis with some further data on programme levels in order to tap into the research dimension of higher education systems.

ASSESSING EQUITY IN ACCESS TO HIGHER EDUCATION

One of the most frequently quoted generalisations in research into post-compulsory education is that expansion has not significantly reduced social class inequalities in access to higher education. Perhaps the strongest empirical support for this thesis comes from the comparative thirteen-country research project reported by Shavit and Blossfeld (1993) who conclude that only two countries, Sweden and the Netherlands, have achieved a significant equalisation among socio-economic groups. This conclusion is based on an analysis of relative chances of different social groups attaining a specific educational level. While, in most countries, students from working class backgrounds have increased their absolute chances of going on to some form of higher education, class inequalities measured in relative terms have remained relatively stable in recent decades. This finding is re-echoed by many other researchers (Halsey, 1993; Kivinen et al 2001). In assessing this conclusion it is necessary to take account of the distinction between relative and absolute changes in levels of participation. In general, social mobility researchers insist on a single interpretation of changes in participation over time. Their focus is on changes in relative levels of participation. While this orthodoxy has been challenged (Hellevik, 1997) it remains the dominant view (Kivinen et al 2002). We have argued elsewhere (Clancy, 2001) that it is necessary to take account of changes both in relative and absolute levels of participation. The former takes account of the extent to which education is a 'positional good' while the latter points to the significance of improvement in participation of any particular group irrespective of how other groups have fared. This analytic distinction has come to the fore in an important recent study, which may lead to a reassessment of the conventional wisdom on this topic (Shavit, Arum & Gamoran, 2007).

Before turning to examine these findings it is appropriate to note that the generally negative conclusions in relation to the failure of educational expansion to reduce social group inequalities is part of a larger sociological literature concerning the reproduction of the class structure in advanced capitalist societies. The traditional measure of a society's openness is the degree to which the attainment of social position is associated with social origin. Contrary to the optimistic predictions of functionalist sociologists such as Parsons (1960) and Kerr et al (1960) that industrialization and modernisation would lead to the triumph of achievement over ascription it is generally believed that the process of social reproduction has not changed significantly. In their authoritative review Erickson and Goldthorpe (1992) concluded that: (1) there were only small differences between nations in their pattern and degree of social fluidity – differences which reflected national peculiarities rather than macro-sociological regularities such as industrialization and modernization and (2) there was very little or no change in fluidity across birth cohorts. This widely accepted thesis has been challenged in more recent work, most notably in a study of *Social Mobility in Europe* (Breen 2004). The main findings from this study of 11 European countries were that, with one or two exceptions, there was a general tendency towards increasing social fluidity over the period 1970 to 2000 and that there was considerable cross-national variation in levels of social fluidity. In relation to the latter it is suggested that in terms of a ranking of countries according to degrees of openness Germany, France and Italy tend to represent the more rigid pole while the Scandinavian countries, particularly Sweden and Norway, together with Hungary, Poland and Israel appear among the most open countries. The Netherlands appear to have become considerable more open in the last 25 years while, over this period, England has gone from being one of the more open to one of the less open countries (Breen and Jonsson 2005: 232). While not included in this study it has been variously claimed that the situation in the US is little different from the general European pattern (Erickson and Goldthorpe, 1992) or that educational inequality in the US is very similar to that of Sweden, one of the most equal countries according to existing studies (Hout & Dohan, 1996).

Returning specifically to our focus on education an important recent study offers a more substantial challenge to the conventional wisdom in respect of the relationship between expansion and equity (Shavit, Arum & Gamoran, 2007)). Noting the pervasiveness of expansion in all of the 15 countries studied (9 from Europe, 4 from Asia, the US and Australia) the authors find that under certain conditions expansion may lead to declining inequality. The authors examine separately tends in inequality in *eligibility* for higher education and in the *transition* from eligible to actual participation in higher education. In respect of inequality of eligibility, it had declined in five countries, was about stable in nine countries and increased in one country. In respect inequality in the transition to higher education the authors report relative stability in six countries, a decline in four countries and an increase in three countries. The authors overall conclusion is that expansion leads to greater inclusion in the sense that even when social selection is stable expansion means that more students from all strata, including those from disadvantaged backgrounds, are carried forward into higher levels of the education system, and for the cohort as whole inequality is reduced. In respect of both eligibility for higher education and transition to higher education, they note that expansion to the point of saturation (rates in excess of 80%) is especially associated with declining inequality.

Quite apart from the particular substantive findings reported, perhaps the most important conclusion which can be drawn for this study is the new interpretation which the authors offer to a familiar set of findings. Previous work, including that of Shavit and Blossfeld (1993), has characterized rising enrolments and stable odds for educational transitions as 'persisting inequality'. This conclusion, they argue, misses an important point; when a given level of education expands we should expect increasing inequality at the next level due to the increasing heterogeneity of the eligible population. Consequently, they suggest, that when inequality in an expanding system is stable rather than on the rise, the system should be regarded as increasingly inclusive because it allows larger proportions of all social strata to attend (ibid: 29). In only one country (Russia) in their sample is there evidence of increasing inequality. This conclusion has important policy implications for all countries which are experiencing rapid expansion of their higher education systems. Expanding higher education systems tend to be increasingly inclusive even when relative advantages are preserved, because they extend a valued good to a broader spectrum of the population.

The papers in this volume make an important contribution to the comparative literature on access and equity in higher education. However a limitation of this and indeed all the mobility research is a reliance on cohort analysis which renders this work being primarily 'historical' and hence not immediately relevant to policy makers in education who require more immediate feedback on policy initiatives. For example, in the Shavit Arum & Gamoran study the most recent data relates to those cohorts who completed higher education in the 1990s and in a few case the last cohort completed higher education in the 1980s. Thus there is an urgent need to collect data on access and equity from those currently in the higher education system and to compare these data with those from earlier enrolment cohorts. This is a major challenge which needs to be addressed in a systematic comparative fashion. Higher education policy makers in all countries have a keen interest in assessing what progress is being made in reducing social inequalities in access. While there is good comparative data available on the elimination of quantitative inequalities in the access of women to higher education and also on the extent of (persisting) generational inequalities, we remain very poorly informed on the changes in social group inequalities and on changing inequalities by ethnic groups and by disability.

Prior to focusing on the potential of comparative research which incorporates data on current and recent enrolments in higher education it is of interest to examine some national data sources to assess the extent to which the very rapid expansion in higher education experienced in most countries has been associated with any lessening of social group inequalities in access. Only a sample of these data will be reported here. We look at some research findings from the US, UK, Ireland, France, Australia, Finland and Norway. In the United States, apart from the work of sociologists working on social mobility, most research on inequalities in educational participation has used data on parents' income, education (NCES, 2001) and ethnicity (NCES, 2002). In this review we focus only on income, looking at levels of participation by family income from 1970 to 2003 (Table A5). Over this period participation has increased for all income groups. For the top income quartile participation has increased from 74% to 80%, while for the lowest income quartile the rate has increased from 28% to 41%. We have calculated the odds ratio for these two groups, which provides a measure of changes in levels of inequality. This analysis suggests that there has been a reduction in inequality of access by income group over the period, but that the pattern of change is uneven. The greatest reduction was achieved between 1970 and 1980. Some of this gain was lost over the next decade. There has been a modest decline in inequality between 1990 and 2000 but this improvement has halted in the early part of this decade.

Table A6 presents data from the UK on higher education by social class from 1960 to 2000. The comparison here is between manual and non-manual classes and the data relates to enrolment by age 21. Overall participation has increased more than six fold with the non-manual participation rate rising from 27% to 48% and the participation rate for the manual groups rising from a low of 5% to 18%. The odds ratios suggest that inequality has declined but, as was the case in the US, the pattern of change has been uneven. The reductions in inequality seem to have occurred between 1970 and 1980 and between 1990 and 1995 with little change evident over the other time periods included here.

In Table A7 we present data from Ireland. The first panel in this table is based on four national studies of access conducted by the author over the period 1980 to 1998. It combines into two categories data for eleven socio-economic groups and compares the changes in the representation of those six groups, which were 'over-represented' in higher education relative to their share of the population in 1980, with the participation of the five groups which were 'under-represented' at this stage. Again the odds ratios suggest that there has been a reduction in inequality over the period, noticeably between 1986 and 1992. The most recent data have to be shown separately in the second panel of this table because of the changes in the national classification of socio-economic and social class groups. The data shown here is based on aggregated social class groups and suggests that there has been a further and significant reduction in inequalities between 1998 and 2004.

We examine next some data from France (Table A8). Here we show the social background of those aged 20/21 in higher education for 1984 and 2002. Over this period the overall rate of participation more than doubled. If we compare the representation of the highest and lowest social group the reduction in social inequalities has been modest; the odds ratio declined from 8.3 to 7.4 over this period. Indeed if we compare the relative position of the top social group with the middle group inequalities actually increased marginally.

In Table A9 we consider the situation in Australia, a country that has a very explicit policy of measuring the performance of a range of equity groups. We confine our attention to the social background of higher education students looking at parents' social class and education. These data are from two national sample cohort studies and measure the rate of participation in higher education at age 19. It would appear that there has been no reduction in social inequalities over the period 1980 to 1999, a period which saw the transition from free tuition to the introduction of an income contingent loan scheme. The consistency of results from the social class and parents' education measures are striking and are further validated by the analysis of enrolment data using the postcodes of students' home residence to measure socio-economic status (James et al 2004).

Table A10 presents some data from Finland and shows the pattern of enrolment of 20–24 year-olds in higher education by fathers' educational level. While these data reveal considerable evidence of continuity in the degree of inequality over much of this period, when we compare students whose parents had a tertiary education with those whose parents had just primary education the odds ratio does show a slow decline over the entire period. The decline through the late 1990s is especially significant. Finally, Table A11 presents some data from Norway and shows the rate of participation in higher education for 1992 and 2002 by parents' education. When we compare the participation of those whose parents had higher education with those whose parents had compulsory schooling only, we note a small decline in inequality.

What can we conclude from this limited review of selected national studies? It allows us to make some tentative generalisations about the changing levels of inequality within countries. In general it would appear that the expansion of higher education enrolments is leading to some reductions in social group inequalities. This is not of course a universal trend and is clearly not inevitable. Furthermore, even when we find evidence of declining inequality the pattern of decline is uneven and can at time be halted or partially reversed. Some countries appear to be more successful than others although, since the time periods covered vary by country and since countries have different starting points with respect to levels of inequalities, the interpretation of cross country differences is problematic.

There is an imperative to move beyond national studies and design comparative research to explore cross-country differences in equity in access to higher education. The most promising development in this area is the evolving EUROSTUDENT (2000; 2005; 2008) project. This research programme, which is now in its third iteration, is coordinated by the Hannover based Higher Education Information System (HIS) with support funding from the German Federal Ministry for Education and Research and the European Commission under the SOCRATES programme. It aims to generate and present internationally-comparable indicators on the social and economic conditions of student life. The number of countries participating has increased from eight in 2000 to eleven in 2005 to twenty-three in 2008. We are especially interested in the data emanating from the EUROSTUDENT surveys relating to the social make-up of the student body although this was not the prime objective of the studies. The scope of these surveys covers a wide range of additional topics such as student demographic characteristics, accommodation, funding and state assistance, living expenses and student spending, student employment, time budgets and internationalisation.

In an earlier paper (Clancy & Goastellec, 2007) we have explored the potential of these data on the basis of an analysis of the findings from the 2005 survey on the occupational and educational background of the parents of higher education students. Subsequently the OECD has included a broadly similar analysis of these data in its *Education at a Glance*, 2007 edition[3]. Only eight of the eleven countries participating in the 2005 study produced the full range of data required on parents' occupational background; this increased to nine in respect of parents' educational background. Because of the variability between countries in the coding of occupations we followed the practice incorporated in the Synopsis of Indicators Report (Eurostudent, 2005) and limited our analysis to the differences in participation between working class (blue collar) and all other occupational groups. Other occupations principally include professional, managerial, other 'white collar' groups, employers and the self-employed. Looking at the findings in respect of fathers' occupational background a clear pattern emerged whereby Germany, Portugal, Austria and France exhibited higher levels of inequality while Spain, The Netherlands, Ireland and Finland exhibited lower levels of inequality. Although these data are less comprehensive in respect of mothers' occupational status, because of lower labour force participation rates, we found a similar distribution of countries which could be classified as having higher and lower levels of inequality.

Perhaps the most striking feature of our analysis is that these country differences were replicated when we examined the educational level of students' fathers and mothers. In this case we compare the percentage of students whose parents have higher education versus those without higher education. It was possible to include Italy in this part of the analysis. Looking first at fathers with and without higher education we found that Portugal, Austria, Germany and France exhibit higher levels of inequality in access to higher education. In contrast Ireland, Spain, Italy, The Netherlands and Finland exhibit lower levels of inequality. With some minor changes in relative ranking within the categories, the pattern of inequality in broadly similar when we rank counties by mothers' education. Because of the consistency of findings between those on occupational status and educational attainment of parents and because of the greater difficulty in achieving comparability in the measurement of occupational status it is not surprising that Usher (2004) should claim that the educational attainment of parents provides an optimum measure of inter-generational inequality in access to higher education.

Because of the recent availability of data from the 2008 EUROSTUDENT survey it is now possible to extend the comparative analysis of inequalities in access to higher education to a larger group of countries utilising the most recent data. Again our focus is on the social make-up of the student body, as reflected in the occupational and educational background of the students' parents. While a total of 23 countries are included in this study the number of countries for which the requisite data are available range from 19 to 22. We have applied the same methodology which we used previously in our analysis of the 2005 data (Clancy & Goastellec, 2007). In respect of parents' occupational background we differentiate between those whose parents are from 'blue-collar' occupations versus those from 'other' occupational groups. Similarly with respect to education we differentiate between students whose parents had higher education versus those students whose parents did not have higher education. Data in respect of these variables are shown separately for both fathers and mothers in Table 5. In calculating the 'relative odds' for each of the 22 countries reported in column 2 the enumerator is the percentage of students' fathers with higher education as a proportion of the percentage of men aged 40–60 in the population with higher education while the denominator is the percentage of students whose parents did not have higher education as a proportion of the percentage of men aged 40–60 in the population without higher education. Comparable data in respect of mothers' educational background are reported in column 3. In columns 4 and 5 we calculate the relative odds in accessing higher education for students from 'other occupational groups' versus students from 'blue collar' groups. These calculations are made separately for students' fathers and mothers. We show in parenthesis in each column the relative ranking of countries on the basis of the relative odds. Finally, on the basis of the average of the sum of the rankings across the four categories we calculate the composite rank for each country. The listing of each country in the table is based on this composite ranking[4]. We suggest that this composite ranking provides a relatively robust indicator of inequality in access to higher education. Those countries with the highest ranking reveal the lowest levels of inequality.

Our preference for a composite measure of inequality follows the same logic which we applied to our choice of measure of participation. We are conscious that the measure of occupational status is less discriminating than we might wish[5] but we are reassured by the high degree of consistency in ranking across the different indicators. Spearman's rank order correlation between the country rankings on the five indicators[6] ranges from $R = .967$ to $.686$. An inspection of the details in each column of the table reveals a few significant discrepancies on the rankings for individual variables. Germany's rank on fathers' education and Spain's rank on fathers' occupation are noticeably lower than on the other variables. Portugal's rank on fathers' occupation is somewhat higher than its rank on the other indicators while in the case of Estonia and Romania the rankings on the educational variables are somewhat higher than on the parental occupational variables.

Turning to the overall findings we note that the countries which have the lowest level of inequality are The Netherlands, Finland, Scotland, and Slovenia. Ireland, Italy and Sweden also have significantly lower levels of inequality. This would also appear to be the case in respect of Switzerland and Norway although in both instances we have no data on parental occupations. In contrast, Bulgaria, Turkey, Portugal, France, Latvia, and Romania have higher levels of inequality. Our more limited data (available only for fathers) in respect of England & Wales would

Table 5. *Inequalities in Access to Higher Education by Parents' Education and Social Background: Analysis of EUROSTUDENT 2008 Data**

Country	Fathers' Higher Education	Mothers' Higher Education	Fathers' Social Class	Mothers' Social Class	Composite Rank
Netherlands	1.65 (2)	1.37 (3)	1.68 (3)	0.79 (3)	1
Switzerland	1.73 (4)	1.19 (1)	NA	NA	NA
Finland	1.75 (5)	1.47 (5)	1.17 (1)	1.04 (4)	2
Scotland	1.33 (1)	1.22 (2)	1.68 (4)	1.69 (9)	3
Slovenia	1.71 (3)	1.59 (6)	1.58 (2)	1.38 (6)	4
Norway	1.75 (6)	1.38 (4)	NA	NA	NA
Ireland	1.65 (7)	1.50 (7)	2.04 (7)	0.49 (2)	5
Italy	1.93 (8)	1.84 (8)	1.97 (6)	0.40 (1)	6
Sweden	2.09 (10)	1.85 (9)	1.36 (5)	1.36 (5)	7
Spain	2.07 (9)	1.90 (10)	4.75 (18)	1.45 (8)	8
Czech R.	2.66 (14)	1.91 (11)	3.11 (9)	2.86 (14)	9
Slovak Rep.	2.62 (13)	2.85 (14)	3.07 (11)	1.71 (10)	10
Germany	3.78 (19)	2.54 (12)	2.11 (8)	2.05 (11)	11
Austria	2.50 (11)	2.62 (13)	2.76 (14)	2.25 (13)	12
Estonia	3.55 (17)	3.24 (17)	2.55 (12)	1.45 (7)	13
Eng & Wales	2.85 (12)	NA	1.79 (15)	NA	NA
Romania	3.86 (21)	4.16 (20)	2.81 (10)	2.08 (12)	14
Latvia	2.89 (15)	2.93 (15)	6.78 (19)	3.29 (15)	15
France	3.24 (16)	3.15 (16)	2.92 (16)	6.14 (18)	16
Portugal	3.78 (20)	3.51 (19)	2.74 (13)	4.99 (17)	17
Turkey	3.62 (18)	3.43 (18)	2.04 (17)	7.43 (19)	18
Bulgaria	5.41 (22)	5.47 (21)	12.77 (20)	4.95 (16)	19

* *Relative odds of accessing higher education where parents have HE versus those without HE and where parents are from 'other' occupational groups versus parents from 'blue collar' occupational groups. Figures in parenthesis refer to country ranking on each of the indicators.*

suggest that it is also among the countries with relative higher levels of inequality in access to higher education. All of the other countries shown in Table 5 occupy an intermediate position on the inequality scale. It is beyond the scope of this paper to seek to identify the factors which may account for this situation [7]. This presents an important challenge for future research in comparative education. A more immediate task is to examine the extent to which these findings are consistent with existing research, limited and all as this may be. It is significant that the results from the most recent survey are consistent with those from the 2005 survey which we described above where we differentiated between countries with 'higher' and 'lower' levels of inequality. If we apply this dichotomy to the present data, the four countries which were classified as having 'higher' levels of inequality in 2005 also demonstrate higher levels of inequality in 2008. Similarly, the countries which were classified as having 'lower' levels of inequality in 2005 also exhibit lower levels of inequality in 2008. Pending the availability of more comparative research, national researchers should be encouraged to assess the extent to which the EUROSTUDENT findings are consistent with other national studies. Such validation would enhance the significance of this research programme and stimulate further analysis of this important data set.

CONCLUSION

This paper seeks to advance the comparative research agenda in respect of access and equity in higher education. Our analysis has been driven by a belief that international comparative research is critical for informed policy development. In our globalised world national policy development is greatly influenced by policy trends in other countries. We have argued that while this instinct to review national policy in the context of an analysis of international trends is deeply embedded in the policy process in many countries, it is frustrated by the lack of appropriate data. We have critically reviewed comparative indicators of participation and pointed to the highly unsatisfactory situation whereby we currently lack an appropriate robust measure to enable us to compare levels of participation in different countries. Having reviewed separately existing measures of entry rates, enrolment rates and output rates we have developed a composite higher education participation index, which facilitates comparison of levels of participation between countries. We argue that the score on this index provides a robust measure of overall participation and that in addition to the usefulness of the summary score, the distribution of scores on the different components of the index draws attention to distinctive features of national higher education systems.

Turning our attention to levels of equity in access to higher education we reviewed the current state of research in this area, in particular drawing attention to some recent research which challenges the conventional wisdom on equity. Contrary to the widely quoted view that expansion has not led to any significant reductions in social class inequalities we examine the findings from an important recent study which concludes that in most countries expansion appears to have led to greater social inclusion. However, we have pointed to the limitations of cohort studies which render the research 'historical' and hence of limited value to policy makers who seek to review the efficacy of current access policies. We argue that it is vital to include in our analysis of this issue data on current student enrolments. In the absence of a substantial body of comparative research we reviewed a selection of national studies which support the tentative generalisation that the expansion of higher education enrolments may indeed be leading to reductions in socio-economic group inequalities in many countries. Because of our emphasis on the importance of having data on current enrolments in higher education and of our insistence on the added value which arises from comparative analysis we have been impressed by the importance of the evolving EUROSTUDENT project which allow us to explore the issue of cross-country differences in equity of access to higher education. In addition to summarising our earlier analysis of the EUROSTUDENT (2005) survey we include an analysis of findings on the social background of students from more than twenty countries from the EUROSTUDENT (2008) study. We calculate a composite measure of inequality in access to higher education based on data on the occupational and educational background of the fathers and mothers of higher education students. We document large differences between countries in the levels of inequality in access to higher education. The high level of consistency in the findings for those countries for which we have data from two rounds of the EUROSTUDENT survey suggest that these differences are not an epiphenomenon. While it is beyond the scope of this paper to explore the genesis of these differences we suggest that this presents a challenge for future research.

We have pointed our elsewhere (Clancy & Goastellec, 2007: 152) that our somewhat more optimistic analysis of the findings of recent research on equity risks being misinterpreted. In concluding that in many countries there have been some reductions in inequality we are not suggesting that we are 'at the end of history'. Very large inequalities persist in all countries even in Scandinavian countries, which have perhaps made most progress. Our analysis should not allow for any complacency. The persistence of large, and in some countries growing, disparities in wealth and opportunity will not be cancelled out by the limited scale of affirmative action that we find in education. However, the differences evident between countries suggest that it is possible to make progress and that enlightened educational and social policy is capable of reducing but not eliminating inequality.

Further caveats are also necessary. Much of our existing evidence is based on social disparities at the point of entry to higher education. There are also significant social differentials in retention and graduation levels. Furthermore, the analysis of aggregate enrolment data does not reflect the social selectivity that exists between different forms of higher education. Limited democratisation in access to higher education is being accompanied by high levels of social selectivity by college, sector and field of study (Clancy, 2001; Duru-Bellat, 2005). The scale of the policy challenge is enormous and comparative researchers can make a substantial contribution by making available good quality data to benchmark comparative achievement and invite policy borrowing from those countries which have made most progress.

NOTES

[1]   The same difficulties apply with the measurement of gross entry rates.
[2]   In the interest of readability some of the tables have been put in an appendix at the end of the paper.
[3]   The OECD report simple odds of students from 'blue collar' families entering higher education while we prefer to use 'relative odds' comparing the relative advantage of students from other occupational groups, vis-à-vis students from 'blue collar' backgrounds.

[4]   We have not calculated a composite rank for Switzerland, Norway or England & Wales because we have data on only two of the four variables. We have, however, included them in the Table, where their relative ranking is that suggested by the limited data which are available.

[5]   The dichotomous measure, of 'blue collar' versus all 'other occupations', is especially problematic for mothers. Indeed in respect of Italy, Ireland and the Netherlands the findings are counter intuitive suggesting that families with mothers from 'blue collar' occupations have higher rates of participation in higher education than families whose mothers came from 'other occupational' groups. Since our focus is on relative country ranking we do not consider that these anomalies constitute a serious limitation of our analysis.

[6]   The rank order correlation coefficient for the two education indicators is .88 while the coefficient for the two occupational indictors is .69. The coefficients for the relationship between fathers' education, and fathers' and mothers' occupation are .72 and .70, respectively, while the correlation between mothers' education, and fathers' and mothers' occupation are .69 and .83, respectively. The correlations between each of the separate indicators and the composite rank score range from .97 (mothers' education) to .76 (fathers' occupation).

[7]   We explore one aspect of this in chapter 6 of this volume where we examine the link between national education structures and levels of participation and equity of access.

BIBLIOGRAPHY

Breen, R. (2004). *Social mobility in Europe*. Oxford: Oxford University Press.

Breen, R., & Jonsson, J. O. (2005). Inequality of opportunity in comparative perspective: Recent research on educational attainment and social mobility. *Annual Review of Sociology, 31*, 223–243.

Clancy, P. (2001). *College entry in focus: A fourth national survey of access to higher education*. Dublin: Higher Education Authority.

Clancy, P., & Goastellec, G. (2007). Exploring access and equity in higher education: Policy and performance in a comparative perspective. *Higher Education Quarterly, 61*(2), 136–154.

Deer, C. (2005). Higher education access and expansion: The French case. *Higher Education Quarterly, 59*(3), 230–241.

DES. (2003). *Widening participation in higher education*. London: Department of Education and Skills.

DEPP. (2005). *Repères et Références Statistiques sur les Enseignements, la Formation et la Recherche*. Paris: DEPP.

Duru-Bellat, M. (2005). *Democratisation of education and reduction in inequalities of opportunities: An obvious link?* Paper presented at European Conference on Educational Research, Dublin.

Erickson, R., & Goldthorpe, J. H. (1992). *The constant flux: A study of class mobility in industrial societies*. Oxford: Clarendon.

Ertl, H. (2005). Higher education in Germany: A case of uneven expansion? *Higher Education Quarterly, 59*(3), 205–229.

EUROSTUDENT. (2008). *Social and economic conditions of student life in Europe: Synopsis of indicators, interim report*. Hannover: HIS Hochschul-Informations-System.

EUROSTUDENT. (2005). *Social and economic conditions of student life in Europe 2005: Synopsis of indicators*. Hannover: HIS Hochschul-Informations-System.

EUROSTUDENT. (2003). *Social and economic conditions of student life in Europe 2003: Synopsis of indicators*. Hannover: HIS Hochschul-Informations-System.

Gradstein, M., & Nikitin, D. (2004). *Education expansion: Evidence and interpretation*. Washington, DC: World Bank Research Working Paper.

Hannum, E., & Buchmann, C. (2003). *The consequences of global educational expansion: Social science perspectives*. Cambridge, MA: American Academy of Arts and Sciences.

Halsey, A. H. (1993). Trends in access and equity in higher education: Britain in international perspective. *Oxford Review of Education, 19*(2), 129–150.

Hout, M., & Dohan, D. P. (1996). Two paths to educational opportunity: Class and educational selection in Sweden and the United States. In R. Erickson & J. O. Jonsson (Eds.), *Can education be equalized?* Boulder, CO: Westview.

James, R., Baldwin, G., Coates, H., Krause, K. L., & McInnis, C. (2004). *Analysis of equity groups in higher education 1991–2002*. Canberra: Department of Education, Science and Training.

Kaiser, F., Hillegers, H., & Legro, I. (2005). *Lining up higher education: Trends in selected statistics in ten Western European countries*. (CHEPS International Higher Education Monitor) Enschede, NL: Centre for Higher Education Policy Studies.

Kaiser, F., & O'Hearn, H. (2005). *Myths and methods on access and participation in higher education in international comparison*. Enschede, NL: Centre for Higher Education Policy Studies.

Kerr, C., Dunlop, T. J., Harbinson, F. H., & Meyers, C. A. (1960). *Industrialism and industrial man*. Cambridge, MA: Harvard University Press.

Kellevik, O. (1997). Class inequalities and egalitarian reform. *Acta Sociologica, 40*, 377–398.

Kivinen, O., Ahola, S., & Hedman, J. (2001). Expansion, education and improving odds? Participation in higher education in Finland in the 1980s and 1990s. *Acta Sociologica, 44*, 171–181.

Kivinen, O., Hedman, J., & Sakari, A. (2002). Changes in differences in participation in expanding higher education: Reply to Hellevik. *Acta Sociologica, 43*, 159–162.

Marks, G. N., Fleming, N., Long, M., & McMillan, J. (2000). *Patterns of participation in year 12 and higher education in Australia: Trends and issue*. Canberra: Australian Council of Education Research.

MOE. (2005). *OECD thematic review of tertiary education: Country background report for Finland*. Helsinki: Ministry of Education Finland.

MOER. (2005). *OECD thematic review of tertiary education: Country background report for Norway*. Bergin: Norwegian Ministry of Education and Research.

Mortenson, T. (2005). *Chance for bachelor's degree by age 24 and family income, 1970–2003*. Retrieved October 11, 2005, from www.postsecondary.org

NCES. (2005). *Comparative indicators of education in the US and other G-8 Countries 2004*. Washington, DC: National Center for Education Statistics.

NCES. (2002). *Digest of education statistics 2002*. Washington, DC: National Centre for Education Statistics.

NCES. (2001). *The condition of education 2001: Students whose parents did not go to college*. Washington, DC: National Centre for Education Statistics.

O'Connell, P., Clancy, D., & McCoy, S. (2006). *Who went to college in 2004?* Dublin: Higher Education Authority.

OECD. (2004). *OECD handbook for internationally comparative education statistics*. Paris: OECD.

OECD. (2007). *Education at a glance 2007*. Paris: OECD.

ONS. (2004). *Focus on social inequalities*. London: Office of National Statistics.

Orfield, G. (2004). *Dropouts in America: Confronting the graduation rate crisis*. Cambridge, MA: Harvard Education Press.

Parsons, T. (1960). *Structure and process in modern societies*. Glenso, IL: Free Press.

Schofer, E., & Meyer, J. W. (2005). The worldwide expansion of higher education in the twentieth century. *American Sociological Review, 70*, 898–920.

Shavit, Y., & Blossfeld, H. P. (1993). *Persistent inequality: Changing educational attainment in thirteen countries*. Boulder, CO: Westview Press.

Shavit, Y., Arum, R., & Gamoran, A. (Eds.). (2007). *Stratification in higher education: A comparative study*. Stanford, CA: Stanford University Press.

UNESCO. (2005). *Global education digest 2005*. Montreal: UNESCO Institute for Statistics.

Usher, A. (2004). *A new measuring stick. Is access to higher education in Canada more equitable?* Toronto, ON: Educational Policy Institute.

Usher, A., & Cervenan, A. (2005). *Global higher education rankings 2005*. Toronto, ON: Educational Policy Institute.

APPENDIX – ADDITIONAL TABLES

*Table A1. Distribution of Higher Education Enrolments, by Age Group,
OECD* Countries, 2003*

Country	Aged 17–19	Aged 20–24	Aged 25–30	Aged 30–39	Aged 40 +	Mean Age	Standard Deviation
Australia	0.19	0.37	0.15	0.16	0.13	27.53	10.16
Austria	0.08	0.47	0.24	0.15	0.05	25.85	7.08
Belgium	0.27	0.52	0.10	0.07	0.03	23.03	6.46
Czech Rep	0.10	0.61	0.18	0.08	0.03	23.98	5.84
Denmark	0.01	0.40	0.35	0.17	0.07	27.82	7.60
Finland	0.04	0.45	0.24	0.16	0.10	27.80	8.80
France	0.25	0.55	0.12	0.09	0.00	22.28	3.92
Germany	0.05	0.45	0.29	0.17	0.04	26.17	6.57
Greece	0.26	0.52	0.20	0.01	0.00	21.93	3.23
Hungary	0.14	0.49	0.20	0.12	0.05	25.15	7.25
Iceland	0.00	0.43	0.24	0.19	0.14	29.38	9.52
Ireland	0.32	0.47	0.11	0.10	0.00	22.08	4.25
Italy	0.13	0.52	0.22	0.13	0.00	24.09	4.82
Korea	0.25	0.56	0.11	0.05	0.02	22.66	5.64
Mexico	0.30	0.53	0.11	0.05	0.01	22.12	5.08
Netherlands	0.18	0.52	0.15	0.08	0.06	24.57	7.68
New Zealand	0.12	0.40	0.13	0.17	0.17	28.89	10.84
Norway	0.04	0.40	0.23	0.19	0.15	29.38	9.81
Poland	0.12	0.64	0.14	0.11	0.00	23.12	3.79
Portugal	0.15	0.49	0.19	0.11	0.05	24.97	7.39
Slovak Rep	0.20	0.57	0.14	0.07	0.03	23.35	6.03
Spain	0.18	0.51	0.19	0.09	0.04	24.25	6.69
Sweden	0.03	0.38	0.23	0.21	0.15	29.81	9.85
Switzerland	0.05	0.44	0.27	0.19	0.05	26.83	7.24
Turkey	0.28	0.61	0.09	0.02	0.00	21.35	3.72
United Kingdom	0.20	0.33	0.12	0.18	0.17	28.75	11.16
United States	0.20	0.38	0.14	0.15	0.13	27.20	10.14

* *Data not available for Canada, Japan and Luxembourg.*

*Table A2. Enrolment Rates In Higher Education By Age Groups
For OECD* Countries 2003*

Country	Age 17–19	Age 20–24	Age 25–29	Age 30–39	Age 40 +
Australia	0.23	0.27	0.11	0.06	0.01
Austria	0.07	0.21	0.10	0.02	0.00
Belgium	0.28	0.30	0.06	0.02	0.00
Czech Rep	0.04	0.23	0.06	0.02	0.00
Denmark	0.01	0.26	0.19	0.04	0.01
Finland	0.06	0.40	0.22	0.07	0.01
France	0.23	0.30	0.06	0.02	0.00
Germany	0.04	0.21	0.14	0.03	0.00
Greece	0.36	0.36	0.13	0.00	0.00
Hungary	0.14	0.25	0.09	0.03	0.00
Iceland	0.00	0.26	0.15	0.06	0.02
Ireland	0.27	0.23	0.06	0.03	0.00
Italy	0.13	0.28	0.10	0.02	0.00
Korea	0.40	0.45	0.09	0.02	0.00
Mexico	0.11	0.12	0.03	0.01	0.00
Netherlands	0.17	0.28	0.08	0.02	0.00
New Zealand	0.13	0.28	0.11	0.06	0.02
Norway	0.05	0.31	0.16	0.06	0.01
Poland	0.11	0.36	0.08	0.04	0.00
Portugal	0.16	0.26	0.09	0.03	0.00
Slovak Rep	0.12	0.19	0.05	0.01	0.00
Spain	0.22	0.30	0.10	0.02	0.00
Sweden	0.04	0.30	0.17	0.07	0.01
Switzerland	0.03	0.19	0.11	0.03	0.00
Turkey	0.10	0.13	0.02	0.00	0.00
United Kingdom	0.20	0.21	0.07	0.05	0.01
United States	0.28	0.31	0.12	0.06	0.02

* *Data not available for Canada, Japan and Luxembourg.*

Table A3. Inter-Correlation between Indicators of Participation in Higher Education

	Gross Enrolment Rate	*Sum of Age Specific Enrolment Rates*	*Enrolment Intensity*	*Population Aged 25–34 with Higher Education*	*Population Aged 35–44 with higher education*	*Overall Index*
Gross Enrolment Rate						
Sum of Age Specific Enrolment Rates	.88					
Enrolment Intensity	.72	.93				
Population Aged 25–34 with Higher Education	.62	.67	.62			
Population Aged 35–44 with higher education	.61	.57	.44	.93		
Overall Index	.93	.89	.81	.92	.86	–

Table A4. Some Correlates of Higher Education Participation Rates

Countries*	Percentage Enrolments Part time	Percentage Enrolment on Type B Programmes	Percentage of Private Expenditure on HE Institutions	Percentage Foreign Students	Percentage Increase in HE Enrolment 1982/02	GDP per Capita: PPPs in US $s 000s
Korea	NA	40	85	<1	228	18.4
Finland	NA	<1	4	3	122	27.8
United States	23	23	55	4	29	36.2
Norway	NA	1	4	5	157	36.7
Sweden	NA	3	10	8	77	28.2
Belgium	17	51	14	11	71	28.6
Australia	39	17	51	19	123	27.7
Greece	3	32	0.4	2	323	19.1
New Zealand	NA	26	38	14	123	22.3
Denmark	3	8	2	9	89	30.0
Spain	42	13	24	3	161	23.2
France	43	24	14	11	85	27.5
Ireland	28	35	14	6	175	32.5
Utd. Kingdom	47	32	28	11	64	28.9
Netherlands	NA	1	22	4	39	29.9
Iceland	46	5	4	4	NA	28.4
Poland	19	1	30	<1	284	11.2
Switzerland	32	20	NA	18	105	32.5
Germany	NA	15	8	11	29	26.7
Hungary	NA	3	21	3	288	14.4
Italy	24	1	21	2	75	26.3
Portugal	45	1	9	4	NA	18.8
Austria	4	11	8	14	57	30.1
Czech Rep.	NA	10	13	4	NA	16.6
Slovak Rep.	32	3	15	1	NA	12.6
Mexico	8	2	29	NA	121	9.4
Turkey	9	30	10	1	580	6.5

* *Countries are ranked in terms of their score on the Higher Education Participation Index.*

Table A5. Participation* in Higher Education in the United States by Family Income, 1970–2000 (in percentages)

	1970	1980	1990	2000	2003
Top Income Quartile	74	63	75	75	80
Third Income Quartile	57	57	64	69	67
Second Income Quartile	47	44	51	56	58
Bottom Income Quartile	28	27	32	35	41
All Income Groups	49	46	53	57	60
Odds Ratios: Top and Bottom Quartiles	7.21	4.59	6.36	5.56	5.75

Source: Adapted from Mortenson (2005).

* *College participation of dependent 18–24 year olds. Odds ratios calculated by the author.*

Table A6. Higher Education Participation* in the UK by Parental Social Class (in percentages)

Social Class	1960	1970	1980	1990	1995	2000
Non-manual	27	32	33	37	47	48
Manual	4	5	7	10	17	18
Total Participation	5	8	12	19	32	33
Odds Ratio	8.9	8.9	6.5	6.3	4.3	4.2

Source: Department of Education and Skills (DES, 2003) and Office of National Statistics (ONS, 2004).

* *Proportion of young people who enter higher education for first time by age 21.*

Table A7. Inequalities in Access to Higher Education in Ireland

1. Participation Rates by Socio-Economic Group, 1980–1998 (in percentages)				
Socio-economic Groups	*1980*	*1986*	*1992*	*1998*
Six Highest Socio-economic Groups	35	43	50	62
Five Lowest Socio-economic Groups	8	11	24	30
All Groups	20	25	36	44
Odds Ratio	6.2	6.1	3.2	3.5
2. Participation Rates by Social Class 1998 and 2004 (in percentages)				
Social Classes	*1998*		*2004*	
Profession/ Managerial/ Technical/ Other Non-Manual	53		60	
Skilled, Semi-Skilled and Unskilled Manual	34		49	
All Social Classes	44		55	
Odds Ratio	2.2		1.6	

Source: Panel 1 Adapted from Clancy (2001): Panel 2 Adapted from O'Connell et al (2006).

Table A8. Participation in Higher Education in France, by Social Background,
1984 and 2002 (in percentages)

Social Groups	*1984*	*2002*
Employers, Executives, Intermediate Occupations	48	76
Employees, Farmers, Craftsmen, Shopkeepers	22	47
Blue Collar Workers	10	30
All Groups	24	50
Odds Ratio: Employers/ Executive etc and Blue Collar Workers	8.3	7.4

Source: DEPP (2005).

Table A9. Participation in Higher Education by Parents' Social Class and Education in Australia in 1980 and 1999 (in percentages)

	1980	1999
Parents' Social Class		
Professional/Managerial/Clerical	28%	39%
Manual Workers	14%	22%
Odds Ratio	2.4	2.3
Parents' Education		
With Higher Education	37%	51%
No Higher Education	19%	29%
Odds Ratio	2.5	2.5

Source: Adapted from G.N. Marks, N. Fleming, M. Long & J. McMillan (2000). Before calculating the odds ratios the author amalgamated the three white-collar and three manual occupational categories.

Table A10. Participation in Higher Education in Finland by Father's Educational Level, 1985 to 2000 (in percentages)

Father's Educational Level	1985	1990	1995	2000
Tertiary Level > 4 years	45.2	47.8	48	43.2
Vocational 11 (3–4 years)	22.9	24.0	25.1	23.6
Vocational 1 (< 3 years)	10.1	10.1	10.7	11.9
Primary	6.4	7.5	8.5	9.5
Odds Ratio: Tertiary/ Primary	12.1	11.3	9.9	7.2

Source: Adapted from MOE (2005).

Table A11. Participation in Higher Education by Parents' Educational Level in Norway in 1992 and 2002 (in percentages)

Parents' Education	1992	2002
Higher Education	36	40
Compulsory School Only	6	8
Odds Ratio	8.8	7.7

Source: Adapted from MOER (2005).

STRUCTURAL DIVERSIFICATION: DOES IT MATTER?

Introduction

In the paper on *Measuring Access and Equity*, (Clancy 2010, see previous chapter), we have argued that comparative research in higher education requires improved measures to quantify levels of access/participation and levels of equity in higher education. Our proposals in respect of each of these dimensions represent merely the first step in a more ambitious comparative research agenda. A more challenging task will be to explain the genesis of the large inter-country differences which we find in levels of access and equity. It is likely that meeting this challenge will require an exploration of a wide range of historical, cultural, economic and social variables which may impinge on higher education. Our focus in this paper is narrower. We explore the extent to which the structure of educational systems may have implications for levels of access and equity. We examine separately differences in the structure of higher systems and in the structure of secondary education and explore whether such differences may impact on levels of access and equity. In the next section of the paper we review the literature on the diversification of higher education systems. This is followed by an examination of the interface between secondary education structures and higher education. In section four we examine empirically the link between system structures and levels of participation. In the next section we examine the relationship between levels of inequality in access to higher education and system structure. The final section of the paper discusses some of the implications of our analysis.

DIVERSIFICATION OF HIGHER EDUCATION SYSTEMS

While massification is probably the defining feature of higher education systems over the last half century the question of structural differentiation has attracted almost as much attention from policy makers. The two processes are of course closely intertwined. The agenda was set by Martin Trow's seminal paper (Trow, 1974) where he argued that while higher education systems expanded their enrolments from elite through mass to universal systems this process set in place a related process of structural differentiation. With more than a hint of ethnocentrism, Trow (1999) argues that while the US had in place the main features of a diversified system long before it reached the phase of mass or universal enrolments, other countries would fail to achieve mass enrolments unless they diversified their systems along the lines of the American model. Since the United States was the first country to achieve mass (meaning enrolments of between 15% and 50% of the age cohort) and universal (enrolments in excess of 50%) it is understandable that the US model has provided a comparative benchmark for other countries. Trow's analysis of the differentiation imperative is consistent with many other analyses. Structural differentiation was a central feature of Parsons & Platt's (1973) analysis of *The American University* and also featured prominently in Burton Clark's (1983) influential analysis of *The Higher Education System*. Drawing principally on Birnbaum (1983), van Vught (1996) has summarised the arguments in favour of diversity arguing that diversified higher education systems are supposed to produce 'higher levels of client orientation (both in relation to the needs of students and the labour market), social mobility, effectiveness, flexibility, innovativeness and stability' (p. 45).

The most visible form of diversification is where new types of higher education institutions are established to complement the longer established universities. These took a variety of forms such as Community Colleges in the US, Polytechnics in the UK, *Fachhochschulen* in Germany and *Instituts Universitaires de Technologie* (IUTs) in France. Typically these new institutions were designed to be more vocationally oriented with little or no provision for research. Diversification also took place within and between universities. One expression of this is the rise of the 'multiversity' (Kerr 1963) or multi-purpose university which Rothblatt (1997: 39) describes as 'carrying out on a single campus the functions of a polytechnic, a normal school, a college of arts and crafts, a technical college, law and medical schools, a business school, research institutes and departments, an American college (even an American upper secondary school) and a sprawling catch-all for undergraduates described as a College of Letters and Science or a College of Arts and Sciences, that is, the attenuated descendant of university colleges'. Another expression of this is the differential ranking of universities in terms of their research standing (Marginson, 2007).

Contrary to the view of those scholars who argue in favour of the superiority and, perhaps, inevitability of greater structural differentiation, others have pointed to the pervasiveness of the counter process of dedifferentiation or isomorphism. Reisman (1956) has pointed to the frequency of lower status institutions seeking to enhance their status by imitating higher status institutions, a process that has become known as 'academic drift'. Birnbaum (1983) found no increase in differentiation in US higher education over a 20 year period (1960–1980) and argued that government policies may be a major factor in decreasing differentiation. Rhoades (1990) has argued that academics have been successful in defending their norms and values and hence have prevented differentiation processes from taking place. Teichler (2006) makes a distinction between collective and individual mobility; in the former case, as exemplified by British polytechnics, an entire group of institutions were re-designated as universities while the latter refers to the movement of a single institution from one category to another.

A variety of categories have been suggested to capture the diversity of higher education systems. In this regard in a recent paper (Kyvik, 2004) reviews the earlier work of Furth (1973), and a collection of more recent analyses such as that by Teichler (1988), Geiger, (1992), Scott (1996) and Kogan (1997). He himself uses Scott's typology which points to the evolution of higher education systems from university-dominated systems, through dual systems, binary systems, unified systems to stratified systems (Kyvik, 2004: 394). In this paper, leaving aside the evolutionary principle, we propose to utilise a simplified model, which differentiates between Unified/Unitary, Binary and Diversified systems. Unified (or unitary) systems embrace both university-dominated systems such as Italy and post-binary systems such as the UK and Australia where non-university institutions have been upgrading to university status or merged with existing universities. Our categorisation of binary also incorporates dual systems since the principal distinction between the two lies in terms of the degree of deliberation surrounding the establishment of binary systems which are designed to complement or perhaps rival universities. Our third category, inspired by the example of the United States, is diversified and is used in preference to 'stratified', the term used by Scott (1996). We refer to countries where higher education is conceived as a total system but where there is a great diversity of institutional types (more than in binary systems) and where different institutions are allocated specific roles within the overall system.

Our three-fold classification refers to system structure only. Since it is also necessary to take account of the degree of hierarchy between higher education institutions within each sector (where there is more than one sector) or within systems where there is only a single sector, we need to add a vertical dimension to allow for an exploration of different levels of stratification. While it is acknowledged that all binary systems embody a hierarchy between sectors, normally with universities at the top of the hierarchy, we are referring here to the degree of stratification of institutions within a sector or within a unified system (Figure 1).

Even if we leave aside the hierarchical dimension, the categorisation of individual countries within the classification systems is not easy. Thus, for example, Sweden is most often defined as having a unified system although Kyvik classifies it as binary; this problem is nicely captured by one Swedish scholar who claims that in the 1980s the Swedish higher education system was 'a hidden binary system' (Dahloff, 1996 cited by Kim, 2004). Similarly France has proved difficult to classify and is excluded from Kyvik's classification of Western European countries. We would classify it as diversified because of the quite separate roles of

Institutional Stratification: Within Sector(s)	System Structure		
	Unified/ Unitary	Binary	Diversified
Strong			
Medium			
Weak			

Figure 1. Classification of Higher Education Systems.

the *Grandes Ecoles*, the universities and the *Instituts Universitaires de Technologie*. It is clear that any classification system is tentative and involves subjective judgment[1]. With these caveats in mind we have classified 27 OECD countries in terms of the structure of their higher education systems (Table 1 below). Our classification follows Kyvik's for 13 of the 15 countries which he categorises. We classify Sweden as 'diversified' and we consider Austria to be still a university dominated system (hence, 'unified') although it does have a small but growing *Fachhochschulen* sector.

Twelve of the 13 countries which we have designated 'binary' are from Europe. We have also classified New Zealand as a binary system. Apart from Australia, all of the other countries classified as having Unified/Unitary systems are from Europe. As already mentioned the higher education system of the US is perhaps the best-known example of a diversified system. This diversity is captured in the evolving Carnegie Classification[2], which in its basic classification differentiates between Doctorate-granting Universities, Master's Colleges and Universities, Baccalaureate Colleges, Associate's Colleges, Special Focus Colleges and Tribal Colleges. The initial version of this classification organised by degree level and specialisation bore marked similarities to another element of Clark Kerr's legacy, the mission differentiation embedded in the 1960 California Master Plan for Higher Education (McCormick, A. & Zhio, C.M., 2005). The diversity of the US system is further enhanced by the mixture of public and private institutions and by the emergence and growth of the for-profit sector. Apart from the US and the French system, mentioned above, we have also classified Mexico and Korea as diversified systems.

A defining feature of the US higher education system is the high level of stratification between institutions, perhaps to a level, which is unique in Western higher education systems. These prestige differentials are determined predominantly by research rankings, whereby the leading US research universities dominate world rankings. In contrast, in the case of France, while the university sector, which guarantees access to all high school graduates, is the largest component of the higher education system, it is not the most prestigious. The *Grandes Ecoles* occupy this position while the selective IUTs occupy an intermediate position in the sectoral hierarchy.

The evolution of binary systems into unified systems as happened in the UK and Australia would seem to signal a decline in prestige differentials between colleges which were previously located in different sectors. However, paradoxically, there is some evidence that the sharing of a common nomenclature is accompanied by increased diversification. One outcome of the research assessment exercise in the UK is an increase in the hierarchical differentiation between institutions all of which carry the title of university. The increased concentration of research funding and academic publications in a select number of universities is leading to a situation whereby some universities are virtually teaching-only universities. The evidence from Australia also suggests that the unified system is not a uniform system. Competitive funding for research and other market oriented steering mechanisms are likely to lead to increased differentiation (Moses, 2004).

The evolution of varying degrees of differentiation and stratification within higher education systems has important implications for equity. One interpretation of the impact of differentiation is that the establishment of new forms of non-university higher education has resulted in democratisation of access, extending the benefits of higher education to previously underrepresented groups. An alternative interpretation focuses on the way in which access to different forms of higher education is structured by class and other social characteristics. It is argued that working class and minority groups are steered into the less noble sector of higher education and ultimately into lower status occupations. It is likely that this 'cooling out' (Clark 1960) function co-exists with the 'educational upgrading' function the outcome being different for different groups of students. This reality is well captured by Dougherty (1994) in his description of the contradictory character of community colleges in the US as both reproducers of inequality and promoters of social mobility. Grubb (2003) has argued that, at least in the US, the upgrading function has dominated over the cooling out function. A recent analysis of the situation in Israel explores the extent to which class and ability structure the allocation of students to different forms of higher education (Ayalon & Yogev 2006). It was found that where second-tier institutions are similar to first-tier ones, in terms of appealing to the traditional clientele of universities, they tend to absorb less able members of privileged social groups or economically established members of otherwise disadvantaged groups. In contrast, second-tier institutions, which are expected to respond to the needs of specific populations, tend to open up higher education to new social groups; these institutions, however, offer only limited opportunities. The general applicability of their findings may be limited by the specificity of the Israeli situation, whereby the differences between the five types of second-tier institutions are partly defined by the differences in the target client group. The more general conclusion however is apposite; the equity implications of diversification are context bound depending on the characteristics of the second-tier institution. If the alternative to enrolment at the less prestigious institution is non-enrolment, diversification carries positive implications. If on the other hand, the existence of newly established institutions prevents members of disadvantaged groups from applying to universities this is likely to increase inequality (ibid).

INTERFACE BETWEEN SECOND LEVEL STRUCTURES AND HIGHER EDUCATION

In any analysis of comparative patterns of access and participation in higher education it is necessary to take account of the structures of secondary education. The interface between the two sectors has been the subject of limited analysis; the most systematic treatment of the topic dates from the mid 1980s in a volume edited by Burton Clark (1985). Clark uses the metaphor of a two-way street to characterise the reciprocal relationship between the two sectors. While acknowledging the downward influence which higher education systems exert on schools at second level we will principally concern ourselves with an analysis of how second levels school structures condition access to higher education. This relationship is especially explicit at a quantitative level in that the output of the second level systems sets the parameter for third level enrolment. For example, it is generally accepted that the stagnation in the rate of entry to higher education in the US is a direct consequence of the failure to increase high school graduation rates, which have remained relatively stable in recent years (Swanson 2004). In contrast, Deer (2005) argues that HE enrolment growth in France is a mechanical phenomenon stemming from the politically encouraged growth in participation at upper secondary level and from the increased success rates at the baccalaureate. However, in addition to the scale of secondary enrolment it is necessary to take account of the way in which second level systems are structured, since not all second level graduates are eligible for higher education. Until the 1960s most European countries had developed a differentiated second level structure, which was variously binary, tripartite or quadripartite in structure, where typically only the graduates of the academic sector were eligible for entry to higher education. This contrasted with the United States, which as early as the first decades to the twentieth century developed a comprehensive second level system which has survived until today. While over the past fifty years many countries have reformed their previously highly stratified second level systems, the continuum of stratified – comprehensive remains the principal axis along which we can locate national differences in the structure of second level systems. These system differences have direct implications for the pattern of access and equity in higher education.

The choice between differentiated and comprehensive structures reflects a central dilemma in the planning of second level provision especially where universal participation has become a policy objective. When only a minority of the age cohort, typically the more able and those from middle class backgrounds, transferred into secondary education it was feasible to provide a predominantly academic programme the purpose of which was to prepare for university entrance and to provide training for those who would enter civil service and other administrative and clerical positions. With increasing social expectations, demanding secondary education for all, there was a need to provide for more diversified curricular pathways catering for the full range of student abilities, motivations and aspirations and the full spectrum of occupational positions which require more highly educated recruits. The provision options were either to provide specialized schools catering for different groups of students with different aptitudes and career aspirations or to provide a single comprehensive school which sought to provide a full range of academic and technical programmes. The latter option allows for varying degrees of within-school curricular tracking by subject or programme. The choices have clear implications for access to higher education. The more differentiated the second level system the more the higher education selection function is lodged at the point of transition between primary and secondary education[3]. The less differentiated the second level structure the more the selection function is shifted upwards towards the point of transition between secondary school and higher education institutions. Comprehensive systems have a later age of selection for higher education increasing the 'zone of articulation' between school and university (Neave, 1987).

The significance of school structure as a determinant of quality and equity has come into fresh relief in the context of recent comparative research, most notably in the Programme for International Student Assessment (PISA) and other cross country research programmes. For example, the analysis of the international differences in performance on Mathematics from the 2003 PISA study concludes that the more differentiated and selective educational systems tend to show much larger differences in school performance but also larger differences between students from more and less advantaged family backgrounds. This analysis suggests that disadvantaged students are more likely to be placed in low status schools with less demanding curricula and lower expectations for their learning. Socially advantaged students are more likely to be placed in high status schools with more demanding curricula. In this sense schools tend to reproduce the existing social hierarchy. In countries with more comprehensive systems the relationship between social background and education performance is weaker, thought not absent. The weaker relationship suggests that schools are making some difference not simply reproducing existing social relationships (OECD, 2005a: 398–406). The 2000 PISA study has been the subject of extensive reanalysis as its findings relate to school factors (OECD, 2005b). Overall it has been found that 35% of variance in reading literacy performance lies between schools and that those countries with highly stratified school systems show the largest between-school variance. Furthermore, school systems with a high degree of institutional differentiation and early selection exhibit larger social disparities whereby educational performance is more dependent on family background. These findings have been replicated by two separate analyses of this data set (Gorard and Smith, 2003: Marks, 2005). An important finding of the analysis of reading literacy performance from the 2000 PISA study, which was not replicated in the analysis of performance in Mathematics in the 2003 PISA study, is that school systems with high levels of institutional differentiation also have lower mean student performance in literacy. Thus quality as well as equity may be partly a function of school structure.

In the PISA studies institutional differentiation is conceived as a continuum not a simple dichotomy, differentiating between stratified and comprehensive systems. For example, in the analysis of the 2000 PISA study the indicator of differentiation is based on a combination of: the number of school types or distinct educational programmes into which students can be sorted; the existence of separate provision of academic and vocational programmes; the age at which selection between tracks is made; and the extent of grade repetition. Furthermore since these studies are based on student assessment at age 15 the systems being assessed relate to that which is experienced at this age. Indeed many systems, which are comprehensive in structure up to the ages of 15 or 16, introduce greater differentiation beyond this age. Some analysts (for example, Marks, 2005) point out that this is inevitable and others such as Clark (1985) have identified 'the lack of differentiation, a minimization of hierarchy and an intolerance of competition' as a major weakness of American secondary schooling. Recent policy changes designed to introduce greater choice and competition to previously comprehensive systems, such as the introduction of Charter Schools in the US and the growth of grant-maintained schools in the UK, have prompted one research team to differentiate between highly marketised comprehensive systems from other fully comprehensive systems. In making this designation Green et al (2003) note that in terms of the equality outcomes these marketised comprehensives have higher levels of inequality, thus having more in common with selective systems rather than fully comprehensive systems. The optimum structuring of second level education remains a contested part of the policy agenda in many countries.

LEVELS OF PARTICIPATION AND SYSTEM STRUCTURE

Central to the functionalist analysis of higher education systems, as exemplified by Trow's thesis, is the view that differentiation is an imperative for the development of mass and universal systems. Thus, it is of interest to look at the relationship between levels of participation in higher education systems and system structure. Drawing on our analysis presented in the previous chapter in our paper on *Measuring Access and Equity* we present in Table 1 data on participation for 27 OECD countries listed in descending order in terms of their score on our Higher Education.

Table 1. Level of Participation in Higher Education and structure of higher education and second level systems for 27 OECD Countries

	Higher Education Participation Index Score	Higher Education System Structure (Provisional Designation)	Level of Differentiation in Structure of Second Level System*
Korea	96.2	Diversified	Medium
Finland	87.5	Binary	Low
United States	84.6	Diversified	Low
Norway	76.8	Binary	Low
Sweden	76.6	Unified	Low
Belgium	74.9	Binary	High
Australia	74.7	Unified	Low
Greece	72.6	Binary	Medium
New Zealand	70.3	Binary	Low
Denmark	69.8	Binary	Low
Spain	69.7	Unified	Low
France	66.1	Diversified	Medium
Ireland	66.0	Binary	Medium
United Kingdom	65.0	Unified	NA
Netherlands	61.1	Binary	High
Iceland	60.8	Unified	Low
Poland	55.0	Binary	Medium

Table 1. (Continued)

Switzerland	53.5	Binary	Medium
Germany	51.1	Binary	High
Hungary	48.7	Binary	High
Italy	46.5	Unified	Medium
Portugal	46.0	Binary	Medium
Austria	42.1	Unified	High
Czech Republic	39.1	Unified	High
Slovak Republic	34.3	Unified	High
Mexico	32.5	Diversified	Medium
Turkey	24.8	Unified	High

* *Adapted from OECD (2005) Education at a Glance. See text for details.*

Participation Index. This table also presents a classification of the structure of the higher education system in each country in the light of our discussion above. We have classified 13 systems as 'binary', 10 systems as 'unified/unitary' and 4 systems as 'diversified'. It is evident that there is only a modest relationship between system structure and levels of participation. This relationship is made more explicit in Table 2, where we classify countries (in 3 groups of nine) as having high, medium or low levels of participation on the basis of their score on our Higher Education Participation Index. Counties with unified systems tend to have lower levels of participation. Half of the countries with unified systems of higher education have lower levels of participation by comparison with about a quarter of counties with binary of diversified systems. Furthermore it is of interest to note that many of the countries with unified systems which have achieved higher rates of participation were previously binary or dual systems. The latter is true of Australia and the UK and arguably is also an appropriate description of the situation in Sweden and Iceland. While conscious of the small number of countries with diversified higher education systems in our sample we cannot conclude from our analysis that these systems have any significant advantages over binary systems in facilitating higher enrolments in higher education. Thus, we are unable to validate Trow's (1999) hypothesis which we discussed above.

More significantly, perhaps, the lack of a more emphatic relationship between the structure of higher education systems and levels of participation suggests that our structural classification may not capture the essential variability of higher education systems. While structures may matter we still haven't identified emphatically what structures impact on levels of participation. In this context it is of interest to note that our findings are consistent with those of Teichler (1997) in a study of six countries (cited by Huisman et al (2003: 26)) and with those of Huisman and his colleagues own study of nine countries. The latter study used a more complex measurement of diversity, which included data on size of institutions, type of control, range of disciplines and degrees, and types of programme organisation.

Table 2. Relationship between Level of Participation in Higher Education
and the Structure of Higher Education System

Level of Participation in Higher Education	Structure of Higher Education System		
	Unified N %	Binary N %	Differentiated N %
High	2 (20)	5 (38)	2 (50)
Medium	3 (30)	5 (38)	1 (25)
Low	5 (50)	3 (23)	1 (25)
All Levels	10 (100)	13 (100)	4 (100)

We turn now to consider the relationship between levels of participation and the structure of the second level system. We draw upon research from the PISA project to catogorise second level systems in terms of the level of differentiation/ stratification. As we noted above the composite measure of stratification used in the PISA study combines four separate indicators[4]. In Table 1 we differentiate between countries which have high, medium and low scores on the stratification index. It is clear that this structural characteristic is strongly related to levels of participation in higher education. Six of the nine countries with the highest levels of participation in higher education have low level of differentiation in their secondary school structure, while two countries have a medium level of different-tiation. Belgium is the only outlier in this group, having achieved a high level of participation in higher education with a highly differentiated second level structure. In contrast six of the countries with a low level of participation in higher education have high levels of differentiation at secondary level, while two countries have medium levels. Countries with medium levels of participation at second level tend to have medium or low scores on the second level differentiation index. The Netherlands is the only exception in this regard.

The differential results from our analysis of these two structural correlates of participation are interesting. It would appear that while the structure of higher education systems is not a very important determinant of levels of participation, the structure of the second level system, which regulates the pipeline of potential recruits, is crucial. The continuing impact of high levels of stratification in the second level system is significant notwithstanding attempts in many countries to blur the distinction between technical and academic courses, typically by making the technical courses more academic, or where technical qualifications are increasingly deemed acceptable for entry into higher education (see Green et al 1999).

LEVELS OF INEQUALITY AND SYSTEM STRUCTURE

We have noted in chapter 5 the absence of comparative data on inequality of access which take account of current enrolments in higher education. We could identify only one comparative research programme, the EUROSTUDENT project, that addresses this issue and even in this case it was not the main focus of the research programme. We have reanalysed these data from the 2005 and 2008 EUROSTUDENT surveys to identify between-country differences in equality of access. In Table 3 we link this analysis to our findings on levels of participation and data on the structure of the educational system in the 13 countries for which we have the relevant data on both participation levels and levels of inequality. These countries are listed on the basis of their score on the Higher Education Participation Index. In column 2 of this table we report the country ranking on levels of inequality. These scores are based on our analysis of the 2008 EUROSTUDENT survey, reported in chapter 5, where we have calculated the average of the sum of the rankings on the separate measures of inequality on fathers' and mothers' educational and occupational background. Taken together these data reveal a modest relationship between participation levels and levels of inequality of access to higher education. The Spearman rank order correlation coefficient is .566, which is statistically significant at the .05 level. Countries with low levels of participation tend to have higher levels of inequality while countries with higher levels of participation tend to have lower levels of inequality in access to higher education. Data in column 3 of Table 3 allows for a similar analysis for eight of the eleven countries which participated in the 2005 EUROSTUDENT study. These rankings are based on an earlier analysis where we calculated the relative odds of accessing higher education based on fathers' occupation and education and mothers' education (Clancy & Goastellec, 2007). As in the case of the previous analysis these data represent the average of the sum of the rankings on the separate measures of inequality on fathers' educational and occupational background and mothers' educational background[5]. Again we find a modest relationship between participation levels and levels of inequality of access to higher education. In this instance the Spearman rank order correlation coefficient is .628, which is statistically significant at the .05 level. Taking accounts of these results from two separate studies we can conclude that although not emphatic, a trend is evident whereby countries with higher levels of participation in higher education tend to have lower levels of inequality.

We also include in Table 3 data on the structure of the higher education and secondary education systems in these countries. Looking at the relationship between our rankings on levels of inequality from EUROSTUDENT 2008 and the structure of the higher education systems we note that three of the five countries with lowest levels of inequality have binary systems; however when we look at the five countries with highest levels of inequality two have binary systems, two have unified systems and one has a diversified system. The three countries with medium levels of inequality have unified systems. When we look at the relationship between rankings on inequality from the 2005 EUROSTUDENT survey and the structure of the higher education systems we find no clear pattern for the eight countries for which we have data. This failure to find a clear link between higher education structure and inequality is perhaps not surprising in view of our failure to find a stronger relationship between the structure of higher education systems and levels of participation.

Table 3. Levels of Inequality, Participation and Educational Structures

	Higher Education Participation Index Score	Inequality of Access: Country Ranking 2008	Inequality of Access: Country Ranking 2005	Higher Education System Structure	Level of Differentiation in Second Level Structure
Finland	87.5	2	4	Binary	Low
Sweden	76.6	5	NA	Unified	Low
Spain	69.7	6	2	Unified	Low
France	66.1	11	5	Diversified	High
Ireland	66.0	3	1	Binary	Low
Netherlands	61.1	1	3	Binary	High
Germany	51.1	9	6	Binary	High
Italy	46.5	4	NA	Unified	Low
Portugal	46.0	12	8	Binary	Low
Austria	42.1	10	7	Unified	High
Czech Rep.	39.1	7	NA	Unified	High
Slovak Rep.	34.3	8	NA	Unified	High
Turkey	24.8	13	NA	Unified	High

We now turn to look at the data on the relationship between the structure of secondary education and inequality of access to higher education. Because of the smaller number of countries for whom we have these data, unlike that reported in Table 1, above, our classification of levels of differentiation in second levels systems is in terms of a simple dichotomy. Seven of the countries are classified as having 'high' levels of differentiation while the other six countries are designated as having 'low' levels of differentiation on the basis of their composite score. Looking first at these findings with respect to the EUROSTUDENT 2008 survey we note that five of the six countries with lower levels of inequality in access to higher education have lower levels of differentiation in their secondary school systems; the exception being the Netherlands. In contrast six of the seven countries which have higher levels of inequality have a highly differentiated second level system. The exception here is Portugal. We observe a similar trend when we examine the findings from the 2005 survey. In this instance, three of the four countries with higher levels of differentiation in the secondary education system exhibit higher levels of inequality while three of the four countries with lower levels of differentiation in the secondary education system exhibit lower levels of inequality in access to higher education. Again, the Netherlands and Portugal are the outliers. While the former has the highest level of differentiation in its second level system it ranks among those countries with the lowest levels of inequality in access to higher education. In contrast, Portugal combines relatively low levels of differentiation at second level with very high levels of inequality in access to higher education. Notwithstanding these exceptions, the consistency of findings drawn from two separate surveys provides strong evidence that the structure of secondary education has significant implications for the levels of inequality by socio-economic group in access to higher education.

DISCUSSION

The search for the optimum structure of higher education systems has attracted the sustained interests of policy makers. This concern is explicable in the light of the continuing expansion of HE systems and the ever-increasing costs of sustaining such systems. International agencies such as UNESCO and OECD, national governments and supra-national institutions such as the European Union have all shown an interest in this topic. This concern of policy makers has not been matched by any significant body of relevant research. We have combined our brief review of the literature on the diversification of higher education systems and the interface with second level systems with an empirical analysis of how system structure relates to levels of participation in higher education and equality of access. In doing so it has been necessary to develop appropriate measures of participation to facilitate comparative analysis (Clancy 2010, chapter 5 in this volume). The relative absence of data on comparative levels of inequality in access to higher education, reflecting current or recent student enrolments, represents a serious lacuna in higher education research that needs to be addressed.

Our empirical analysis of the relationship between the structure of educational systems and levels of participation in higher education and levels of inequality in access does not provide for a simple unequivocal answer. We find strong evidence that the structure of secondary education systems is a significant determinant of both levels of participation and levels of inequality. Countries which have highly differentiated second level systems have lower overall levels of participation in higher education and higher levels of inequality of access by socio-economic group. Second level education structures do matter. Our findings are much less emphatic when we examine the effect of higher education structures. While we found that both binary and diversified systems tend to have higher levels of participation in higher education than unitary/unified systems, higher education structure is not significantly related to level of inequality in access to higher education. Notwithstanding data limitations we feel that our failure to identify a stronger relationship between higher education structures and levels of participation and the absence of any relationship with equity call for a serious stocktaking. Either we conclude that higher education structure does not matter or we revisit our conceptual categories. Since we have established that second level structure does matter and does affect the pattern of higher education participation we conclude that we need to revisit our analytic categories which relate to our understanding of the structural features of higher education systems.

The most obvious limitation about our categories for defining the structure of higher education systems is that they are not pure categories. If we consider the unified system in the UK as an example, Scott (1996) has noted the tendency for binary systems to reproduce themselves. This is most obvious in the emergence of Further Education Colleges as significant providers of higher education, with expectations of further expansion of this sector. By the mid 1990s Further Education colleges enrolled 13% of all students in higher education in the UK (Parry 2003: 322) and in Scotland, by 2001, over half of Scottish higher education entrants began their studies in the further education sector (Morgan-Khlein 2003: 338). Yet we, and all other commentators, describe the UK system as unified, notwithstanding this significant element which lies outside the formal higher education sector. There is a similar ambiguity about the other post-binary system, Australia, which is reproducing elements of a binary system in the Technical and Further Education (TAFE) institutions' contribution to tertiary education. We have already referred to the difficulty of categorizing Sweden, which we have designated as a unified system, despite its hidden binary elements. We have designated Austria as a unified system although in recent years it has introduced a small but growing non-university sector. It is possible to enter some caveats about most of our country classifications. It is also of interest to note that the system classification of unified/binary/diversified does not appear to bear any consistent relationship to the widely used OECD categorization of systems in terms of the distribution of enrolments between Type A and Type B higher education programmes (Table 4). Programmes which are largely theoretically based and designed to provide quailfications for entry into advanced research programmes and professions with high skill requirements are defined as Type A programmes while Type B programmes are more occupationally oriented, typically of shorter duration, and lead to direct labour market access. Of the 13 systems which we have classified as binary, six have very low levels (5% or less) of enrolment on Type B programmes, five have relatively high percentages (20% plus) on Type B programmes while three countries report moderate levels of enrolment on these programmes. Of the ten countries with a unified system of higher education, four have medium levels of enrolment on Type B programmes, four have low levels of enrolment on Type B higher education programmes while two have a high level of enrolment on these programmes. However three of the four countries which we classified as having diversified higher education systems report a high percentage of enrolments on Type B programmes. The lack of clear unambiguous classifications has caused some commentators to invoke the concept to 'fuzziness' to characterise the fluidity of boundaries between sectors in many countries (Huisman & Kaiser 2001). Similarly, Scott (1996) has argued that the increasing complexity of the environments in which all higher education institutions operate and the demands made upon them require levels of institutional differentiation which go beyond sectorisation.

The results of our analysis give credence to Teichler's (2006) view that there appears to be no international consensus on the appropriate extent of structural differentiation within higher education systems. Similar conclusions have been reached by Scott (1996) and Green et al (1999), in respect of the absence of a

Table 4. Classification of Structure of Higher Education Systems and Percentages of Enrolments on Type B Programmes

	Higher Education System Structure	*Percentage Enrolment on Type B Programmes*
Australia	Unified	17
Austria	Unified	11
Belgium	Binary	51
Czech Republic	Unified	10
Denmark	Binary	8
Finland	Binary	<1
France	Diversified	24
Germany	Binary	15
Greece	Binary	32
Hungary	Binary	3
Iceland	Unified	5
Ireland	Binary	35
Italy	Unified	1
Korea	Diversified	40
Mexico	Diversified	2
Netherlands	Binary	1
New Zealand	Binary	26
Norway	Binary	1
Poland	Binary	1
Portugal	Binary	1
Slovak Republic	Unified	3
Spain	Unified	13
Sweden	Unified	3
Switzerland	Binary	20
United Kingdom	Unified	32
United States	Diversified	23
Turkey	Unified	30

Europe-wide model for the organisation of higher education. The long established interest in various forms of horizontal differentiation is now complemented by a heightened interest in vertical differentiation especially as it relates to research activity. Whether this will lead to the emergence of a small number of research-intensive universities or looser networks of centres of excellence or networks of excellence, which may be discipline specific, remains to be resolved (Teichler (2006). The outcome is likely to be partly determined by the operation of market mechanisms whereby research funding is increasingly allocated following a competitive bidding process. In respect of study programmes it may be that, at least in Europe, the impact of the Bologna process, which seeks to institutionalise the Bachelors/ Masters distinction, may make the differentiation by programme level more important than sectoral differences. In combination the trend towards greater research selectivity and towards a differentiation of study programmes by level would suggest that vertical differentiation will become more significant than horizontal differentiation.

The absence of an international convergence in relation to the structure of higher education systems which have achieved 'universal' levels of enrolment would seem to question the validity of Trow's convergence thesis. Clearly Trow underestimated the variety of structural forms which are compatible with universal levels of enrolment. However, at a deeper level his emphasis on diversification seems to have been well placed. The analytical challenge is to conceptualise and measure the nature of this diversification which characterises higher education systems and to explore the linkages between such characteristics and their consequences whether this is in terms of levels of expansion and inequality or in respect of other outcomes.

NOTES

[1]   In a few cases we invoked the assistance of 'local' experts to assist us where our own knowledge was limited and where we could not locate appropriate analytical descriptions of the higher education systems.

[2]   The first version of the classification was published in 1973 and has been subject to various revisions, most recently in 2005 see (www.carnegiefoudantion.org/classifications accessed 27/06/08).

[3]   This does not preclude some students who fail to follow and complete the college preparatory pathway accessing higher education through non-standard entry routes.

[4]   The composite score is derived by averaging the standardised score (around a mean of zero and a standard deviation of 1) on each of the four separate indicators.

[5]   Mothers' occupational background is not included in this composite measure.

BIBLIOGRAPHY

Ayalon, H., & Yogev, A. (2006). Stratification in the expanded system of higher education in Israel. *Higher Education Policy, 19*, 187–203.

Birnbaum, R. (1983). *Maintaining diversity in higher education*. San Francisco: Jossey-Bass.

Clancy, P. (2010). Measuring access and equity from a comparative perspective. In H. Eggins (Ed.), *Access and equity in higher education: Comparative perspectives* (chap. 5). Rotterdam: Sense Publishers.

Clancy, P., & Goastellec, G. (2007). Exploring access and equity in higher education: Policy and performance in a comparative perspective. *Higher Education Quarterly, 61*(2), 136–154.

Clark, B. R. (1960). The cooling-out function in higher education. *American Journal of Sociology, 65*, 569–576.

Clark, B. R. (1983). *The higher education system: Academic organization in cross-national perspective*. Berkeley, CA: University of California Press.

Clark, B. R. (1985). *The school and university*. Berkeley, CA: University of California Press.

Dahllof, U. (1996). Conditional conclusions in a Scandinavian comparative perspective. In U. Dahllof & S. Selander (Eds.), *Expanding colleges and new universities* (Vol. 56). Uppsala: Almqvist & Wiksell, Uppsala Studies in Education.

Deer, C. (2005). Higher education access and expansion: The French case. *Higher Education Quarterly, 59*(3), 230–241.

Dougherty, K. J. (1994). *The contradictory college*. Albany, NY: State University of New York Press.

EUROSTUDENT. (2008). *Social and economic conditions of student life in Europe 2005: Synopsis of indicators*. Hannover: HIS Hochschul-Unformations-System.

EUROSTUDENT. (2005). *Social and economic conditions of student life in Europe 2005: Synopsis of indicators*. Hannover: HIS Hochschul-Unformations-System.

Furth, D. (Ed.). (1973). *Short-cycle higher education: A search for identity*. Paris: OECD.

Geiger, R. (1992). The institutional fabric of the higher education system, introduction. In B. R. Clark & G. Neave (Eds.), *The encyclopaedia of higher education*. Oxford: Pergamon Press.

Grubb, N. (2003). *The roles of tertiary colleges and institutes: Trade-offs in the restructuring postsecondary education*. Paris: OECD.

Gorard, S., & Smith, E. (2003). An international comparison of equity in education systems. *Comparative Education, 40*(1), 15–28.

Green, A., Wolf, A., & Leney, T. (1999). *Convergence and divergence in European education and training systems*. London: Institute of Education.

Green, A., Preston, J., & Sabates, R. (2003). Education, equality and social cohesion: A distributional approach. *Compare, 33*(4), 453–470.

Huiseman, J., & Kaiser, F. (2001). *Fixed and fuzzy boundaries in higher education: A comparative study of (binary) structures in nine countries*. Twente: CHEPS.

Huiseman, J., Kaiser, F., & Vossensteyn, H. (2003). The relations between access, diversity and participation: The search for the weakest link? In M. Tight (Ed.), *Access and exclusion*. Amsterdam: Elsevier.

Kerr, C. (1963). *The uses of a university*. Cambridge, MA: Harvard University Press.

Kim, L. (2004). Massification in a uniform system of higher education – The Swedish Dilemma. In I. Fagerlind & G. Stromqmist (Eds.), *Reforming higher education in Nordic countries*. Paris: International Institute for Educational Plannning.

Kogan, M. (1997). Diversification in higher education: Differences and commonalities. *Minerva, 35*, 47–62.

Kyvik, S. (2004). Structural changes in higher education systems in Western Europe. *Higher Education in Europe, 29*(3), 393–406.

McCormick, A., & Zhio, C. M. (2005, September/October). Rethinking and reframing the Carnegie classification. *Change*.

Marginson, S. (2007). Global University rankings. In S. Marginson (Ed.), *Prospects of higher education: Globalisation, market competition, public goods and the future of the University*. Rotterdam: Sense Publishers.

Marks, G. N. (2005). Cross-national differences and accounting for social class inequalities in education. *International Sociology, 20*(4), 483–505.

Morgan-Klein. (2003). Scottish higher education and the FE-HE Nexus. *Higher Education Quarterly, 57*(4), 338–354.

Moses, I. (2004, April 29–30). *Unified national system or uniform national system? The Australian Experience*, paper delivered at CHE conference, Berlin.

Neave, G. (1987). Interfaces between secondary and tertiary education. *Higher Education in Europe, 12*(2), 5–19.

OECD. (2005a). *Education at a glance 2005*. Paris: OECD.

OECD. (2005b). *School factors related to quality and equity: Results from PISA 2000*. Paris: OECD.

Parry, G. (2005). Mass higher education and the English: Wherein the colleges? *Higher Education Quarterly, 57*(4), 308–337.

Parsons, T., & Platt, G. M. (1973). *The American University*. Cambridge, MA: Harvard University Press.

Reisman, D. (1956). *Constraint and variety in American education*. Lincoln, NE: University of Nebraska University Press.

Rhoades, G. (1990). Political competition and differentiation in higher education. In J. C. Alexander & P. Colony (Eds.), *Differentiation theory and social change*. New York: Columbia University Press.

Rothblatt, S. (1997). *The modern university and its discontents: The fate of Newman's legacies in Britain and America*. Cambridge: Cambridge University Press.

Scott, P. (1996). Unified and binary systems of higher education in Europe. In A. Burgen (Ed.), *Goals and purposes of higher education in the 21st century*. London: Jessica Kingsley.

Swanson, C. B. (2004). *High school graduation, completion, and dropout (GCD) indicators*. Washington, DC: The Urban Institute.

Teichler, U. (1988). *Changing patterns of higher the education system: The experience of three decades*. London: Jessica Kingsley.

Teichler, T. (1997). Reforms as a response to massification of higher education: A comparative view. In A. Arimoto (Ed.), *Academic reforms in the world: Situation and perspective in the massification stage of higher education*. Hiroshima University: Research Institute for Higher Education.

Teichler, U. (2006). Changing views in Europe about diversification in higher education. In *Transitions to mass higher education systems: International comparisons and perspectives*. Haifa, Israel: The S. Neaman Institute.

Trow, M. (1974). Problems in the transition from Elite to mass higher education. In OECD (Ed.), *Policies for higher education*. Paris: OECD.

Trow, M. (1999). From mass higher education to universal access: The American advantage. *Minerva, 37*, 303–328.

Van Vught, F. (1996). Isomorphism in higher education? towards a theory of differentiation and diversity in higher education systems. In L. Goedegebuure, V. L. Meek, O. Kivinen, & R. Rinne (Eds.), *The mockers and the mocked: Comparative perspectives on differentiation convergence and diversity in higher education*. Oxford: Pergamon.

INTERVENTION STRATEGIES: HANDLING COMPLEXITY

The pattern of interventions, and their drivers, is complex. On the one hand, governments are concerned to establish social justice, of which social mobility and a level playing field for those considering higher education is a part. This also has some economic benefits for a country in that an expansion in the number of graduates will bring more skills to the labour market and enable the individual country to play an active part in the 'knowledge society'. On the other hand, the majority of countries can no longer meet the cost of providing tuition for the high numbers of students, so 'cost-sharing' has been introduced, whereby students are expected to contribute towards the cost of their own university education. Care then has to be taken that those from lower socio-economic groups are not precluded from entering higher education. Policies to widen participation and improve access for disadvantaged groups remain important, as do policies to retain those students through to successful completion of their studies.

Almost all countries in our study were involved in setting in train interventions to widen access. These can arguably be seen as falling into four distinct groups: government policy to monitor and oversee higher education; financial interventions; structural interventions; and 'aspirational' interventions. The first, which can be viewed as 'overarching', is the specific setting up of government bodies to oversee the provision of higher education. This has taken a range of forms, from the establishment of national blueprints for the higher education system, to setting up national Committees with specific remits to report on the system and make recommendations for its future shape. White Papers have commonly been used and Education Acts have translated the desired changes into law. On occasion, separate agencies or buffer bodies have been set up to fulfil particular aspects of the law.

The second group, financial interventions, are frequently used to encourage and support students from underprivileged backgrounds, disabled students, ethnic minorities, and, in some countries, female students and geographically isolated populations. The range of interventions takes into account local and cultural factors. Financial support from a range of sources can be targeted at individual students, or at institutions. In the latter case, institutions themselves can be offered financial incentives to accept more students from disadvantaged backgrounds. Structural interventions, the third group, are common. Governments introduce new qualifications to meet the needs of the twenty-first century, thereby widening participation. They also set new admission criteria, encourage the establishment of new institutions, particularly in the private sector, and bring about mergers of existing institutions. The fourth group of interventions to widen access can be termed 'aspirational'. Here the interventions are designed with specific groups in mind: they can be, for instance, targeted to raise the awareness of those from families with no experience of higher education, or aimed that those from geographically isolated and underprivileged areas. These initiatives can be organised by governments, institutions or charitable foundations. Programmes can be offered for individuals or for groups of institutions.

One separate group of interventions which needs comment are those concerned with retention and completion. The drive to produce a larger graduate cohort depends on two aspects of a country's higher education system: the need to improve access and widen participation, and the necessity to retain as high a percentage as possible of higher education students in the system so that they successfully graduate. In some countries access is not a problem: the major concern is the low retention rate of those who do enter the system, thereby depressing the potential graduation rates. Interventions to address this problem range from the provision of financial incentives to targeted support systems (see chapter 8).

GOVERNMENT POLICIES

It is clear that important policy White Papers have set out, in many countries, a blueprint for the development of higher education. In South Africa a National Plan for Higher Education was published in 2001, developed from a report 'Towards a new Higher Education Landscape' published by the Council on Higher Education (2000). As a result a number of important changes have taken place: several institutions have been merged, and an expanding private sector has been established. In 2005 the Regional University Association was set up which has the task of setting student tuition fees on a regional basis.

In Israel, the Knesset (Israeli Parliament) passed the Council for Higher Education Act in 1958 whereby the Council for Higher Education was established to oversee the higher education system. A Planning and Budgeting Committee was established by the Council in 1974 whose role was to allocate money to the various institutions, and to plan and monitor the development of the system. As a result many new institutions were founded. Under its auspices teacher training colleges were upgraded to enable them to offer B.Ed and M.Ed degrees, and private law schools were set up. In 1991 the Council of Higher Education took powers to validate the private colleges.

Ethiopia set out an Education and Training Policy in 1994 which instituted a range of initiatives aimed at ensuring national development and competitiveness. This was followed in 1997 by a document 'Future Directions of Higher Education in Ethiopia', a White Paper on Higher Education Capacity Building (2002) and, in 2003, a Higher Education Proclamation. Under this latter proclamation, the Higher Education Relevance and Quality Assurance Agency was established, along with the Ethiopian Higher Education Strategy Centre. Major reforms affecting provision have been brought in: a graduate tax; the encouragement of private provision; with a resultant expansion of both private and public provision. (By 2006, there were 34 private university colleges offering degrees.) The influence of the World Bank has been considerable, and can be viewed as a major factor in facilitating reform. The consultative dialogues in which the World Bank takes part have encouraged a wide range of stakeholders to contribute, and helped to build a consensus.

The Irish government published a White Paper in 1995 'Charting our Education Future' which stated that a major objective was to promote equality of access to higher education, irrespective of social class, age or disability, for all who had the capacity to benefit from it (p. 102). A number of government sponsored advisory reports followed, including one in 2001 by the Action Group on Access which recommended the development of a co-ordinated framework to promote access for the socially disadvantaged, mature students and those with disabilities. As a result the National Access Office for Equity of Access to Higher Education was established, with a remit to draw up policy proposals and oversee the implementation of agreed measures. Its Action Plan (2005–2007) stated that in addition to the target groups already identified, participation targets should also be set for members of the Traveller Community and for ethnic minority groups. The Higher Education Authority, the body which provides funding for the higher education institutions, is charged with facilitating these recommendations.

The first statements relating to government policy on access and equity in the UK are found in the Robbins Report (1963), a wide-ranging report produced under the chairmanship of Lord Robbins. The Committee stated that 'courses of higher education should be available for all those who are qualified by ability and attainment to pursue them and who wish to do so' (Robbins, 1963, 7–8). The growth of higher education was recommended and as a result a group of new universities were established, grants were made more widely available and numbers expanded.

The next major report was called for following the abolition of the binary line in 1992 when the polytechnics, along with some other higher education institutions, became part of the mainstream university system. The early 90s had seen an unprecedented growth in student numbers. A National Committee of Inquiry into Higher Education was established with bipartisan support in 1996 to make recommendations 'on how the purposes, shape, structure, size and funding of higher education, including support for students, should develop to meet the needs of the United Kingdom over the next 20 years'. The Report, chaired by Ron Dearing, was entitled 'Higher Education in the Learning Society' considered a wide range of issues. It noted that students from lower socio-economic groups were failing to access higher education because of poor qualifications, low aspiration levels and flawed educational decision-making (Dearing 1997, 101–113). The Report suggested that a national strategy of widening participation needed to be developed: this would be a key factor in promoting economic prosperity in the UK.

Vietnam has likewise witnessed a developing interest in higher education. At the 7th Congress of the Communist Party of Vietnam (CPV) in 1986, it was stated that 'education in general and higher education in particular is considered as the first national priority policy'. In 1993 the Central Committee of the CPV issued a Decision relating to the Reform of Education whereby the university structure was reorganised and enrolment increased, especially from ethnic minority regions. In 2001 the Prime Minister approved the Higher Education System Planning Period

2001–2010, and a National Education Development Strategy 2001–2010, which proposed a number of policies relating to access and equity. In 2005 a further Government Decision was issued to continue the reform of Vietnam Higher Education through the period 2006–2020. Since then there has been a considerable injection of funding by the World Bank, with a number of reforms facilitating access. The Ministry of Education and Training (MOET), which is directly responsible for higher education, has set clear principles of equity in access and excellence in performance from which stem a number of recent reforms.

The effect of the Bologna Declaration and following agreements, which have been signed by the Ministers of Higher Education for the majority of European countries, has been particularly noticeable in France. These agreements have established a European Higher Education Area and a common European framework of a harmonised degree structure with three cycles, quality assurance and student mobility. In 1989 the French government published its 'Code de l'Education' which states 'the first cycle of higher education is open to all high school graduates'. The introduction of more elements of the common framework have helped further moves towards reform. These are ongoing: President Sarkozy is currently intent upon enabling a more equitable system to be established.

FINANCIAL INTERVENTIONS

Every country in our study has initiated some form of financial intervention to attract more students to study in higher education, particularly from disadvantaged groups, and a number have established interventions before the age of higher education entrance.

An example of a successful intervention before the age of admission to higher education is found in the UK. An ongoing problem has been the loss of talented pupils at age 16 from underprivileged groups. These pupils entered the labour market while their more affluent peers remained in full-time education until the age of 18, and were thus able to gain the qualifications for entrance to higher education. Those already in the labour market were commonly denied that opportunity. A scheme, the Education Maintenance Allowance, has therefore been developed which provides a financial incentive to the family to keep their children in full-time education. It became available for all 16 year olds studying in England from September 2004. Prior to its national rolling out, it was piloted in ten Local Education Authorities in England in September 1999, with the piloting further extended in September of the following year. By the first term of the 2005–2006 academic year, over 380,000 young people had received an EMA payment.

The EMA's objective is to help support young people to continue their education after GCSEs (General Certificate of Secondary Education) on academic or vocational courses that involve at least 12 hours' guided learning each week. The allowance is a weekly payment of £30, £20 or £10 depending on the household income (see table below). In addition, there are also £100 bonuses to reward good performance and progression on the course, though these are likely to be curtailed in 2010, as a result of the financial crisis. If the student was applying for 2006–2007, for instance, then the allowance was based on the total household income for the tax year ending March 2006. The amounts were:

Household income per annum	Weekly EMA
up to £20,817	£30 a week
£20,818 – £25,521	£20 a week
£25,522 – £30,810	£10 a week

The EMA payments are only available to students who have had no gap in their education; they must have come straight from secondary school to sixth-form or Further Education college. If they decide to go out and get a job instead, they will not be able to claim EMA (although they may be able to apply for an Adult Learning Grant instead).

Continued receipt of the allowance and the bonuses is dependant on young people complying with the terms of the learning agreement between them, their parents and their school or college. This agreement sets out conditions relating to young people's attendance, behaviour and performance. Any unauthorised absences will cause the student to lose that week's allowance. Decisions regarding whether an EMA payment should be made for a particular week are taken by the college or school, but according to guidelines set by the government.

Thorough evaluation of the EMA concluded in 2005 indicated that it has been effective in increasing participation and retention in full-time post-16 education, and has had a positive impact on young people from lower income families, and on young men in particular, who have shown an increased retention of 5.5%.

TUITION FEES

The complexity of the situation relating to government policy on widening participation is aptly illustrated by decisions with regard to the imposition of tuition fees, some of which have only been introduced recently. On the one hand, every country is seeing the demand for higher education rising steadily, with more and more students choosing to study. The costs to the individual governments in providing places has risen in line with demand. The phenomenon of 'massification' of higher education is seen in all countries. As a result, driven by economic necessity, the majority of countries have introduced tuition fees, thus potentially exacerbating the problem of ensuring that students from disadvantaged backgrounds are encouraged to apply for higher education without the anxiety of carrying a huge debt burden through future years.

Costs for higher education commonly break down into costs for maintenance, and costs for tuition. France and Ireland still offer free tuition, while the majority of the countries studied have instituted some form of cost-sharing, with students contributing to the costs of their own higher education by making use of grants and loans. All the countries in the study made some effort to cover the costs of students drawn from the lowest socio-economic groups.

A change in England and Northern Ireland, instituted during 2006, was the introduction of variable tuition fees for all students, but capped at an annual maximum of £3000. The fees are paid on the students' behalf by government, and are repaid after they graduate. When their annual income has reached a threshold of £15,000 they will repay the money through the national tax system. A special bursary scheme for students from low-income families is provided, and some grants towards living costs are available. Scotland, meanwhile, has abolished tuition fees.

Ireland, as mentioned previously, also has no tuition fees for undergraduate programmes, in line with the aim of the White Paper (1995) which stated that its aim was to 'remove important financial and psychological barriers to participation at third level.' Additionally, those from very low income families are able to qualify for a top-up grant which matches the personal rate of Unemployment Assistance, an important psychological point: studying is supported at the same level as unemployment. Targeted funding is also available for institutions to enable them to reduce inequalities.

France, too, has free tuition but the 'grandes ecoles' are able to set fees. Need-based grants are available for all higher education institutions for years 1–4, and a merit-based grant for year 5. Extra funding is made available to institutions in education priority areas to enable students to work in small groups and have access to better resources.

Ethiopia, Vietnam, South Africa and Israel all have tuition fees. In Israel the tuition is kept low, and special stipends, loans and fellowships are available. In South Africa tuition fees vary from 10,000 – 25,000 Rands a year. A National Student Financial Aid Scheme provides needy students with loans to study in public institutions of which up to 40% can become bursaries, dependent on academic achievement. The loans available range from 2000 to 30,000 Rands a year. Banks also offer loans, and a number of companies offer bursaries, sometimes with the expectation that on completion of one's studies, the person will work for the company. Merit-based awards are also provided by most South African universities. Vietnam introduced tuition fees and charges for such items as examination entry as early as 1986. However, there is an extensive range of student scholarships, some of which are merit-based, while others are for students from low socio-economic areas, from minority groups, from families of war veterans and for those from low-income families who perform well in higher education. A student loan scheme was introduced in 2000.

A more detailed discussion of the wide variety of student financial support is explored in chapter 8.

INSTITUTIONAL FINANCIAL INTERVENTIONS

Whereas the majority of the financial interventions to promote access are targeted at students (Chapter 8), some countries have set up specific government agencies or buffer bodies whose aim is to provide incentives to higher education institutions to widen participation. Corrales (2006) argues that incentives and pressures on institutions are symptomatic of massification, and linked to the drive by governments to expand the numbers of skilled professional workers in the labour market.

England provides an interesting example of this trend. Under the terms of the 2004 Education Act a radical shift was made in student financing, namely the introduction of tuition fees. Another aspect of this Act, however, was the establishment of an Office for Fair Access, whose aim was to promote widening participation and greater access. Universities were able to charge up to £3000 per year in tuition fees for their undergraduate courses. If higher education institutions charge the maximum fee, they must provide bursaries of £300 to low-income students to supplement state-funded grants and loans. The Secretary of State's letter of Guidance to OFFA, 2004, makes the aims clear:

> 'The philosophy behind the creation of OFFA is that institutions that decide to raise their fees above the current standard level should plan how they will safeguard and promote access. In particular, there is an expectation that they will plough some of their extra income back into bursaries and other financial support for students, and outreach work'

All institutions who charge more than £2700 in tuition must submit an Access Agreement to OFFA for approval. Each Access Agreement sets out how each institution would 'safeguard and promote fair access' (OFFA 2007a) particularly for low-income students. The result has been that there has been a marked growth in the number of scholarships and non-mandatory bursaries offered by the institutions. Students from disadvantaged backgrounds (where household income is £17,500 p.a. or less) are entitled to a full government maintenance grant of £2700 plus the mandatory bursary of £300. Institutions, on the other hand, can offer a range of their own bursaries and scholarships. They can even set their own terms and conditions.

Thus higher education institutions are themselves playing a new and significant role in providing 'institutional aid'. Only recently are evaluations being undertaken of the new system: while it appears to have partly achieved its goal in widening access, it has brought about unanticipated consequences. The historic inequities across higher education institutions appear to remain, particularly in those institutions where bursaries and scholarships are used a competitive tool: this is frequently described as 'merit aid'. OFFA is now undertaking research into the overall effects of these approaches, and it may well be that changes will be introduced into the system.

One can argue that, in reality, the system in the UK has a number of aspects in common with that in the US. Federal and State governments are also concerned with the necessity to broaden access. While much of the focus of attention has been on financial and non-financial support for individuals (Chapter 8), there are now a number of institutions who themselves provide aid. According to the College Board's 'Trends in Student Aid', some $23 billion in aid was distributed by colleges and universities in 2003–4, mainly in the form of grants. Concerns have been raised , in view of the large rise in student aid in recent years, that the continuing use of merit to ration scarce existing resources means that more institutional aid is going to fairly affluent students. About 25% of students enrolled in public colleges and universities and 60% of those in private institutions receive institutional grant aid.

In recent years several US higher education institutions, particularly the well-endowed Ivy League universities, have created their own programmes to increase participation from low- income students. Princeton, Harvard, Stanford and Yale all have such programmes. Princeton was the first to establish a scheme, which replaces loans with grants, distributed solely on the basis of financial need. It offers no merit aid. A financial aid counsellor assesses each individual's situation and meets 100% of the calculated need of each aid applicant. As a result the number of students on financial aid has risen from 38% in 1998, the start of the scheme, to 54% in 2006. Public institutions, such as University of North Carolina-Chapel Hill, and the University of Virginia, have now developed their own programmes, with the aim of keeping higher education affordable for every student, regardless of family income. Clearly it is only universities with sizable endowments who can offer such programmes, and the numbers involved are tiny in comparison to the mass of students from low socio-economic backgrounds who attend institutions with little or no endowments. Institutional aid is thus highly beneficial to those who are able to access the programmes, but the effect is to strengthen further the elite institutions, and emphasise the discrepancies between the few with such schemes, and the many without.

One other source of funding should be mentioned: the money provided by private benefactors, usually through charities established specifically to offer financial or other support to students and institutions e.g. ISEF in Israel, The Bill and Melissa Gates Foundation in the US, Chuck Feeny's foundation in Irish universities.

STRUCTURAL CHANGES

The concern of governments to restructure their higher education systems, and introduce new programmes and new admission criteria, is a feature of the range of interventions found in our study. The drivers are twofold: the need to widen participation, and the wish to expand research and labour capacity. This is combined with a concern to maintain and enhance the quality of the programmes while expanding the system.

Recently some governments have introduced structural changes in the range of courses available. The European Higher Education Area, which has been established by the Ministers of Education, developed from the Bologna Agreement, has introduced, as previously mentioned, three cycles of higher education. The first, normally of three years' duration, leads to a Bachelor's Degree; the second, normally of two years' length, leads to a Master's Degree; and the third leads to Doctorate level. This new degree structure enables a much more efficient pipeline of students to be established. The shorter three-year period of study to the Bachelor's Degree brings students to the labour market more quickly and thus benefits the economy.

Ireland has developed a large technological sector, which is linked to the expansion of vocational and technological education to meet the employment opportunities offered by the 21st century. It has also restructured the high school certificates that provide entry to higher education. The traditional Leaving Certificate Programme, which in 2003 about 65% students followed, has been supplemented by a Vocational Programme Leaving Certificate, established in 1989 and restructured in 1994. This certificate also provides for higher education entry. In 2003 29% of students took this. The only Irish programme not providing entry to higher education is the Applied Programme Leaving Certificate but this attracts only 6% of students. Ireland is remarkable in that over 90% of Irish students now follow pre-entry courses which lead directly to higher education, thus considerably expanding the pool of those who are able to participate in higher education.

The level of high school completion worldwide appears to be one of the keys to the ability of a country to expand its higher education system. Ethiopia has not yet achieved universal primary school completion, a factor which is bound to affect the numbers able to benefit from higher education. Both Vietnam and South Africa have found that the numbers completing secondary level studies are not yet maximised, and this affects the cohort able to benefit from university.

A somewhat different structural initiative has been developed by the UK. The recognition that the introduction of new, flexible routes into higher education would be likely to benefit those from underrepresented groups has led to the development of Foundation Degrees, which offer a means of gaining a degree in a vocational subject equivalent to two years of an Honours Degree. It is a new type of degree, first delivered in 2001 and the only major new Higher Education qualification introduced in England in the last 25 years. The creation of the new Foundation Degree qualification was announced by the (then) Secretary of State for Education, David Blunkett in his speech 'Modernising higher education: meeting the global challenge':

> If we are to become a leading knowledge-based economy we must create new routes into higher education and new forms of provision. Our historic skills deficit lies in people with intermediate skills – including highly-qualified technicians. We have to develop new higher education opportunities at this level, orientated strongly to the employability skills, specialist knowledge and broad understanding needed in the new economy. We therefore intend to create new two year Foundation Degrees to help meet our objective that half of all young people benefit from higher education by the age of 30. [Blunkett, 2000]

It is clear, therefore, that the government's higher education participation target of 50% did play a role in originating the Foundation Degree. The Prospectus, published in July 2000, set out the key national policy aims to:
- address shortages of intermediate level skills in the national and regional economies;
- enhance the employability of students;
- widen participation in higher education and contribute to lifelong learning;
- rationalise and enhance the quality of provision below honours degree level.

Initially the Foundation Degree was seen as a hybrid of vocational and academic education: its key distinction from other qualifications lay in the integration of work-based learning into the programme of study. Employer involvement is a key feature: employers are fully involved in the design and regular review of Foundation Degree programmes. The work-based learning component enables students to earn a living whilst studying, thus widening participation. Modes of study are flexible, and a range of progression routes are available. The delivery of the programmes involves a network of partnerships which can include higher and further education institutions, professional bodies, and government agencies concerned with Skills and Regional Development.

Although Foundation Degrees are relatively new qualifications, they are becoming increasingly popular. In 2001 the first Foundation Degrees attracted 4,000 students. In 2004/05 this increased to around 38,000 people. Figures from the HE Students Early Statistics Survey (HEFCE, 2005) for 2005–06 recorded nearly 47,000 students studying for Foundation Degrees. These are split almost equally between full-time and part-time students and those studying as part of their professional development. In 2009 there were 1700 Foundation Degree courses available, with a further 900 at the planning stage. The range of subjects is extensive, covering such subject areas as veterinary nursing, e-commerce, health, social care, and forensic science. In 2005 the Quality Assurance Agency (QAA) reported that 'Foundation Degrees are successful in providing a new award at intermediate level ... which links and integrates work-based learning and academic studies'.

The development of the Internet has brought about a massive expansion in access to knowledge, which can arguably be seen as a structural change of a different order. Massachusetts Institute of Technology offers open courseware on the net: the main users are Chinese. Journals are commonly available on the net, with articles which can be downloaded quickly and easily. The Chinese are frequently the heaviest users. Thus one can access new information and pursue one's studies in new technological environments. The Open University in the UK pioneered the provision of programmes delivered via modern technology – television, CDRoms, and web-based delivery. A number of other institutions worldwide have adopted similar approaches.

New types of institutions have been established to meet modern demands. The US has developed large numbers of corporate universities. Perhaps the best known is the University of Phoenix, which provides courses over a range of employment related areas, using IT and tutorial methods. France founded a network of institutions, the Institut Universitaire Technologie, to train students in modern technology. Access is highly competitive.

ASPIRATION

The final group of government interventions is aimed at heightening potential students' awareness of higher education and encouraging them to take part in it, particularly those from disadvantaged groups within the community. Every country is concerned to raise the aspirations of their young people. Many set targets for the percentage of the age cohort that the government would like to see enter higher education. Other countries have established specific initiatives to widen the participation of particular groups.

There are three types of aspirational interventions: programmes for individuals offered prior to higher education entrance; programmes for groups of institutions; and programmes developed by individual institutions, under pressure from governments and funding bodies, often with financial incentives, to raise pupils' awareness of higher education and encourage them to aspire to it.

Ethiopia has developed a policy of affirmative action towards women students, those from disadvantaged backgrounds and those from isolated regions. Degree programmes have grown, with a wider range of disciplines now made available in several regions. Access to the internet has expanded. Special libraries have been established for women's use, and an office set up specifically to offer support to women. This has had some effect: the percentage of women in higher education rose from 20.2% in 1996/7 to 25.2% in 2003/4.

Vietnam also has as one of its main aims the wish to offer equal opportunities to women and ethnic minorities. The open university network has been expanded to 'provide more opportunities for those from low socio-economic background.' By 2004/5 there had been a marked improvement in the percentage of women students (47.79%).

Both Ethiopia and Vietnam have introduced measures to encourage the growth in numbers of those eligible to enter university. In Ethiopia those students who complete the two year preparatory classes in grades 11 and 12, or those who follow a three year technical and vocational education and training programme, are eligible to enter any higher education programme. In Vietnam the selection criteria varies for different groups, with a separate benchmark being used for students from mountainous areas, remote areas, and very low social and economic backgrounds. Some universities also offer special foundation courses for ethnic minority groups, which allow direct entry to the degree course.

Israel has set a target of 50% age participation rate in the next decade (in 2004 it was 41%). A one year access course has been developed for students from disadvantaged backgrounds and for new immigrants. Successful completion of this offers entry to higher education. In 2004 over 14000 students took the course.

'Bashaar', a non-profit organisation established by a group of faculty members from all the universities in Israel, have developed a number of programmes for high school students to get them interested in the pursuit of knowledge and to value learning, knowledge and rational thinking. Over the period 2004–2008 about 300 faculty members from a wide range of disciplines (natural sciences, advanced technology, humanities and social sciences) have been involved, reaching some 55,000 students, often in remote areas and including Arab, Druze, and Bedouin as well as Israeli Jewish peoples. The programme is carried out in close cooperation with the Ministry of Education.

The ISEF Foundation, founded in 1977, aims to narrow Israel's wide social and economic gaps by providing equal access to higher education for capable young Israelis from disadvantaged communities. (Less than 50% of Israeli teenagers achieve their high school diploma.) The 800 annual beneficiaries of scholarships are drawn from such groups as immigrant families from less developed countries, Ethiopians, and Druze. The scholarships are based solely on criteria of financial need and scholastic and leadership potential. To date some $40 million has been invested by ISEF in their initiative. They offer an on-campus network of assistance which nurtures the ISEF scholars and enables them to complete their studies. Over 90% of these earn their degrees. In impoverished areas they run education projects to encourage young people to believe in their capacity to succeed, to finish high school and go on to higher education.

France has set a target that 80% of the age group should graduate from high school. In 2003 62.4% did so, and hence were qualified to enter higher education, but of these 21% did not go on to higher education in the following year. Students have the right to free entry to higher education institutions in the geographic area where they previously studied. Certain institutions, however, such as 'grandes ecoles' and engineering schools, have tough selection criteria. There are examples, though, of affirmative action to allow admission of students from disadvantaged backgrounds to gain entry to a 'grande ecole'.

Ireland, too, has set a target of 90% high school completion (currently 82–84% of the age cohort). Considerable, and successful, efforts have been made to expand vocational education, as previously mentioned. A wide range of outreach initiatives have been developed: these include teams working with selected secondary schools in their catchment areas to foster college-going aspirations and counter early drop-out from secondary school; supervised evening study programmes; supplementary tuition by university students; summer schools to familiarise second level students with higher education; and briefing sessions for parents.

Most Irish higher education institutions have developed access programmes to prepare admission for non-standard students. A pool of reserved places for those from disadvantaged backgrounds, disabled students, and mature students is available. Once this group enters higher education there is additional support provided to enable them to achieve success.

The English initiative has much in common with the range of mechanisms found in Ireland. The integrated national Aimhigher programme was developed in response to a government objective to increase participation in higher education in England to 50% of the 18–30 year old cohort by 2010. The White Paper 'The Future of Higher Education' (2003a) followed by 'Widening Participation in Higher Education' (2003b) made a commitment to bring 'Excellence Challenge' and 'Aimhigher: Partnerships for Progression' together 'to deliver a coherent national outreach programme to be called Aimhigher' (DfES 2003b). Hence, the national Aimhigher programme was launched on August 1, 2004.

The national integrated Aimhigher is an outreach programme. It brings partners together in order to reach out to schools and communities to encourage commitment to learning, to stimulate aspirations, to help raise attainment so that learners can realise ambitions, and to work across the school-college-HEI boundaries to break down the barriers to access. The programme promotes regional and sub-regional partnerships between higher education institutions, schools, colleges, employers

and other agencies to encourage interest in higher education and support admission into higher education. These partnerships aim to increase participation in each geographical area and to address low rates of participation by students from lower socio-economic groups, low participation neighbourhoods and by those with disabilities. The main purpose of Aimhigher is to:
- Raise aspirations and motivation to enter HE among young people in schools, further education and workplace learning, who are from under-represented groups
- Raise the attainment of potential HE students, who are from under-represented groups, so that they gain the academic or vocational qualifications and learning skills that will enable them to enter HE
- Strengthen progression routes into HE via vocational courses, including Apprenticeships, whether they are delivered in schools, colleges or the workplace
- Raise students' aspirations to enter HE and to apply to the institution and/or course best able to match their abilities
- Improve the attainment, aspirations, motivation and self-esteem of gifted and talented young people aged 14–19; and the quality of identification, provision and support for those students in schools and colleges (www.aimhigher.ac.uk/practitioner).

Activities are offered at three levels: national, regional and area:

- Offering information, advice and guidance to potential HE students and their teachers and families so that learners are well advised about their future
- Organising summer schools, taster days, master classes and mentoring schemes to raise the aspirations and attainment of young people with the potential to enter HE
- Working with employers and training providers to progress students onto vocational routes to HE
- Working to encourage those already in the workplace to become full-time, part-time or distance learning students

The evaluation of Aimhigher, which is in itself a long-term, complex initiative, has drawn on a longitudinal tracking study, combined with quality indicators and secondary data. Individual students are targeted and tracked over time.

The indications are positive: the findings in one study showed that at the start of the initiative those who had neither parent with HE experience were less well informed about HE, less likely to aspire to HE by year 11, less likely to progress to study at a higher level and less likely to study A levels (the qualification for higher education entrance).

Recent Aimhigher evaluations have focussed upon assessing the impact on the individual in terms of awareness, aspiration, attainment and educational progression towards higher education. Another issue is the long-term nature of Aimhigher. The partnerships work with young people at the age of 13 or 14 to make sure that they become aware of HE before they begin to specialise. It is then four or five years to their entry to HE. Many from under-represented groups take a less direct route, often not enrolling in HE until their mid-20s (Gilchrist, Phillips and Ross 2003).

The findings for one particular region are instructive:

a) the social class gap between higher education applicants appears to be closing. In 1997 66% of those who applied to HE came from upper social groups though these were only 42% of the region's population. But by 2004, the proportion of applicants from those groups had dropped to 59 per cent. Between 2000 and 2004 those applicants from lower social groups and those whose group was not known or classified rose by 25%.

b) The extent to which the programme was reaching those who were intended to benefit was examined i.e. to 'operate most intensively in disadvantaged areas' (HEFCE 2004a: p. 3). It was found that 80 % of the parents/carers had no experience of HE: the programme was thus to a large extent meeting the specification (Hatt, Baxter and Tate 2005).

c) The impact of Aimhigher activities on raising awareness of higher education has been marked. Pre- and post-event questionnaires make this clear. Indeed, over the years there has been a growth in background HE awareness. In 2001, the Aimhigher regional partnership reported that only 20–30% of summer school participants, before the event, had considered they had enough information to make a decision about HE; by 2005, 54 % felt they had.

d) The tracking study found that information relating to local or vocational opportunities was less well understood. Knowledge about vocational routes into and through higher education remains poor.

e) One particular initiative that has been effective in raising aspiration for HE has been that involving current HE Having students work as ambassadors, mentors and tutors has been successful (NFER 2002; HEFCE 2003; Austin and Hatt 2005). After one such event, 82% of pupils wished to go on to university, in contrast to 31% before it began.

f) There has been a steady rise in attainment: 52% of pupils in 2000 gained at least 5 A-Cs; 55% in 2004, which is considered the benchmark for those entering higher education.

g) The Aimhigher programme appears to be having an effect on educational progression. The tracking study shows that the Aimhigher sample were more likely to remain in post compulsory education (after 16) than the regional or national average. At age 16, 91% of the sample remained in education, whereas the national average was around 70%. Likewise those involved in Aimhigher were almost all studying level 3 qualifications (A level or equivalent) – 86%.

Efforts are continuing. The UK government established a Cabinet Office Social Exclusion Taskforce which published a short study in December 2008: '*Aspiration and attainment amongst young people in deprived communities.* It explored the potential to raise the attainment of young people in deprived communities by raising aspirations and changing attitudes within the communities themselves. Their findings indicate that although young people in some very deprived communities, notably ethnically diverse urban neighbourhoods, had high aspirations, young people in other areas, particularly traditional working class communities in ex-industrial areas, had low aspirations which may well affect their ability to achieve their potential.

The key age range appears to be 11–14. Although aspirations varied by gender, ethnicity, social class and area, white boys have the lowest aspirations. As a result of this analysis and discussion paper, the government published the *New Opportunities White Paper* (Jan 2009) which announced that an Inspiring Communities programme would be established to develop a new approach to raising the aspirations and educational attainment of young people in deprived areas. Fifteen neighbourhoods were announced in August 2009. These will be funded in order to support neighbourhood partnerships which will deliver a programme of activities working with young people, their parents and the communities, in order to create new opportunities, broaden horizons and develop self-efficacy and self-esteem. The partnerships include schools, councils, third sector organisations, parents and young people. Local businesses are also encouraged to take part.

The US is also moving forward in translating the available research on widening participation into practice. Under the Obama administration, considerable attention is being directed towards understanding the situation of those from disadvantaged groups, and providing guidance to remedy the US position where only 7% of those from the lowest social groups access higher education. The administration has now set a target of 60% participation in higher education by 2025. In order to achieve this it will be necessary to increase the numbers of students from low socio-economic backgrounds, to improve their preparedness for higher education, and help them to apply for and complete their college courses successfully.

A major problem in the US lies in the fact that students from such backgrounds are not sufficiently academically prepared to enable them to enter a four-year college (Cabrera et al 2005). Other research also showed that low income students from a Latino background were frequently placed in high school maths courses that were unlikely to result in being prepared for a four-year college course (Swail, Cabrera, Lee and Williams 2005).

Further research (Cabrera et al. 2006) led to the finding that one of the comprehensive intervention programmes established by the US Department of Education appears to be showing very positive results. The programme, entitled Gaining Early Awareness and Readiness for Undergraduate Programs (GEAR UP) is aimed at nearly a million low-income middle school students and their families in deprived areas. They are supported by partnerships of schools, colleges and universities, community organisations and local businesses. These partnerships work with whole classes, beginning no later than age 13 and remaining with the group throughout high school. The partnership works to raise the pupils' and parents' awareness of college as an option, raise their college aspirations, and improve their level of preparedness for college, both academically and financially. The improvement in maths achievement has been significant. Such interventions as this programme can provide access to forms of cultural and social capital which would not normally be available to students from low income backgrounds. It is also becoming clear that such interventions need to begin at the latest by age 14, and preferably earlier.

The Institute of Education Sciences (IES) publishes regular reports and guides related to the issue of understanding what enables those from deprived backgrounds to be successful, and how best to achieve such success. One recent report based on statistical analysis (July 2009) is a study of Pell Grant recipients: *A Profile of Successful Pell Grant Recipients: Time to Bachelor's Degree and Early Graduate School Enrollment.* In September 2009 IES published a Practice Guide entitled *Helping Students Navigate the Path to College: What High Schools Can Do.* The research base for the guide rests on a thorough search of studies evaluating College access interventions and practices. The panel of experts argues that every student should leave high school with the necessary skills to enable him/her to attend a two- or four-year institution. The guide proposes a strategy addressing four areas of development: 'curriculum, assessment, aspirations and hands-on assistance with college entry activities' (p.7).

The recommendations are as follows:

- Offer courses and curricula that prepare students for college-level work, and ensure that students understand what constitutes a college-ready curriculum by ninth grade.
- Utilize assessment measures throughout high school so that students are aware of how prepared they are for college, and assist them in overcoming deficiencies as they are identified.
- Surround students with adults and peers who build and support their college-going aspirations.
- Engage and assist students in completing critical steps for college entry.
- Increase families' financial awareness, and help students apply for financial aid.

The guide calls itself a workbook, and the suggestions are both practical and possible. Schools will need to dedicate much time and effort to the task, but it shows a way forward that can be followed if there is sufficient will.

CONCLUSION

It is clear that recent worldwide research on the many aspects of access and equity is leading to an enhanced understanding of what can be done to improve levels of access to higher education, particularly for those from disadvantaged groups. The interventions discussed in this chapter illustrate the range of approaches being explored by governments worldwide. Evaluations carried out so far appear to show that these initiatives are having a beneficial effect.

BIBLIOGRAPHY

Austin, M., & Hatt, S. (2005). The messengers are the message: A study of the effects of employing HE student ambassadors to work with school students. *Widening Participation and Lifelong Learning, 7*(1), 22.

Blunkett, D. (2000, February). *Modernising higher education: Facing the global challenge.* Speech at the University of Greenwich.

Cabinet Office Social Exclusion Task Force. (2008). *Aspiration and attainment amongst young people in deprived communities: Analysis and discussion paper.* London: Cabinet Office.

Cabrera, A. F., Burkum, K. R., & La Nasa, S. M. (2005). Pathways to a four-year degree: Determinants of transfer and degree completion. In A. Seidman (Ed.), *College student retention: A formula for success* (pp. 155–214). Westport, CT: Praeger.

Cabrera, A. F., Deil-Amen, R., Prahbu, R., Terenzini, P. T., Lee, C., & Franklin R. E. (2006). Increasing the college preparedness of at-risk students. *Journal of Latinos and Education, 5*(2), 79–97.

Committee on Higher Education. (1963). *Higher education: Report of the committee under the Chairmanship of Lord Robbins 1961–1963*. London: HMSO.

Council on Higher Education. (2000). *Policy report: Towards a new higher education landscape: Meeting the equity, quality and social development imperatives of South Africa in the twenty-first century*. Pretoria: CHE.

Department of Education. (1995). *Charting our education future: Government white paper on education*. Dublin: Stationery Office.

Department for Education and Skills (DfES). (2003a). *The future of higher education*. DfES White Paper. London: HMSO.

Department for Education and Skills (DfES). (2003b). *Widening participation in higher education*. DfES White Paper. London: HMSO.

Dodgson, R., & Whitham, H. (2004, September). *Learner experience of foundation degrees in the north east of England: Access, support and retention*. Draft report.

Duke, C., & Layer, G. (2005). *Widening participation. Which way forward for English higher education?* London: NIACE.

Federal Democratic Republic of Ethiopia. (2002). *Capacity building strategy and programs*. Addis Ababa: FDRE.

Federal Democratic Republic of Ethiopia. (2003). *Higher education proclamation No 351/2003*. Addis Ababa: FDRE.

Gilchrist, R., Phillips, D., & Ross, A. (2003). Participation and potential participation in UK higher education. In L. Archer, M. Hutchings, & A. Ross (Eds.), *Higher education and social class: Issues of exclusion and inclusion* (Vol. 75). London: RoutledgeFalmer.

Hatt, S., Baxter, A., & Tate, J. (2005). Who benefits from widening participation: A study of targeting in the South-West of England. *Journal of Further and Higher Education 29*(4), 341–352.

HEFCE. (2004a). *Aimhigher: Guidance notes for integration*. HEFCE 2004/08. Bristol: HEFCE.

Jackson, C., & Tunnah, E. (2005). *The information, advice and guidance needs of Foundation Degree students – report of an AGCAS survey*. Association of Graduate Careers Advisory Services. Retrieved June 17, 2020, from http://www.agcas.org.uk/publications/other_publications/fd/docs/fdsurvey_report_complete.pdf

Middleton, S., Maguire, S., Perren, K., Rennison, J., Battistin, E., Emmerson, C., et al. (2005). *Evaluation of education maintenance allowance pilots: Young people aged 16–19 years final report of the quantitative evaluation*. Research Report 678, Department for Education and Skill.

Ministry of Education, Ethiopia. (1997). *The future directions of higher education*. Addis Ababa: MOE.

National Committee of Inquiry into Higher Education, chaired by R. Dearing (1997) *Higher Education in the Learning Society*. London: HMSO.

National Office for Equity of Access to Higher Education in Ireland. (2005). *Achieving equity of access to higher education in Ireland: Action plan 2005–2007*. Dublin: Higher Education Authority.

National Office for Equity of Access to Higher Education. (2006). *Towards the best education for all: An evaluation of access programmes in higher education in Ireland*. Dublin: Higher Education Authority.

Putnam, R. D. (1995). Bowling alone: America's declining social capital. *Journal of democracy, 6*, 65–78.

Schuller, T. (1997). Relations between human and social capital. In *A national strategy for lifelong learning*. Newcastle.

Swail, W. S., Cabrera, A. F., Lee, C., & Williams, A. (2005). *Latino students and the educational pipeline*. Washington, DC: Education Policy Institute.

Tierney, W. G., Bailey, T., Constantine, J., Finkelstein, N., & Hurd, N. F. (2009). *Helping students navigate theb path to college: What high schools can do: A practical guide* (NCEE#2009–4066).

Washington, DC: National Center for Education Evaluation and Regional Assistance, Institute of Education Sciences, U.S. Department of Education.

Turock, I., Kintrea, K., St. Clair, R., & Benjamin, A. (2008). *Shaping aspirations: The role of parents, place and poverty: Interim Report*. Glasgow: Department of Urban Studies.

QAA. (2001). *The framework for higher education qualifications in England, Wales and Northern Ireland*.

QAA. (2004). *Foundation degree qualification benchmark*. Retrieved from www.aimhigher.ac.uk

STUDENT SUPPORT MECHANISMS

Introduction

Higher education systems have expanded enormously in recent years all over the world. Most governments view the widening of access to higher education as a crucial imperative for the future development of their nations in a globalised, knowledge-based society. Access rates vary greatly between countries, and various socio-economic groups are unequally represented in any given country. One of the greatest challenges facing many governments today is how to enhance equity and broaden access to higher education for people from all walks of life.

Many studies which examine equity issues in higher education focus mainly on access policies. Rarely do they relate to policies directed to encourage persistence in studies and to increase graduation rates by providing appropriate student support mechanisms. Obviously, support systems are immensely important for students from disadvantaged backgrounds. This chapter examines the intricate relations between access and equity in eight countries: USA, UK, Ireland, France, Viet Nam, Ethiopia, Israel and South Africa. It relates to the various support mechanisms offered in each of the examined countries by governments, non-governmental organisations (NGOs) and by higher education institutions themselves. The nature of the support considered in this chapter is primarily financial, with some reference to learning support and to counselling. The latter part of the chapter provides a critical review of retention rates in the eight countries.

Support systems can be manifested through a variety of financial forms (grants, loans, subsidies for housing, food, travelling etc.) or offered as a supportive intervention in the learning/teaching process or through counselling networks aimed at facilitating the social and psychological well-being of students, as well as dealing with special needs of students, such as learning disabilities.

It is worth mentioning that the availability of data for conducting the comparative analysis in this chapter is somewhat problematic. Each country has its own system of statistics, some of which are restricted and not open to researchers. Thus, the analysis below and the conclusions and recommendations at the end of the chapter should be interpreted with caution. Nevertheless, it is hoped that policy makers, academics and other stakeholders in higher education systems will gain important insights as to the array of student support systems offered in the eight countries, which encompass both developed and developing ones.

GOVERNMENT SUPPORT SCHEMES

In all the eight countries mentioned above, regardless of economic status, the Government generally is the main provider of financial support for university students. Unfortunately, it is hard to give a "fair" comparison as to which national government provides the most, as the market value of currency in each country varies depending on the purchasing power in that country. Hence this report makes an attempt to give an analysis of the various forms of support for tuition and cost of living without ranking the value of those supports. Similar analysis is applied to the consideration of learning support and counselling for higher education students, and to the improvement of student retention and graduation rates, focussing on the undergraduate level.

The United States, which is one of the wealthiest countries in the world, is ranked fourth in the level of grants to university students among the 16 countries surveyed (Belgium-Flemish, Belgium-French, Ireland, Finland, Netherlands, Germany, Sweden, Italy, Austria, France, Canada, Australia, United Kingdom, Japan and New Zealand). (Usher and Cervenan, 2005) Approximately half of the grants higher education students received were from Government; these were income-based and targeted at students from low-income backgrounds. The rest were pre-dominantly from educational institutions, and from NGOs. In the US the average student grant was equal to roughly half of average educational costs, which covered tuition fees, educational materials and maintenance (Usher and Cervenan, 2005: p. 20). The recently passed Bill (March 2010) is likely, however, to bring about an adjustment in these figures.

The USA

Many people may think that in the United States higher education is less affordable due to high tuition costs, but *"the fact is: compared to much of Europe, North American students' assistance programs are reasonably generous"* (Usher and Cervenan, 2005: p. 20). In the US, support for higher education students varies from state to state, as does the cost of university education. The figures for 2003/04 show that undergraduates paid a mean of $17,150 in fees, with financial aid contributing a mean of $7,000 per individual (Heller 2009). However, the cost of public higher education varies widely because the state has authority over public education within its boundaries. Costs are higher in the Northeastern states, and less expensive in the Southwest and Western states. Besides the cost of tuition, other costs such as room and board significantly increase the expense of attending the US Northeastern universities in comparison with those in the rest of the country (Swail, 2004:16).

The federal Pell Grant programme which was established in 1972 constitutes the largest grant programme in the US and provides need-based grants for low-income undergraduate students. However, with increases in tuition fees during 1980s–1990s, the value of the grant had lost considerable purchasing power. An early decision of the Obama administration in 2009 was to raise the level of each Pell grant in line with inflation, thereby raising its ability to offer support to needy US students.

The maximum Pell Grant for July 1 2009 to June 30 2010 is $5350. These are considered to provide a foundation of federal financial aid to which aid from other federal and non-federal sources might be added. These include the Supplementary Educational Opportunity programmes (SEOG) and the Leveraging Educational Assistance Program (LEAP), which matches state funding to that provided by individual states.

France

The forms of aid available to French higher education students are varied. In an analysis of Government support in relation to access and equity for higher education students, the distinctive characteristic is that tuition is free for all levels of study including degree level, apart from "Les Grandes Ecoles" – the elite higher education institutions which set fees themselves. Besides free tuition for everyone, the French Government provides first to fourth year students with need-based scholarships/ fellowships which are calculated on the basis of a national scale taking into account the family income, the number of children in the family and the distance between the family residence and the university. But for fifth year students, scholarships are awarded on the basis of merit. Further, there are a number of direct and indirect kinds of social grants to assist students in covering the cost of transport and accommo- dation. For example, needy students can benefit from a low cost room (about a hundred euros a month) in a student residence. Additionally, some needy students can benefit from subsidised health care and insurance and reduced-cost food and other expenses (Deer, 2005: p. 238). In some regions, fellowships are available from local authorities on the basis of family income (Goastellec 2006). In 2003, over half a million students benefited from some form of government financial aid (Deer 2005). 60% of the students having a fellowship come from blue-collar families or unemployed parents. These students are exempt from registration fees and social security fees. Depending on the family income, they receive between €1188 and €3263 a year. There is also a merit fellowship scheme for students who are preparing for specific governmental examinations, 50% of whom come from low income families. For graduate students, merit based fellowships are available in limited numbers, and about 28.7% of all the students receive a fellowship (Goastellec, 2006). The total amount of aid for higher education in France has been increased, reflecting the need for more students to gain access to higher education. About €2M are distributed annually to poorer students in the form of means-tested, academic or merit-related grants. In 2003, 28% of the university student population received this kind of grant. Interest-free loans and bursaries were also provided to 20% of students in 1990, rising to 30% in 2003. (Deer, 2005: p. 240).

Ireland

Irish third level institutions, in contrast to the French ones, traditionally charged tuition fees. But from the late 1960s to 1995, a means-tested grant scheme was available to cover the cost of tuition (except for the Institute of Technology where tuition was free) and to provide some support to cover maintenance costs. These grant schemes were administered by Local Authorities but were financed by central government. Initially these needs-based grant schemes also had merit criteria. Gradually the academic merit criteria were relaxed so that any student who had gained admission to a university or other approved college was deemed to have met the ability threshold.

The issue of assessing eligibility for gaining means-tested support has always been controversial, principally because of a perception that it favoured the self-employed who could, through 'creative accounting' manipulate their reported income to qualify for a state grant. A government appointed advisory group recommended the adoption of a variant of the Australian system, whereby a capital test would be introduced to supplement the income test (Advisory Committee on Third-Level Student Support, 1993). This recommendation was rejected by the Government which feared the electoral consequences of alienating the self-employed especially the powerful farmers' lobby. Instead in 1995, at a time when many other Western European countries were contemplating the introduction of tuition fees, the Irish government abolished tuition fees for all undergraduate programmes. This populist decision was partly justified on the basis that it would 'remove important financial and psychological barriers to participation at third level' (Ireland Department of Education, 1995: 101).

However, many have questioned the decision on equity grounds. Students from disadvantaged backgrounds were no better off since they would have already qualified for a state grant to cover tuition fees and their entitlements for maintenance support had not changed. A raising of the income threshold governing eligibility for state grants would have helped those on modest income levels who were previously ineligible for support. This would not have involved substituting public expenditure on higher education for existing private expenditure by families who were well positioned to meet existing tuition fee levels. This is a particular concern of university leaders who have seen their own direct funding significantly reduced, apparently to pay for the higher state contribution made to fund student tuition. Additionally, the level of means-tested grant (based on parental income) depends on whether the student is deemed to be capable of living at home, operationally defined as being within a 15 mile radius of the institution. Such students get the 'adjacent rate' which is half the full rate. If students' homes are more than 15 miles from the institution, they are eligible for the full grant. Subsequently, in recent years, a 'top-up' grant has been introduced for students whose family income is very low, principally those in receipt of Social Welfare payments. The maximum grant payable in 2005/6 was €3,020 for the basic maintenance grant or €5,355 for those in receipt of the top-up grant (matching the maximum personal rate of Unemployment Assistance. Furthermore, free medical services for students are determined by family income. Unlike the situation in many Continental European countries, Irish higher education students get little indirect cost of living support (Clancy, 2006).

Postgraduate students in Ireland are required to pay tuition fees. However, if these students meet the means test requirement (based on parental income) their grant will cover this tuition fee and they can draw the same level of maintenance grant as for undergraduates. There is also a large range of ability-based grants available for doctoral study, but competitively. Some of these come from the National Research Council and some from the Universities' own resources.

The UK

The student support schemes in the United Kingdom are different in England, Scotland and Wales. However, data obtained in this research covered only England and Scotland. In England a somewhat similar tuition policy to that in France had been operated until 1998 i.e. that undergraduate students received free tuition. In addition, 50% of living expenses were covered by a mortgage-type loan and 50% by either grant or parental contribution (Barr, 2002). However, with a growing demand for higher education and limited public funds available to finance this growth, the student financial support system in England has passed through radical changes since 1998 with the emphasis placed on the concept of 'cost-sharing'. In other words, students and their families are being required to make greater contributions to the cost of their higher education. This has resulted in less generous student support, the substitution of maintenance grants by loans and the introduction of means-tested tuition fee contributions. A student loan scheme was added to the student support system of maintenance grants in 1990. The success of the new system resulted in a partial replacement of the maintenance grants with loans in the mid-1990s. Finally, all maintenance grants were abolished and replaced with loans in 1999. However, the 2004 Higher Education Act introduced a tuition fee set by each university to a maximum of £3000 (£3225 2009). A range of bursaries can be applied for, including needs-based bursaries, the details of which are decided by each institution. Loans continue to be available, which can amount to £4745 per year for living costs as well as £3225 per year for tuition fees (Barr, 2004). Repayment of loans is deferred until the student graduates and his/her income reaches £15.000 (Eggins 2006). Obligations are placed on institutions to attract and support disadvantaged students. The University of the West of England, for instance, offers three types of undergraduate bursaries: a guaranteed payment of £1000 for UK undergraduate students who have completed a recognised Access course and who are liable for the tuition fee of £3225; an Income-assessed bursary of up to £1000 for full-time UK students whose annual income is £25000 or less; and a Care Leaver Bursary of £1000 for students who have been in local authority care for a minimum of 3 months from the age of 14. Other means of student support offered by institutions include the following:
– The Parental Learning Allowance - grants to help with course-related costs for students who have dependant children.
– Childcare Grant - grants available to students with registered or accredited childcare.
– Adult Dependent Grant - grants for students with a spouse/adult dependant who is wholly or mainly financially dependant upon them.
– Disabled Student Allowance - these additional allowances are for students who have a disability, long term health condition or dyslexia; and they are not means-tested.

Scotland maintains a student support scheme different from that in the rest of UK. In 2006/2007 it introduced flat fees of £1,700 (Medicine courses - £2,700), but these do not have to be paid by eligible full-time Scottish students and EU citizens. The fees are paid for them by the Student Awards Agency for Scotland (SAAS), where they have to apply to have their fees to be paid. After graduating, however, students in Scotland are expected to contribute £2,000 to the graduate endowment in recognition of the benefits they have gained from higher education. Those Scottish students studying in the universities and colleges in England, Wales and Northern Ireland can apply to SAAS for a loan of up to £3,000 which is repayable after graduation on an income-contingent basis. In addition such students qualify for a new income-assessed support package to cover their living expenses (Eggins, 2006).

Israel

The Israeli higher education system consisted in 2009 of 70 higher education institutions, 10 of which are private (Council for Higher Education, 2009). The tuition in all public higher education institutions is monitored by the Council of Higher Education (Guri-Rosenblit, 2006), and in all public institutions is approximately $2,500 per year for all fields of study. But in the private colleges, students pay a much higher tuition fee ranging from $3,500 to $9,000 per year. To help cover the tuition fees, the government provides financial support to students at public institutions through special stipends and fellowships. The stipends and fellowships are given to students at all degree levels of studies based on the socio-economic situation of individual students, including parameters related to the parents' income, the size of the family, the size of the apartment in which the family lives, the location where the student comes from, etc. The second type of fellowship is merit-based, granted mainly to outstanding students. Additionally, there are other kinds of fellowships which are based on service to the community for 8 hours per week (i.e., tutoring for weak students in schools, helping old people, being a "brother" or "sister" to children who lost one of their parents in terrorist acts or wars, etc.). On the basis of serving the community, the students are exempted from 50% tuition fees.

Altogether, about 30% of the undergraduate students get various types of fellowships. The fellowships generally range from 50% to 100% of the tuition fees. There are unfortunately almost no fellowships for students that help cover living expenses, except for doctoral students. Besides the financial support offered to students, has established the Ministry of Education preparatory programmes for students from disadvantaged backgrounds or for newcomers ("Mehinot"). The one year course of study enables candidates, who either have a low average grade point in the "Bagrut" or who come from other countries, to get a "substitute" diploma for enrolment at the universities. Thousands of students study in these "Mehinot" each year, particularly students from outlying areas and from lower socio-academic groups. Statistically, in 2007, 18,054 students studied in the Mehinot (Central Bureau of Statistics, 2008).

Since 2006 some efforts have been made to "revolutionise" the system of university tuition and student support mechanisms in Israel. The former Minister of Education was willing to adopt the Australian model, in which students are given generous loans at the start of their undergraduate studies, and asked to pay back the loan after completing their degree, based on their income. Such loans might have enabled many of the Israeli students to study full-time. Currently, 74% of the student population in Israel works full- or part-time concurrently with their studies (Guri-Rosenblit, 2006). Unfortunately, the scheme has not been enacted so far.. .

Ethiopia

Ethiopia is a developing country with a very low percentage of the population accessing higher education, but the tuition policy for undergraduate studies at higher education institutions before 1993 was similar to the French policy in that all students received free tuition. In addition, they were given free accommodation and food at the institution they enrolled in. The issues of broadening access to higher education for a much greater proportion of the population, and the availability of funds to cover the costs of tuition, accommodation and food were a challenge to the Ethiopian Government. The inappropriateness of covering the tuition, accommodation, and food costs for such a small proportion of the age cohort - the university students - is very clear and has become increasingly questionable (Yizengaw, 2006). Further, in practice, a significant number of students were enrolled in fee-paying programmes at evening and summer courses at public institutions. In the 2003–04 academic years, for example, 53,780 students (31.2% of total national higher education enrolments, or in other words, 45.9% of those at public institutions) enrolled on fee-paying evening courses and summer programmes at public institutions. Thus, the number of fee-paying students, including those at both public and private institutions, accounts for approximately 54% of the higher education student population. Those students were not only paying tuition fees but also paid, out of their own pocket, the full cost of their food, accommodation, and transportation. To deal with such a clear injustice, a "cost sharing tuition fee" policy was introduced by the Proclamation of 2003 that requires students to pay about 15% of costs related to education after graduation from their salaries in the form of tax. All students now pay costs related to services for their accommodation and food. Students who come from a very impoverished background are provided with a monthly allowance to cover living expenses. More support for females and disabled students is provided by Ethiopian Government policy in that they are given priority in their choices in higher education studies (Yizengaw, 2007).

South Africa

Tuition policy in South Africa, in contrast to that in Ethiopia, is that all students have to pay tuition fees. These range from about 10,000 to 25,000 Rands a year for undergraduate studies, depending on the field of study. Professional and specialised degrees are more expensive, as well as private college tuition (Goastellec, 2006). To help cover tuition fee costs in general, financial aid to students exists at several levels. At the national level, the National Student Financial Aid Scheme (NSFAS), a statutory body funded by the Department of Education, provides economically needy students with loans to study at public institutions. Depending on their further academic achievement, part of their loan can be converted into a bursary (40% of the loan at the most). These loan-wavers range from 2,000 to 30,000 Rands a year. There are also some need-based fellowships covering some living expenses for undergraduate students.

Vietnam

Vietnam is one of the developing countries that has experienced major changes in higher education policies from the very beginning of the foundation of the country up to the present. From Independence Day on 2nd September,1945, the Vietnamese Government provided free education for everyone. Students at higher education institutions received free tuition with stipends/scholarships to cover their board, books and living expenses. At the time of the Renovation in 1987, the Vietnamese Government realized the necessity of introducing tuition fees for higher education studies. As a result, higher education institutions were permitted to charge fees, subject to Government regulations on fee levels. Certain categories of students paid reduced fees or were exempted from paying them. Regulations for the use of the tuition fees collected were laid down by Government with the requirement to report the revenue to the line ministry or the provincial government that oversaw the institutions' operations. From 1995, fees can also be charged for special services, such as matriculation, examinations, accommodation and graduation. The fees charged for these services are not regulated and may be set at full cost-recovery. However, current policies on fees and fee exemptions do not take family income into account in determining how much students pay, while specific categories of students, including war invalids, orphans and ethnic minorities, are granted fee exemptions. In the interest of equity objectives, the Vietnamese Government does provide scholarships; furthermore, it has recently established a student loan scheme, on a pilot basis, to assist students whose families cannot afford the fees or other private costs of public education.

Besides open access to the Vietnam higher education system within the country for eligible students, the Vietnamese Government regulates policies concerned with sending students abroad for higher education studies on foreign scholarships or on Government scholarships. In 1951, the first group of students was sent abroad to the Soviet Union, and then to other former socialist countries. These countries trained over 30,000 undergraduates, 13.500 postgraduates, 25,000 technicians and thousands of other scientists (WES, 2000, p.12). In 1989, with the collapse of the former Soviet Union, Vietnamese students from all of the socialist countries in Eastern Europe returned home. Consequently, there were few full scholarships available to study overseas. It is estimated that, from late 1990 to the present, each year there are about 10 Canadian Government scholarships, 70 scholarships to study in the UK, 200 for France, and 150 for Australia. Thailand offers 70 short-term scholarships and 10 long-term scholarships, the Japanese Government offers about 60 scholarships, and the US about 30 Fulbright Fellowships for masters degree students. There are currently about 20 doctoral scholarships annually from the Vietnam Education Foundation (VEF). Additionally, scholarships are offered directly by foreign universities, foundations or corporations to Vietnamese students to undertake their undergraduate and postgraduate studies overseas. The Vietnamese Government also provides financial assistance to send Vietnamese students abroad for undergraduate and postgraduate study. The numbers studying abroad have expanded exponentially in recent years – part of a worldwide trend. The latest figures for Vietnamese students in the US, for instance, show a rise of 45% for 2008/09, with 12823 studying there (World University News 2009). Students are sent to some 29 countries to pursue their studies. Since 2006, the Government has been offering 400 scholarships annually to study abroad of which 50% is for doctoral students, 25% for masters students and the rest for under-graduates.

Among the targeted groups mentioned above, Vietnamese students from ethnic minority groups and from remote or mountainous areas have received special attention. In 1989, the Vietnamese Government issued special edicts which confirmed their policies for ethnic minorities in Viet Nam. These are equity, unity, and support for the general development of the country. During the period from 1990–1995, the Ministry of Education (MOET) aimed to recruit a certain number of ethnic minority students to higher education every year and also to expand the network of secondary schools in mountainous and remote areas. In the same period, three university foundation schools were established in three regions (North, Central and South) of Vietnam. According to the statistics, from 1990–1995, there were 4.876 ethnic minority undergraduates studying at 25 universities and colleges, accounting for 88.9% of the expected figures. From 1996–1998, there were 2,312 new undergraduate enrolments from ethnic minorities which accounted for 78% of the targeted figures. From 1999–2005, more privileges were allocated to the ethnic minority and to those from low socio-economic backgrounds with the result that there were 7,288 new undergraduate enrolments from those targeted groups (MOET). MOET confirmed that about 80% of the graduates returned to work in their geographical areas. These policies have been continued since 2005.

NON-GOVERNMENTAL SUPPORT

Based on the data available, it appears that support for higher education students from bodies other than government across developed and developing countries is not as extensive as that from Governments. Furthermore, there exist differences between developed countries and developing countries in the forms and in the amount of support from these sources.

Among the eight countries considered here, students in the USA, though facing high tuition fees, appear to receive more financial support from bodies not linked to government than students in the other countries. In addition to the main financial support from the federal government and state government, several agencies also provide grants to higher education students, but these are usually smaller than those from the Governments. Banks and several state providers also offer unsubsidised sources of loan support; in 2003 non-Federal loans amounted to $4.0 billion (Heller 2009).

Since, as noted above, tuition is free to all eligible students in France, bodies such as banks and some insurance companies offer loans to students to cover living expenses. This is, however, not as widespread a practice as in the US.

As in France, Irish higher education students get little indirect cost of living support in comparison to many Continental European countries. However, a few institutions and Foundations in Ireland do offer a small number of both merit and need-based scholarships to students.

It is apparent that financial support from non-governmental sources for students in most of the developed countries is not as generous as that from Governmental sources. In Israel potential higher education students are provided with some special fellowships by philanthropic organisations. Private banks also offer various loans to students, but the majority of students do not take them up.

The situation in developing countries is that support from NGOs is much less than in the developed ones. Indeed, in some countries it is very rare. In Ethiopia the role of the NGOs seems to be blurred. Available data show that students can benefit from financial support from projects funded by foreign countries which provide monies to NGOs operating in Ethiopia or to Ethiopian Government organisations, such as a project funded by the Belgian government, NORAD (Yizengaw, 2006).

By comparison, it seems that non-governmental bodies operating in South Africa appear to be more active in relation to providing financial support to higher education students (Cooper and Subotzky 2001). These are either in the form of loans provided directly by the banks or bursaries with attached conditions offered by some companies, e.g. working for the company after graduation. Most major banking institutions offer student loans at attractive interest rates, which may decrease for consecutive years of study, and are to be repaid when students graduate or start to work. Furthermore, companies may offer bursaries that cover tuition fees, accommodation costs, books and travel costs to academically promising students. Furthermore, many church groups and religious organisations offer bursaries to their members (financial assistance webpage of University of the Witwatersrand, Johannesburg).

Viet Nam, a developing country in South East Asia, has undergone rapid development with investment from foreign non-governmental bodies together with the growth of local private enterprises. These organisations, such as Toyota, East and West, FPT (local) and numerous private donors offer either merit-based scholarships or need-based scholarships. As a result, for more than a decade now, higher education students in Viet Nam have received financial support from such bodies operating in Viet Nam to cover either their tuition and/or living expenses. Some private companies also offer merit-based tuition fees and some maintenance costs on condition that students will work for the company after graduation (Nguyen, 2006).

INSTITUTIONAL SUPPORT SCHEMES

Besides the financial support from Governments and various non-governmental organisations, institutional support to students is very essential, as it is the institution itself that understands its students' circumstances and what they really need to advance in their study at the institution. Support for higher education students varies from institution to institution and from country to country regardless of whether it is a developed or developing country. Institutional support comes in various forms including financial support, learning support and counselling.

Most public universities in the US provide their students with some form of financial support such as grants, scholarships, bursaries or tuition discounts. Those funds come either from endowments or special contributions from institutional contributors. According to Heller's findings (2009), the total grants from all sources (the federal government, states, charitable bodies and institutions) available to students came to some $23.9 billion. Besides the financial support, US institutions, both public and private, offer various kinds of learning support such as tutoring in essay writing and mathematical skills, and language centres for those whose language competency needs improving. Counselling is normally available for any student who is suffering emotional or academic problems. These services can be accessed by all students, including female students, international students and ethnic minority students.

French universities make a number of university residences available to their students at a very reasonable cost, thus reducing the financial burden to their students. Most French universities/institutions also provide their students with tutoring in the form of senior students assisting junior students to tackle problems in their studies (senior students eventually get paid for their tutoring work). Each university town has a Centre of Information which provides open access to students for information on the availability of university curricula and professional opportunities.

In Ireland, in addition to the Government-funded higher education grant schemes, most universities/institutions offer a small number of merit-based scholarships to attract high achieving students. However, none of these alternative sources of student financial support rivals the importance of Government support which constitutes the overwhelming source of student aid. Limited medical and counselling services are also provided to students as well. Learning support within the institution is available principally for those who are non-standard admissions, e.g. students from disadvantaged backgrounds, students with disabilities and mature students. Counselling services are available for all students but are somewhat limited.

In England, besides the Government grants and loans offered in a number of forms to English students, institutions also provide students with various means of financial support. Details of the bursaries offered by the University of West of England, as an example, have been given earlier in this chapter (http://info.uwe.ac.uk/money/).

In relation to the financial support students receive from the Government and from institutions, the Higher Education Funding Council for England (HEFCE) emphasises that institutional policies should be developed to support achievement and success of students when they are at the institutions (HEFCE 2003). Hence HEFCE can direct funds to individual institutions for student support to enhance the student retention rate. A number of programmes relating to student support include extended induction programmes preparing students for the approaches to teaching and learning adopted in higher education, and enabling deficiencies in skills and knowledge to be identified and rectified; workshop support; tutor support; and peer support groups (Greenbank & Hill, 2006: p. 152); at later stages in their studies, students continue to be provided with support in further developing their skills and knowledge to progress successfully through courses. Career management skills, personal development profiles, and career education are also included.

In Israel, as mentioned earlier, student support schemes are mainly monitored by the Council for Higher Education or sponsored by the Ministry of Education. However, most universities and other higher education institutions in Israel offer extensive counselling services and operate special centres geared towards assisting students with learning disabilities or social and psychological stress.

Institutional support to students in Ethiopia is different from that in Israel, reflecting the difference in priorities and economic and cultural perspectives. Ethiopian higher education students, in addition to receiving financial support from Government and NGOs, are provided with more finance based on the family's economic situation, which is examined and analysed by the Students' Councils. Furthermore, some other forms of support are available e.g. orientation programmes, and free scheduled tutorial programmes for those who wish to take them. In particular, special tutorial support workshops are offered in many universities focussing on female students and those from disadvantaged backgrounds. A number of universities have established libraries near the dormitories of female students, providing a special service for them. Furthermore, a special office that follows up issues related to female students has been established in almost all universities/ institutions. The Quarterly Reports of the Presidents of All Universities, submitted to the Ministry of Education, list the most important student support mechanisms implemented in Ethiopian universities as the following: the establishment of student councils, clubs (HIV/AIDS, arts, etc.), offices for men and for women, tutorials, financial support for needy students, orientation, affirmative action, assertiveness training, and the priority placement of female students and disabled students according to their choices, among others. Each academic is expected to have a number of students to supervise during their study at the university until they graduate, so that the students can discuss both educational and personal issues with their supervisor, including practical training and recreational facilities, health services, consultation hours, external placements, and extension of library hours.

In South Africa, in addition to the National Student Financial Aid Scheme, most universities provide the best students with bursaries or grants, regardless of their economic background. There is no requirement to repay a scholarship or merit-based award at the end of the studies. For example at the University of the Witwatersrand, Johannesburg, institutional scholarships include a number of types in the first year; examples include Vice-Chancellor's Scholarships, Academic

Excellence Scholarships, University Council Entrance Scholarships, University Council Entrance Merit Awards, Sport Scholarships and National Olympiad Winners. In addition, learning support and counselling are also available in the form of bridging classes and tutoring for all those who need them.

Vietnamese higher education institutions/universities all offer various forms of support to their own students. However this varies from city to city and from province to province, and more or less depends on the size and the location of each institution. Most universities offer some financial support for students based on merit, and some also provide fellowships based on need depending on the resources the university can raise each year. Additionally, based on the examination and analysis of individual cases recommended by the University Student Council and the University Student Association, special grants to cover living expenses are provided for students who experience difficult circumstances, such as sickness, accidents or some natural disaster. Further, every university provides learning support and counselling to every student who is in need, with special attention paid to minority and female students.

STUDENT RETENTION AND REASONS FOR A LOW RATE OF RETENTION

Equity in higher education is not only a matter of an open access policy it is also a matter of staying in higher education and progressing successfully. This matter has been considered at institutional level and national level in all the eight countries studied in this research, but to different degrees depending on the focus of the priority of each national government, and the average retention rate of the national higher education system and individual institutional cases within the national higher education system. Student retention rates vary from country to country, from field to field, and from institution to institution. Reasons for high or low retention rates also differ; however, common reasons are identified and addressed in this section.

In the USA, retention strategies became more prominent after the 1970s but, although their application at institutional level has increased over the past decades, attrition rates continue to be relatively high. Data collected by ACT over the past 20 years indicated little change in five-year graduation rates for combined Bachelor's, Master's, and Ph.D. granting institutions (ranging from a high of 54.6% to a low of 50.9%) with a 2003 rate of 51.6% (ACT, 2004). A study by the Pell Institute, *Moving Beyond Access: College Success for Low-Income, First Generation Students* (2008) by Jennifer Engle and Vincent Tinto, provided evidence that those from deprived backgrounds were nearly four times more likely to leave higher education after the first year than students who were not low income and first generation in college After six years of study, only 11 percent of this group had earned bachelor's degrees, compared with 55 per cent of more advantaged groups. An ACT survey of more than 1,000 two- and four-year colleges and universities showed that a number of schools had no specific plans or goals in place to improve student retention and degree completion; and that colleges tended to put the blame for dropping out primarily on students, rather than on themselves. Data reveal that up to one-fourth of all students at four-year colleges do not return for their second year studies. According to the National Centre for Education Statistics, dropout rates are particularly high for African American and Hispanic students; other student populations at greater risk of dropping out include those referred to above who are the first in their family to attend college and are low income, and also those who have limited English proficiency, and are non-traditional students, such as returning adult students. Reasons for fairly low retention rates differ across institutions and states. According to the findings of one survey (ACT, 2004), college officials believed that both student and institution characteristics might affect a student's decision to drop out; and they pointed out 13 student characteristics in which lack of motivation, inadequate preparation, inadequate financial resources and poor study skills were felt to have significantly contributed to student attrition. Surprisingly, in contrast, only two institutional characteristics were identified as making a significant impact on attrition, the amount of financial aid available and the ability of the student to fit in with the environment of the institution.

In France access to, and especially retention in, higher education studies is highly dependent on the social origins, gender and even geographical origins of students (Deer, 2005). The data concerning student retention published by the DEP (Direction de l'evaluation et de la prospective, *Reperes et References Statistiques*, edition 2004) for the Ministry do not allow direct information to be obtained about its level. It was only possible to ascertain that, after the first year of study, 24.3% of the first year student population left higher education, and 9.8% changed direction. Of those who pursue their studies after the first year, 75.7% obtain the 2nd year Diploma (DEUG) within 2 to 5 years (Goastellec 2006). Thus the rate of achievement in two years of higher education studies is about 45%, and 20.7% over three years. From these figures, it is calculated that approximately 58% of students enrolling in higher education institutions graduate within 5 years. However, the completion rates differ according to the field of study. Excluding those who drop out in the first year, the retention rate is the lowest in Law, Economics and Languages (66.2%, 71.2% and 72.4% respectively), and the highest in Humanities, (84.6%), Sciences (81%), and Human Sciences (79.8%). Some 80% of high school graduates (which were 498400) enrolled in higher education studies; however, the one year Licence course had a retention rate of 58.2%. Such a drop-out rate after the first year is due to academically under-prepared students and an inappropriate course of study. For those undertaking study at Master's and Doctoral level, financial difficulties often add to the causes of dropping out. In order to improve the completion rate at different levels of higher education study, the French Government and the institutions themselves have launched several initiatives: students are expected to graduate within a certain amount of time, and tutoring will be provided for those who require it, in order for them to attain this goal.

In Ireland, the issue of student retention has been the focus of a number of studies and has attracted the attention of policy makers. In general the attrition rate at university is low by comparative standards. The most comprehensive national study (Morgan et al, 2001) gives a figure of 83% completion; of those 82% complete within the expected time with the remaining graduating late. Non-completion rates vary by field of study, being highest in Computer Science (27%), Science (22%) and Engineering & Architecture (20%). In general, fields of study which require the highest level of student achievement for entry have the highest completion rates, while those areas of study which admit students with more modest levels of achievement have lower completion rates. In addition to the national study, many individual universities and colleges have commissioned their own studies to identify the scale of the problems with a view to adopting institutional policies to maximise graduation rates.

In comparison with the universities, the scale of attrition at the Institutes of Technology is much larger and has given rise to considerable concern by policy makers. One study of first year students in three Institutes of Technology revealed an average non-completion rate of 37% among first year students (Healy et al, 1999). A more recent study of non-completion in the Technological Sector (The Institutes of Technology) reports much higher completion rates –defined as graduating within the standard duration of the course plus one year. This study of the full sector reports a completion rate of 70% for students on sub-degree courses and a completion rate of 87% for degree courses. The latter rate includes both 'ab-initio' and 'add-on' courses so that students who enter after already gaining a Higher Diploma would be expected to have higher completion rates (CIRCA GROUP "Completion Rates for Students Taking Full-time Programs of Study in Institutes of Technology", Council of Directors of Institutes of Technology and Dublin Institute of Technology, 2006.) The study conducted by Healy et al (1999) that attempted to find reasons for non-completion rates indicated that non-completion was associated with several reasons as follows:
– Low grades in the Leaving Certificate Examination;
– Unclear career aspirations;
– Lack of information and guidance on course and career options;
– Unsuitable course choices,
– Difficulty with some or all of the subjects;
– Financial and work related problems.

Many individual universities and college have commissioned their own studies to identify the scale of the problem with a view to adopting institutional policies to maximise graduation rates. Besides the reasons mentioned above, institutional factors also played a role in the student retention rate, in particular:
– Lack of facilities and support services;
– Poor communication between staff and students.

There is no large-scale study which links attrition rates with the social characteristics of students. To maximise the completion rate at different levels of studies, several individual institutions have monitored the progress of students from disadvantaged backgrounds who were admitted through the non-standard direct entry route. The results of these small-scale studies have generally shown that, where institutions offer additional support, such students have retention and graduation rates which match the average for standard intake students.

The United Kingdom has a long history of a relatively high proportion of students who, having obtained a place in university or college, complete their courses and achieve the standard necessary to obtain the qualification for which they have been studying. It still has one of the highest graduation rates in the OECD, about 83% compared to an OECD average of 70%. (The highest retention rate is in Japan - 90%). Despite the high retention rates, in recent years there has been evidence of an increasing number of students who do not complete their studies. According to the House of Commons' Sixth Report (2001) non-completion rates in the UK in 1999 were slightly over 17 percent. In general terms it can be said that about one in six students who entered higher education left without completing their degree. Non-completion rates vary significantly by the subject of study from 2 percent in Medicine, Dentistry and Veterinary Science to 11 percent in Engineering and Technology (HEFCE 00/40). More recent data from the Higher Education Statistics Agency, (HESA, 2005) show that non-completion rates for each UK country in 2003/04 were: 15.4% - for England; 11.3% - for Wales; 10.9% - for Scotland; and 9.9% - for Northern Ireland. Reasons affecting students' decisions to withdraw from higher education include the following problems:

– Financial reasons (inability to pay tuition fees and living expenses);
– Academic problems – course suitability (mismatch between students' expectations of HE and their actual experiences when studying).
– Lack of support that institutions provide for students, especially during their first year of studies.

It is often assumed that non-traditional students are at a greater risk of non-completion than traditional entrants to higher education. Evidence suggests that students attending state schools achieve better in higher education than students from independent schools after other factors are taken into account (HEFCE 03/32). However, pupils from failing inner city schools are disadvantaged by having poorer preparation for higher education studies.

In Israel, the average completion rate at first degree level at Israeli universities is around 70% (after 5 years of study). Non-completion rates vary greatly by field of study, being highest in Humanities (39%) and Science (33%), and the lowest in Law (17%) and Engineering & Architecture (16%) (Central Bureau of Statistics, 2004). The retention rate at second degree level is lower than for Bachelor studies and is about 55% (5 years from the start of the second degree). The non-completion rate at second degree level is highest in Humanities (59%), and lowest in Social Sciences (37%) and Agriculture (32%). The relatively low completion rates at the second degree level are related to the heavy research orientation of master level studies in Israel, with a requirement for a thesis which resembles in many respects a PhD dissertation in many other higher education systems. It also explains the attractiveness of universities abroad which offer MA studies in 1 or 2 years. The retention rate at doctoral level is even lower, with only 29% of those who started doctoral studies in 1993/4 having completed them within five years of the start of their studies (Central Bureau of Statistics 2004). The highest completion rate is in Engineering & Architecture (46.6%), and the lowest in Humanities (19.6%).

Although a very small percentage of the population attends university in Ethiopia, many drop out during their first year of university education. Although there are some signs of improvement in the recent years, there are still significant numbers of students who leave universities before graduation or before completing the programmes. Female students, in particular, exhibit a tendency to drop out from many universities. Retention and completion rates differ from discipline to discipline, with most of the Sciences and Engineering programmes having lower rates of retention. However, retention figures need to be collected systematically and collated statistically to describe the causes and remedial measures required.

This has not yet been done. The main reason for the high drop-out rate in the first year at undergraduate level could be that, during the first year, students find it hard to adapt to the new study environment. In addition, the faculty currently perceives the high failure rate of first-year students as a measure of quality and standards. Similarly, this is also the reason for much non-completion at master and doctoral levels. In order to improve the completion rate at different levels of study, institutions have introduced tutorial support and remedial classes for needy students.

Based on extracts from the Quarterly Reports of the Presidents of All Universities submitted to the Ministry of Education, Ethiopian higher education suffers a number of problems:

Problems which need to be addressed
- Insensitivity or poor awareness of beneficiaries;
- Lack of clear policy and guidelines,
- Lack of experience,
- Resource constraints,
- Poor faculty commitment and motivation,
- Misconception and mindset,
- Lack of qualified personnel,
- Limited support from the government

Solutions suggested from the reports
Development of clear policies and strategies for
- funding and implementation of strategies
- increasing female role models in universities
- maximising an awareness of what is available
- inclusion of male students in the need- based support scheme
- starting affirmative actions at lower levels of education;Institutional commitment
- proper planning with appropriate strategies
- staff training and professional development programmes,
- employment of professional counsellors,
- understanding of common/shared vision and goals among staff and faculty and institution leaders
- peer tutorials and counselling programmes for students;

CHAPTER 8

Data on student retention in South Africa are unfortunately not available for this research. However, it is known that the main reason for the low retention rate is financial difficulty. A number of strategies have been conducted by the Government and institutions in South African to improve the rate of graduation, e.g. centralisation of the registration process to access universities and benefit from financial help, bridging classes and tutoring, and work with high schools to better prepare the students for higher education entrance.

In Viet Nam, studies of the issue of student retention at higher education institutions are few, partly due to the nature of the very highly competitive university entrance examination. As a result, once students get a place at a higher education institution, they try their best to fulfil all the requirements to obtain the degree for which they have enrolled. The number of students who drop out during their study at higher education institutions are not reported nationally, but kept within each institution, except for a survey conducted by the National Higher Education Project in 2002. The statistics from the survey concerning percentage of students who dropped out are reported in Table 1 below.

Table 1. Statistics from the Survey in 2002 (the Higher Education Project Data)

	Number*	Sample**	% surveyed	Average size of students	% of drop-outs	% of student repeated
National General Statistics	**198**	**185**	**93.43**	**5,852**	**4.49**	**2.00**
1. Types of ownership						
– Public	175	164	93.71	5,917	3.91	1.18
– Semi-public	6	6	100.00	5,368	10.59	17.44
– Private	17	15	88.24	5,325	6.50	2.15
2. Types of structure						
– Multi-disciplinary – National University	2	2	100.00	58,250	6.31	2.46
– Regional multi-disciplinary university	3	3	100.00	41,890	4.76	1.54
– Public university	55	53	96.36	10,427	3.49	0.74
– Provincial university	3	3	100.00	5,125	1.65	0.35
– Private university	17	16	94.12	6,113	6.78	2.47
– College	118	108	91.53	1,616	4.21	5.32

* *Number of institutions in 2002*
** *Number of institutions surveyed in 2002*

It is seen clearly in Table 1 that from the 2002 national comprehensive survey, 4.5% of the student population dropped out during their studies at higher education. However, the drop-out rates varied by types of institution, which indicates whether

students have to pay all their tuition and other related expenses. It should also be noted that it is easier to get a place at private universities than at public ones. A further complication concerns students who dropped their studies at private universities and re-started their study at public ones, as students are allowed by national regulations to take university entrance examinations twice. Table 1 also indicates that the drop-out rates varied between types of institutional structures. It is reported that the academic standards required by national universities are higher than those from regional ones, and regional universities, in turn, required academically higher standards than provincial ones: this could explain the difference in drop-out rates. From the result of the survey, it could be concluded that the students dropped out of their higher education studies for the following reasons:
- Financial problems
- Highly demanding academic requirements
- Change of their choice of higher institutions

The rate of graduation at the first graduation examination, according to MOET, is generally 90% for undergraduates and more than 90% for post-graduates. Students are allowed by MOET regulations to re-take the graduation examinations once and re-defend their thesis/project (for the fields of studies requiring thesis/ project defend) once.

CONCLUSIONS AND RECOMMENDATIONS

This chapter has dealt with issues of student support and student retention in the eight countries. Both are of major importance in relation to access and equity. Of the eight countries, various forms of support have been made available to higher education students, though the types and amount of support differ from country to country and, within any one country, from state to state, from city/province to city/province and from institution to institution. Based on the data available for this research and the analysis above, it could be said that US higher education students, though facing high tuition fees and other related costs of education, receive the widest range of financial aid from a number of sources, with the most from federal government and state government, followed by institutional grants and scholarships. On average, the total grants US students received cover roughly 50% of the bill in the US (Swail, 2004: p.34). All the countries studied offer some form of grants, which in some countries will cover a large percentage of the cost, particularly for those from disadvantaged backgrounds. Besides grants, the other form of financial support seen in the developed countries are various types of loan which help cover the cost of university education for students in general, though the forms of loans offered differ; and sources for loans also vary. The percentage of students who applied for loans also varied from country to country, with the US at the top. Loan financing, however, has been severely criticised, as its effects are difficult to ascertain; *"the prospect of debt probably deters some less advantaged young people from considering postsecondary education. There is also evidence that financial aid in the form of loans is less effective than grant aid in helping students to stay in college and get their degrees"* (Gladieux, 2003: p. 5).

In the developing countries such as Ethiopia and Viet Nam, grants from the national governments are considerably less in comparison with the amount US students receive from their federal and state governments. Foreign and local NGOs operating within each national territory play some role in providing students with some financial support, but this is constrained and unstable because of limited resources. Loans and bursaries from banks and private companies with conditions attached are other forms of financial support available to students in these countries. However, a loan is not the form that is welcomed by most students in developing countries, though a number of students in Viet Nam make use of this financial source during their studies at higher education institutions.

Learning support and counselling are the two other forms of support higher education students received in the eight countries. Nevertheless, these differ from institution to institution even within an individual national territory, depending on the particular needs of students in each institution, and on the resources of the institution. Where comparisons are possible among the eight countries, learning support and counselling in general also differ, given differences in national priorities, cultural and economic backgrounds and resources available in each country.

Retention can be considered as a consequence of the learning support and counselling in place at each institution. Retention rates vary with the field of study and from institution to institution with national average retention rates markedly differing. The drop-out rates after the first year of study at higher education institutions are high; this is a matter that challenges higher education globally. It appears from the above analysis that, in general, the tendency is for the retention rate to be high at the institutions that recruit students with high achievement at senior high school or with high scores in university entrance examinations. Unfortunately, what we do not know is whether those institutions provide more support and counselling to their students than the ones with lower retention rates do for theirs. This is an issue that is still open for further research.

In summary, higher education students in the eight countries covered in this research do receive various forms of financial support as well as learning support and counselling from their national government, state government, provincial authorities and institutions. NGOs play a role but it is not as significant as that of governments. Institutional support is vital as institutions understand their students' variety of needs, especially in the areas of learning and counselling. There is no doubt that financial support, learning support and counselling play significant roles in enhancing access, equity and success in higher education globally. However, the questions "Has that support actually determined the number of enrolments of people from various backgrounds? Is it significant in retaining them in higher education and enabling them to graduate in timely fashion? And to what extent does each type of support affect access and retention in higher education?" must wait for future exploration and discussion elsewhere.

However, what is seen from the above analysis is that "free education to everyone at levels of higher education studies" appears to favour the "rich people" over those with low incomes. Financial difficulties often affect studies. Consequently, access to higher education and the ability to maintain their studies is of most concern to low-income students. It was pointed out in the research conducted by Gladieux (2003: p.3) that "chances of a college education remain sharply unequal in the U.S. As in virtually every country of the world, participation in higher education - rates of entry and completion, as well as type and prestige of institution attended - is closely associated with socio-economic status". Gladieux also noted that strategies were being applied that were strengthening academic preparation for low-income and minority students as well as making higher education more affordable. The key question of access and equity relevant to this chapter is that the high cost of tertiary level education not only refers to tuition fees but also to other costs associated with it such as living expenses for students during their time in higher education.

This issue is a decisive factor for low-income students. Would it be solved by grants which are non-repayable or by loans with high risk of debts for those who come from poor background families? Grants based on need-based analysis, which are non-repayable, would appear to be the best answer to the question, given the current forms of financial support available to higher education students all over the world. Nevertheless, transparency and appropriate methods of allocation and criteria for need-based analysis are matters that policy makers, stakeholders, and educators should pay attention to.

Much international research has been conducted on access and equity to higher education, but less research on support for students once they have gained entry to institutions. It is clear that such support is essential to help retain them and enable them to be successful, thus enhancing the retention rate. The issue of low retention rates is still alarming not only within the US (Lotkowski et al, 2004), but globally. There is a need for investment in research in this area to empirically identify what would be the most economic and effective initiatives. Based on research in the field (Tinto 2004), (Lotkowski et al, 2004), (Engle and Tinto 2008) which examined the need analysis above, and the important role that student support and consequential student retention contribute to the success of an institution, it is recommended to higher education institutions worldwide that,

— Institutions should have policies and resources (financial, academic, social and cultural) in place to provide students with adequate support at the institution;

— Institutions should be able to recognise differences among their student population so that support strategies at each institution can reflect and meet the needs (academic and non-academic) of individual students, since they have many different reasons for dropping-out;

— Institutions should focus on retention programmes such as first year orientation, tutorials on learning skills, and mentoring to enhance students' understanding of the institutional culture;

— Evaluation of support/retention programmes and use of the evaluation outcomes for the improvement of these programmes and the support process should be undertaken;

— Social support programmes should be provided for those students who are away from home for the first time, are from ethnic or minority groups, or from low

socio-economic background. Such programmes increase the students' self-confidence and their involvement with the institution;
- Retention programmes should be developed to acknowledge a range of academic and non-academic factors;
- Student participation and attendance is an important indicator of any possible problems, thus keeping a record of student profiles will help in predicting potential difficulties;
- The student profile should be used to develop programmes to meet the needs of students;
- Institutions should take responsibility for their students to ensure that they are progressing with appropriate support from the institution;

To policy makers, governments, international actors and donors, it is recommended that:
- Every country should be encouraged to establish a national statistical database to collect data annually and systematically, as in the US, to which policy makers and researchers can have access. This would be of potential benefit to the Government and to society in the sense that decisions would be made that are based on sound research findings; and international comparison could be facilitated;
- More investment should be provided to enhance research capacity to identify best practices so that lessons could be drawn and the implication of such research made widely available;
- An evaluation should be made of what effect grants/loans and other support is on access and retention rates. Thus intervention strategies could be developed to solve the issues identified;
- As the costs of higher education increase, national governments and state/local governments should work more closely together with educators and students. It is essential that their voices be heard so that the students' variety of needs can be identified appropriately, allowing more informed consideration of the policies of allocation and/or criteria for grants and learning support to higher education students.

BIBLIOGRAPHY

ACT. (2004b). *Tracking charts compiled from ACT institutional data file.* Retrieved from http://www.act.org/path/policy/reports/retain.html

ACT. (2004a). *What works in student retention* (Appendix 1). Retrieved from http://www.act.org/path/policy/reports/retain.html

Advisory Committee on Third-Level Student Support. (1993). *Third level student support.* Dublin: Stationery Office.

Barr, N. (2002). *Funding higher education: Policies for access and quality.* House of Commons Education and Skills Committee, Post-16 Student Support.

Central Bureau of Statistics. (2008). *Education and culture - Selected data, based on the statistical abstract of Israel* (Vol. 59). Jerusalem: State of Israel Central Bureau of Statistics.

Clancy, P. (2006). *Access and equity: National report of Ireland.* An internal paper, New Century Scholars Program of Fulbright.

Cooper, D., & Subotzsky, G. (2001). *The Skewed revolution: Trends in South African higher education: 1988-1998.* Cape Town: Education Policy Unit, University of the Western Cape.

Council for Higher Education. (2009). *Website of the Israel Council for Higher Education.* Retrieved from http://www.che.org.il/english.aspx

Deer, C. (2005, July). Higher education access and expansion: The French experience. *Higher Education Quarterly, 59*(3), 230–241

Department for Education and Skills. (2003a). *The future of higher education.* Cm5735. London: HMSO.

Direction de l'évaluation et de la prospective, Repères et Références Statistiques, édition 2004.

Eggins, H. (2006). *Access and equity: National report of United Kingdom.* An internal paper, New Century Scholars Program of Fulbright.

Engle, J., & Tinto, V. (2008). *Moving beyond access: College success for low-income, first-generation students.* Washington, DC: The Pell Institute for the Study of Opportunity in Higher Education.

Gladieux, L. E. (2003). *Student assistance the American way.* Washington, DC: Educational Policy Institute, Inc.

Goastellec, G. (2006). *Access and equity: National report of France.* An internal paper, New Century Scholars Program of Fulbright.

Greenbank, P. (2006, April). The evolution of government policy on widening participation. *Higher Education Quarterly, 60*(2), 141–166.

Guri-Rosenblit, S. (2006). *Access and equity: National report of Israel.* An internal paper, New Century Scholars Program of Fulbright.

Healy, M., Carpenter, A., & Lynch, K. (1999). *Non-completion in higher education: A study of first year students in three institutes of technology.* Carlow: Institute of Technology.

HEFCE. (2003). *Performance indicators for higher education, 00/40.* Bristol: HEFCE.

HEFCE. (2003). *Schooling effects on higher education achievement, 03/32.* Bristol: HEFCE.

Heller, D. (2009, March). *Access to higher education in the United States: Issues and challenges.* Paper presented at Staffordshire University.

HESA. (2005). *Performance indicators in higher education 2003/04.* Cheltenham: Higher Education Statistics Agency.

House of Commons Education and Employment Committee Sixth Report. (2001). *Higher education: Student retention.* HC 124. Retrieved from http://info.uwe.ac.uk/money/; http://www.edu.net.vn

Ireland Department of Education. (1965). *Investment in education.* Report of the Survey Team appointed by the Minister for Education. Dublin: Stationery Office.

Lotkowski, V. A., Robbins, S. B., & Richard, J. N. (2004). *The role of academic and non-academic factors in improving college retention: ACT policy report.* ACT inc.

Ministère de l'Education Nationale et de la Recherche, (?) et Références Statistiques sur la formation et la recherche, Paris, 2004.

Morgan, M., Flanagan, R., & Kellaghan, T. (2001). *A study of non-completion in undergraduate university courses.* Dublin: Higher Education Authority.

Nguyen, P. N. (2006). *Access and equity: National report of Viet Nam.* An internal paper, New Century Scholars Program of Fulbright.

Roberts, D. V., et al. (2005, June 27–29). *Funding for success in higher education: A mechanism to meet national challenges?* Communication at the SAARDHE congress, The African University in the 21st century, Durban.

Swail, W. S. (2004). *The affordability of university education: A perspective from both sides of the 49th parallel.* Washington, DC: Educational Policy Institute, Inc.

Tinto, V. (2004). *Student retention and graduation: Facing the truth, living with the consequences.* Washington, DC: The Pell Institute.

Usher, A., & Cervenan, A. (2005). *Global higher education rankings 2005.* Toronto, ON: Educational Policy Institute.

WES. (2000, May/June). *World Education News & Reviews, 13*(3), p. 1–14.

Yizengaw, T. (2006). *Access and equity: National report of Ethiopia.* An internal paper, New Century Scholars Program of Fulbright.

Yizengaw, T. A. (2007). *The Ethiopian higher education: Creating space for reform.* Addis Ababa: Yizengaw.

CONTRIBUTORS

Patrick Clancy is Associate Professor of Sociology and former Dean of the Faculty of Human Sciences at University College Dublin. His publications include *College Entry in Focus* (Dublin: HEA, 2001) the fourth in his series of national studies of access to higher education in Ireland, and *Irish Society: Sociological Perspectives* (Dublin: IPA, 1995) one of three jointly edited books on Irish society. He has served on a variety of national advisory and policy groups on higher education and is a founder member, and currently a member of the Board of Governors of the *Consortium of Higher Education Researchers* (CHER). He has recently edited (with David Dill) *The Research Mission of the University*, the first volume of a new series sponsored by CHER and published by Sense Publishers in 2010.

Address: UCD School of Sociology, University College Dublin, Belfield, Dublin 4, Ireland, e-mail: patrick.clancy@ucd.ie

Heather Eggins is Visiting Professor at the Institute for Education Policy Research, Staffordshire University, Visiting Professor at Strathclyde University and a senior member of Lucy Cavendish College, University of Cambridge. She recently served as a consultant to UNESCO. She is also a member of the Governing Council of the University of Northampton. Her research interests are in higher education policy, with a particular interest in access issues and globalisation. Her publications include a number of edited books, and articles on higher education e.g. *Globalization and Reform in Higher Education* (Maidenhead, SRHE, 2003). She was Editor of *Higher Education Quarterly*, 2004–2007.

Address: Institute for Education Policy Research, Staffordshire University, Brindley Building, Leek Road, Stoke-on-Trent, ST4 2DF, United Kingdom, e-mail: heggins@btinternet.com

Gaële Goastellec is a sociologist, researcher and Head of the higher education research unit on comparative higher education policies at the Observatory for Science, Policy and Society, University of Lausanne. She has been a visiting researcher at the Universityof Witwatersrand, South Africa, New York University and the Centre de Sociologie des Organisations, Paris. She has contributed to many academic journals on the issue of access to higher education.

Address: OSPS, Bâtiment Vidy 350, CH-1015 Lausanne, Switzerland, e-mail: gaele.goastellec@unil.ch

Mary-Louise Kearney is a Consultant, Institutional Management of Higher Education (IMHE) Programme, OECD Director, The UNESCO Forum on Higher Education, Research and Knowledge (2006–2009). She was also Director of the Division for Relations with National Commissions and New Partnerships in UNESCO's Sector for External Relations and Co-operation. She was involved in the WCHE of 1998 and 2009 and is a Vice President of the Society for Research into Higher Education.

Address: OECD, 2 rue Andre-Pascal, 75775, Paris, CEDEX 16, France.

Phuong Nga Nguyen is the Director of the Center for Education Quality Assurance and Research Development, Vietnam National University, Hanoi (CEQARD). She is the Chief quality Officer of the ASEAN University Network (AUN). She completed her PhD in Education majoring in assessment and evaluation at the University of Melbourne, Australia in 1998, and was a Fulbright Visiting Scholar working at Massachusetts University, Amherst, MA, in 2002–2003. She has served as the principle researcher and team leader of a number of projects on testing, measurement, evaluation and accreditation in education, and has received numerous research grants in those fields and in higher education governance. She has also been a consultant in the areas of evaluation and accreditation for development projects from primary education to Higher education funded by the World Bank, as well as by bilateral donors such as AusAID, and the Vietnam-Netherlands Higher Education Project. She is the author of more than 36 articles and the author or co-author of several monographs published in Vietnam and abroad.

Address: Centre for Education Quality Assurance and Research Development, Vietnam National University Hanoi, 144, Xuan Thuy Road, Cau Giay District, Hanoi, Vietnam, e-mail: nganp@vnu.edu.vn.

Sarah Guri-Rosenblit is Professor and the Director of International Academic Outreach and the Head of Graduate Studies in Education at the Open University of Israel. She got her PhD from Stanford University in 1984 in education and political science. Her areas of expertise are focused on comparative research of higher education systems, distance education and e-learning. She has published books and dozens of articles in these fields. She served as a member of the Scientific Committee of Europe and North America in the UNESCO Forum of Higher Education, Research and Knowledge. Her recent book on *Digital Technologies in Higher Education: Sweeping Expectations and Actual Effects* was published in March 2009 by Nova Science in New York.

Address: Director, International Academic Outreach, Education and Psychology Department, P.O. Box 808, 1, University Road, Raanana 43107, Israel, e-mail: saragu@openu.ac.il.

Teshome Yizengaw Alemneh is currently serving as a Program Officer managing the Africa Initiative Program of the Higher Education for Development (HED). He is responsible for creating requests for applications (RFAs), planning grants and managing several partnership projects for sub-Saharan Africa, and was involved in designing the Africa-U.S. Higher Education Initiative. Dr. Alemneh has researched and written extensively about the challenges of higher education reform in Africa. His most recent book is *The Ethiopian Higher Education: Creating Space for Reform* 2007. He was also an Associate Professor of soil sciences and land suitability assessment in Addis Ababa. He holds a PhD in Earth Sciences and Land Evaluation from Ghent University in Belgium. He has a strong background in developing national strategies and development programs for education, particularly higher education. Dr. Alemneh has extensive experience in higher education policy and management of the implementation of strategies during his position as Deputy Minister of Higher Education in Ethiopia from 2001–2005.

Address: HED, One Dupont Circle NW, Suite 420, Washington DC 20036-1110, USA, e-mail: talemneh@hedprogram.org

GLOBAL PERSPECTIVES ON HIGHER EDUCATION

Volume 1
WOMEN'S UNIVERSITIES AND COLLEGES
An International Handbook
Francesca B. Purcell, Robin Matross Helms, and Laura Rumbley (Eds.)
ISBN 978-90-77874-58-5 hardback
ISBN 978-90-77874-02-8 paperback

Volume 2
PRIVATE HIGHER EDUCATION
A Global Revolution
Philip G. Altbach and D. C. Levy (Eds.)
ISBN 978-90-77874-59-2 hardback
ISBN 978-90-77874-08-0 paperback

Volume 3
FINANCING HIGHER EDUCATION
Cost-Sharing in International perspective
D. Bruce Johnstone
ISBN 978-90-8790-016-8 hardback
ISBN 978-90-8790-015-1 paperback

Volume 4
UNIVERSITY COLLABORATION FOR INNOVATION
Lessons from the Cambridge-MIT Institute
David Good, Suzanne Greenwald, Roy Cox, and Megan Goldman (Eds.)
ISBN 978-90-8790-040-3 hardback
ISBN 978-90-8790-039-7 paperback

Volume 5
HIGHER EDUCATION
A Worldwide Inventory of Centers and Programs
Philip G. Altbach, Leslie A. Bozeman, Natia Janashia, and Laura E. Rumbley
ISBN 978-90-8790-052-6 hardback
ISBN 978-90-8790-049-6 paperback

Volume 6
FUTURE OF THE AMERICAN PUBLIC RESEARCH UNIVERSITY
R. L. Geiger, C. L. Colbeck, R. L. Williams, and C. K. Anderson (Eds.)
ISBN 978-90-8790-048-9 hardback
ISBN 978-90-8790-047-2 paperback

Volume 7
TRADITION AND TRANSITION
The International Imperative in Higher Education
Philip G. Altbach
ISBN 978-90-8790-054-4 hardback
ISBN 978-90-8790-053-3 paperback

Volume 15
BUYING YOUR WAY INTO HEAVEN: EDUCATION AND CORRUPTION IN
INTERNATIONAL PERSPECTIVE
Stephen P. Heyneman (Ed.)
ISBN 978-90-8790-728-0 hardback
ISBN 978-90-8790-727-3 paperback

Volume 16
HIGHER EDUCATION AND THE WORLD OF WORK
Ulrich Teichler
ISBN 978-90-8790-755-6 hardback
ISBN 978-90-8790-754-9 paperback

Volume 17
FINANCING ACCESS AND EQUITY IN HIGHER EDUCATION
Jane Knight (Ed.)
ISBN 978-90-8790-767-9 hardback
ISBN 978-90-8790-766-2 paperback

Volume 18
UNIVERSITY RANKINGS, DIVERSITY, AND THE NEW LANDSCAPE OF HIGHER
EDUCATION
Barbara M. Kehm and Bjørn Stensaker (Eds.)
ISBN 978-90-8790-815-7 hardback
ISBN 978-90-8790-814-0 paperback

Volume 19
HIGHER EDUCATION IN EAST ASIA: NEOLIBERALISM AND THE
PROFESSORIATE
Gregory S. Poole and Ya-chen Chen (Eds.)
ISBN 978-94-6091-127-9 hardback
ISBN 978-94-6091-126-2 paperback

Volume 20
ACCESS AND EQUITY: COMPARATIVE PERSPECTIVES
Heather Eggins (Ed.)
ISBN 978-94-6091-185-9 hardback
ISBN 978-94-6091-184-2 paperback

Lightning Source UK Ltd.
Milton Keynes UK
13 January 2011
165613UK00001B/37/P